The
Black Family
in the
United States

Recent Titles in
Bibliographies and Indexes in Afro-American and African Studies

Black-Jewish Relations in the United States: A Selected Bibliography
Lenwood G. Davis, compiler

Black Immigration and Ethnicity in the United States: An
Annotated Bibliography
Center for Afroamerican and African Studies, The University of Michigan

Blacks in the American Armed Forces, 1776-1983: A Bibliography
Lenwood G. Davis and George Hill, compilers

Education of the Black Adult in the United States: An Annotated Bibliography
Leo McGee and Harvey G. Neufeldt, compilers

A Guide to the Archives of Hampton Institute
Fritz J. Malval, compiler

A Bibliographical Guide to Black Studies Programs in the United States:
An Annotated Bibliography
Lenwood G. Davis and George Hill, compilers

Wole Soyinka: A Bibliography of Primary and Secondary Sources
James Gibbs, Ketu H. Katrak, and Henry Louis Gates, Jr., compilers

Afro-American Demography and Urban Issues: A Bibliography
R. A. Obudho and Jeannine B. Scott, compilers

Afro-American Reference: An Annotated Bibliography of Selected Resources
Nathaniel Davis, compiler and editor

The Afro-American Short Story: A Comprehensive, Annotated Index with
Selected Commentaries
Preston M. Yancy, compiler

Black Labor in America, 1865-1983: A Selected Annotated Bibliography
Joseph Wilson, compiler and editor

Martin Luther King, Jr.: An Annotated Bibliography
Sherman E. Pyatt, compiler

Blacks in the Humanities, 1750-1984: A Selected Annotated Bibliography
Donald Franklin Joyce, compiler

The Black Family in the United States

A Revised, Updated,
Selectively Annotated Bibliography

Compiled by
Lenwood G. Davis

Bibliographies and Indexes in Afro-American and African Studies,
Number 14

Greenwood Press
New York • Westport, Connecticut • London

Library of Congress Cataloging-in-Publication Data

Davis, Lenwood G.
  The Black family in the United States.

  (Bibliographies and indexes in Afro-American and
African studies, ISSN 0742-6925 ; no. 14)
  Includes index.
  1. Afro-American families – Bibliography. I. Title.
II. Series.
Z1361.N39D355   1986   016.3068'5'08996073   86-9926
[E185.86]
ISBN 0-313-25237-8 (lib. bdg. : alk. paper)

Library of Congress Catalog Card Number: 86-9926
ISBN: 0-313-25237-8
ISSN: 0742-6925

First published in 1986

Greenwood Press, Inc.
88 Post Road West, Westport, Connecticut 06881

Printed in the United States of America

The paper used in this book complies with the
Permanent Paper Standard issued by the National
Information Standards Organization (Z39.48-1984).

10 9 8 7 6 5 4 3 2

Contents

ARTICLES (continued)

DISSERTATIONS   175

DISSERTATIONS (continued)

Preface

This annotated bibliography is a revision of the one that I published in 1978. Since that time, a number of reports, books, pamphlets, articles, and essays on the Black family have been published. This updated book, like the earlier one, is primarily designed as a reference for those who want to know more about the Black family in the United States.

This book differs from the earlier one in many respects. One hundred references have been added to the section on Major Works. Twenty-one new sources were added to the section on General Works. Further, special attention was devoted to the section dealing with the "Black Family and Slavery." The previous bibliography listed eighteen books on the subject; this work discusses thirty-two. The previous book listed one hundred forty-four articles; this work discusses over two hundred seventy. Special attention was given to dissertations. The earlier book listed seventy-six; this bibliography over one hundred. This book includes several topics that were either not fully developed or not mentioned earlier: abortion, adoption, alcoholism, illegitimacy, aging, genocide, homosexuality, polygamy, prisons, public policy, racism, sterilization, stress, sickle cell disease, and military families. Some attention has been given to autobiographies and autobiographical works. These works give us insights into how Blacks felt about the larger community. These books tell of their achievements, aspirations, dreams, and hopes, of their pains, disappointments, and sufferings, and of racism in this country. They give us a more accurate understanding and appreciation of Black family members and their innermost feelings and thoughts. This book includes works published as recently as 1985. Because of the current proliferation of materials on the Black family, however, the user must consult various indexes to see what is presently available.

It must be stated that the compiler has attempted to discuss all aspects of the historical evolution of the Black family from Africa, through slavery, to contemporary times. Not only are the roles of the mother, father, children, and grandparents in Black families discussed, but their roles are compared to those in non-Black families.

It should be pointed out that this bibliography is neither comprehensive nor definitive. This work is, however, the most up-to-date book that chronicles and assesses other works on the Black family. It is the compiler's hope that this book will help others to better understand and appreciate past, present, and hopefully future developments in the Black family.

Although many people and institutions assisted me in this endeavor, I must acknowledge special thanks and appreciation to the following: Janie Miller Harris, Barbara Manns, Lora A. Poyner, and Cheryl L. Love. I would like to thank Martha Rokahr for typing the final copy of the manuscript. Several libraries also assisted me: The Schomburg Center for Research in Black Culture; the Moorland Spingarn Research Center, the University of North Carolina at Chapel Hill Library; Duke University Library; University of Tennessee Library; University of North Carolina at Greensboro Library; Wake Forest University Library; Winston-Salem State University Library; University of Maryland Library; New York Public Library; and the Library of Congress. Without their assistance, this work would not have been completed. I take full responsibility, however, for all errors, and would appreciate being informed of any necessary corrections or omissions.

The
Black Family
in the
United States

Major Books

1. Aptheker, Bettina. <u>Woman's Legacy: Essays on Race, Sex, and Class in American History</u>. Amherst, MA: University of Massachusetts Press, 1982, pp. 129-151.

   Chapter 7 is entitled "The Matriarchal Mirage: The Moynihan Connection Historical Perspective." The writer argues that the ideological themes such as the Moynihan idea of the Black matriarch come as the result of some felt need on the part of men who write them. This assumption-namely that ideology derives from social conditions-led Mrs. Aptheker to look for changes in the social conditions of Black women in the post-World War II period that might help to explain the origin and popularity of the Moynihan myth. According to the author, she found much cause to rejoice in writing this essay "in the collective strength of Black woman, and the power which that strength bestows upon all of us."

2. Aschenbrenner, Joyce. <u>Lifelines: Black Families in Chicago</u>. New York: Holt, Rinehart and Winston, Inc., 1975. 146 pp.

   This is a study of ten individuals and their extended families in Chicago. The author provides detailed information based on observation and interviews on the social drama in Black family life in the context of Black culture in one Northern urban center. The writer stresses the extended kin group rather than the nuclear family that is the norm among middle-class whites. She shows how the consanguineal relationships are emphasized, as much as, or more than the nuclear ones in social and economic interaction, and how the mother-daughter tie is of particular significance, suggests the author.

3. Auletta, Ken. <u>The Underclass</u>. New York: Random House, 1982, pp. 39, 41, 68, 81, 194, 199, 258, 254-268.

   In Chapter 20 the writer discusses "Has There Been Progress in "War on Poverty"? It was pointed out that sixteen years after the Moynihan Report appeared, few local or federal efforts have addressed the role of family structure in perpetuating poverty. It was pointed

Auletta:

out that since Moynihan wrote his report, Black out-of-wedlock
births have risen from 23.6 percent of all births in 1962 to 55 percent in 1979, and over 70 percent in many urban ghettos. (White
out-of-wedlock births have also risen, but these total just 9 percent of all white births.) The proportion of Black and Puerto Rican
families headed by women doubled. AFDC rolls swelled from 3 million
in 1960 to 10.8 million in 1980, and the number of Black children
supported by welfare rose from 14 to 36 percent, asserts the author.
The reasons that this issue has remained submerged are varied. Un-
derstandably many people fear that pointing out family weakness will
ease the pressure on government to do more to help the poor, according to Auletta. Or as Martin Luther King, Jr., who agrees with Moynihan that the conditions of the Black family were a "social cata-
strophe," said at the time of the Moynihan Report, "the danger will
be that problems will be attributed to innate Negro weakness and
used to justify neglect and rationalize oppression." Thus, those
who oppose further government and societal efforts will cite evidence that the "solution" to poverty must come from the individual,
not from society, concludes the writer.

4. Bass, Barbara Ann, Gail Elizabeth Wyatt and Gloria Johnson Powell,
    Editors. The Afro-American Family: Assessment, Treatment, and
    Research Issues. New York: Grume and Stratton, 1982. 364 pp.

This work was the outgrowth of a seminar held in 1974 at UCLA Center for the Health Sciences. The three editors are Black females on
the faculty of UCLA. Like the seminar, this book was created from a
growing need to offer information to mental health professionals
about the assessment and psychiatric treatment of Afro-Americans and
relevant research issues. The following essays are included in this
collection: Joan E. Johnson, "The Afro-American Family: A Historical Overview"; "The Survey of Afro-American Behavior: Its Development and Use in Research" was penned by the Editors, Wyatt, Powell
and Bass; Hector F. Myers contributed "Research on the Afro-American
Family: A Critical Review"; "The Validity of Sociocultural Factors
in the Assessment and Treatment of Afro-Americans," was essayed by
Barbara Ann Bass; Lewis M. King, added "The Assessment of Afro-
American Families: Issues in Search of Theory"; Editor Wyatt wrote
"Alternatives to the Use of Standardized Test with Afro-American
Children" and "Sociocultural Assessment of Home and School Visits
in Psychiatric Evaluations of Afro-American Children and Families";
Editor Powell authored "Overview of Epidemiology of Mental Illness
Among Afro-Americans" and "A Six-City Study of School Desegregation
and Self-Concept Among Afro-American Junior High School Students: A
Preliminary Study With Implications for Mental Health"; "The Deli-
very of Mental Health Services to Afro-Americans and Their Families:
Translating Theory into Practice" was written by Barbara Bryant
Solomon; "Transference and Countertransference in Interracial Psychotherapy" was essayed by Ralph Greenson, Ellis Toney, Perry Lim,
and Annelisa Romero; Helen A. Mendes did "The Role of Religion in
Psychotherapy with Afro-Americans", "Improving Intervention Strategies with Minority Group Adolescents" was authored by Yvonne B. Fer-
guson; Lewis M. King wrote "Suicide from a 'Black Reality'"

Bass, et al.:

Perspective"; "Television, Self-Esteem, and The Afro-American Child: Some Implications for Mental Health Professionals" was presented by Gordon L. Berry; Editor Wyatt wrote "Identifying Stereotypes of Afro-American Sexuality and Their Impact Upon Sexual Behavior"; and Editor Bass concluded the book with "Interracial Dating and Marital Relationships: A Lecture". References follow each essay and an index rounds out this book.

5. Bernard, Jessie. Marriage and Family Among Negroes. Englewood Cliffs, NJ: Prentice-Hall, Inc., 1966. 160 pp.

The writer stresses the influence that the unique history of Black people in America has had upon their family life and it reveals a great range of marriage patterns -- including stable husband-wife relationship as well as families which have become matriarchies by default. The author investigates such factors as the forced adaptation to white culture, the retreat of the husband/father, and the presence of "two cultures" within Black people. She depicts the achievements as well as the problems of Black families of all types. Dr. Bernard stresses that data on Black families should not be viewed merely as deviance from a white norm. The best mirror of Black life, she concludes, is the Black himself....

6. Berry, Mary Frances and John W. Blassingame. Long Memory: The Black Experience in America. New York: Oxford University Press, 1982, pp. 8, 70-113.

Chapter 3 is entitled "Family and Church: Enduring Institutions". The authors point out that one of the most important causes of family disorganization is generally overlooked by students. Poor health in the Black community and the extremely high death rate among Black males probably accounted for more family disorganization than any other factor except economic oppression declare the writers. The authors argue that much of the strength of the Black woman and the Afro-American family can be attributed to their roots in the Black church.

7. Bianchi, Suzanne M. Household Composition and Racial Inequality. New Brunswick, NJ: Rutgers University Press, 1981, pp. 3, 5, 10-12, 35-37, 43-58, 59-65, 73-80, 81-87, 105-110, 112-134, 136-137, 145.

Much of the data on the Black family in this book has appeared elsewhere. The author attempts to provide insight into effective strategies for eliminating racial inequalities in economic well-being, inequalities that truly remain a "case for national action." Dr. Bianchi concludes, in part: "...blacks will not fully achieve equality in American society until they are as successful as whites in passing on advantages to their children...."

8. Billingsley, Andrew. Black Families and the Struggle of Survival.
    New York: Friendship Press, 1974. 95 pp.

    This book was written and published for the Committee on Ministries
    with Black families, of the Black Christian Education Project of
    the National Council of Churches. The author sees the goal of the
    Black family life to be able to produce competent individuals who
    can conquer some major aspects of their inner and outer environ-
    ments in order to survive to perpetuate the race and make some con-
    tribution to the larger society....

9. _____. Black Families in White America. Englewood Cliffs,
    NJ: Prentice-Hall, Inc., 1968. 218 pp.

    Dr. Billingsley describes some of the major dimensions of Black
    family life, so that some of the problems and potentials associa-
    ted with different patterns can be more clearly understood and more
    accurately perceived. The author also traces the implications of
    those approaches which may be taken by Blacks themselves, by other
    individuals and organizations interested in Black life and affairs,
    as well as by the governmental agencies whose responsibility it is
    to provide leadership in the development of a viable interracial,
    pluralistic, and democratic society....

10. Billingsley, Andrew and Jeanne M. Giovannoni. Children of the
    Storm: Black Children and American Child Welfare. New York:
    Harcourt, Brace, Jovanovich, 1972. 263 pp.

    Various references are made to Black children and their importance
    in the Black family structure throughout this book. The research-
    ers state that the 1970 United States Census showed that most Black
    children live with both their parents. The proportion of Black
    children growing up in these favorable circumstances ranges from
    60 to 95 percent, depending on such factors as geography and eco-
    nomic status. This simple fact, well known within the Black com-
    munity, has been true with minor variations, for a hundred years,
    ever since the end of slavery. And yet, much of child welfare the-
    ory, planning and programs, and almost all child welfare institu-
    tions are predicated on the assumption that children will be liv-
    ing apart from their parents, argue the authors. They conclude:
    "When Black children are given any special theoretical attention
    at all, and where they are considered as having any parents at all
    (that is, not primarily in need of homes), they are considered as
    having only one parent, namely a mother. A cursory examination of
    the literature and of actual practice will show the pervasiveness
    of this orientation in child welfare...."

11. Blassingame, John W. Slave Testimony: Two Centuries of Letters,
    Speeches, Interviews, and Autobiographies. Baton Rouge: Louisiana
    State University Press, 1977. pp. 12-13, 18-23, 116-119, 145-146,
    164-167, 171-174, 185-190, 211-219, 235-240, 263-265, 325-326, 348-
    349, 385-394, 597.

Blassingame:

The following topics relating to the slave family are discussed:
"Affection among members of the slave family", "Escape of slave
family", "Purchasing freedom of slave family", "Reunion of slave
family", "Search for members of slave family", "Separating members
of slave family", "Mothers and wives of slaves", "Visiting slave
family."

12. Blood, Robert O., Jr. and Donald M. Wolfe. Husbands and Wives:
The Dynamics of Married Living. Glencoe, IL: Free Press, 1960,
pp. 34-36, 66, 91-93, 108-110, 144, 171-172, 182, 195-197, 214-215,
223-224, 255, 272.

The authors rely mainly on E. Franklin Frazier's study on the Black
family in this work. They point out the differences between Black
and White families is the cumulative result of the discrimination
in jobs, the segregated housing, and the poor schooling of Black
men. Hence, they conclude such factors undermine the morale of the
Black male, weakening his position in the eyes of his family to the
place where it is easy for him to desert altogether. Faced with an
undependable husband, the Black wife has become accustomed to having to hold the family together by hard work and responsible decision-making....

13. Bracey, John H. Jr., August Meier and Elliot Rudwick, Editors.
Black Matriarchy: Myth or Reality? Belmont, CA: Wadsworth
Publishing Co., 1971. 217 pp.

All of the essays have been published previously. The articles
are by E. Franklin Frazier, Melville J. Herskovits, Charles S.
Johnson, Lee Rainwater, Elliot Liebow, Daniel P. Moynihan, Hylan
Lewis, Elizabeth Herzog, Herbert H. Hyman, John Shelton Reed, and
Virginia Heyer Young. The editors state that the purpose of this
volume is to illustrate the major point of view concerning the
existence, extent, and nature of a Black matriarchy. Students of
the Black family can then see what the issues are, what the evidence is, and what conclusions can be drawn, suggest the editors.

14. Bromley, David and Charles F. Longino, Jr., Editors. White Racism
and Black Americans. Cambridge, MA: Schenkman Publishing Co.,
1972, pp. 197-290.

The following essays are in this collection: Daniel P. Moynihan,
"The Tangle of Pathology"; William Ryan, "Savage Discovery: The
Moynihan Report"; Lee Rainwater, "Crucible of Identity: The
Negro Lower-Class" and Robert Hill, "The Strengths of Black Fami-
lies." All of these essays have appeared throughout this work.

15. Borchert, James. <u>Alley Life in Washington: Family, Community, Re-</u>
     <u>ligion, and Folklife in the City, 1850-1970</u>. Urbana, IL: Univer-
     sity of Illinois Press, 1980, pp. 57-99.

     Chapter 2 is entitled "Alley Families". The writer observed that
     the alley family was not the "broken," disordered, and irrelevant
     institution that most studies have found. Its order, form, and va-
     lues often differed from those of the mainstream, although certain-
     ly many alley residents approached mainstream values to varying ex-
     tents. The alley family was more flexible than the "ideal" main-
     stream family, if only because its available resources were so
     scarce: to survive, alley families had to expand the numbers of
     people, both related and unrelated, who could help in times of
     need. Certainly similarities between the slave and alley families
     suggest that this continues a practice developed much earlier.
     Simple analysis of family form based on census data therefore pro-
     vides little insight into the real functions of the alley family,
     states Dr. Borchert. He concludes: "Moreover, the existence of rela-
     ted family units in the same or nearby alleys must certainly alter
     the description of the family as only or largely nuclear -- especi-
     ally since these family units, while living apart, acted as exten-
     ded kinship networks, sharing in housework and providing rooms or
     other necessary assistance. Even country relatives were not isola-
     ted from their alley kin, because births, deaths, and family prob-
     lems brought them together...."

16. Burgess, Ernest W. and Harvey J. Locke, <u>The Family: From Institu-</u>
     <u>tion to Companionship</u>. New York: American Book Co., 1963, pp. 77-
     98.

     Chapter 5 discusses "The Negro Family." The authors argue that
     Black family behavior needs to be seen in the perspective of race
     relations as they find expression in slavery, in a caste system, in
     economic and political discrimination, and in residential segrega-
     tion. Even more significant is an appreciation of racial attitudes
     and opinions as they involve conceptions of the role and the beha-
     vior of the whites and of the Blacks. These often include mistakes
     in fact and in interpretation. The writers conclude, chief among
     the mistakes in facts is the tendency to think of Blacks in terms
     of categories and stereotypes. They discuss the history of the
     Black family from Africa to the modern city.

17. Carson, Josephine. <u>Silent Voices: The Southern Negro Woman Today</u>.
     New York: Dell Publishing Co., Inc., 1966. 273 pp.

     The author makes various references to the Black woman and the very
     important role that she plays in the Black family. The author sur-
     mises that Black women could at this moment lead white women to see
     their power and influence. They (Black women), continues the wri-
     ter, have known total repression, abuse, hopelessness, humiliation,
     and endless labor. Miss Carson concludes that they know the human
     race, Americans especially, by way of the back door. We must seek
     them out and aid them and listen to them....

18. Chestang, Leon W. Child Welfare Strategy in the Coming Years.
    Washington, DC: United States Government Printing Office, HEW,
    1979, pp. 169-194.

    There is one section in this work called "The Delivery of Child
    Welfare Services to Minority Group Children and Their Families".
    This essay flows from an analysis that suggests that the child wel-
    fare problems of Black and other minority-group children and fami-
    lies stem from their condition in society, a condition characteri-
    zed by social injustice, discriminatory practices, and the inabili-
    ty of members of these groups to influence the social systems, in-
    cluding child welfare, that impinge on their lives. The author
    argues that, fundamentally, the needs and problems of minority-
    group children, as these concern child welfare, parallel those of
    all children and families in society. He concludes: "Minority sta-
    tus, however, heightens the needs and, in large measure, gives rise
    to many of the unique social problems faced by these groups.
    Therefore, the proposals for improvement focus on these groups.
    However, not until the twin barriers of poverty and racism are re-
    moved will any of the efforts outlined here deal effectively with
    the problems they address. For basic effectiveness, the active
    support of the federal government and public and private advocacy
    groups is crucial. Through the solution of minority-group child
    welfare problems, not only will the lives of these children and
    families be improved, but the quality of life for all members of
    society will be enhanced."

19. Clark, Ann L., Editor. Culture and Childbearing. Philadelphia,
    PA: Davis Co., 1981, pp. 68-95.

    Betty Greathouse and Velvet G. Miller penned Chapter 4 entitled
    "The Black American." The authors basically describe the Black
    family life and childbearing practices in the preslavery, slavery,
    and postslavery periods. Professors Greathouse and Miller dis-
    cussed: Family Structure (Nuclear family, Extended family, Aug-
    mented family, Single parent family). Family size, planning,
    strengths, and childbearing are also discussed.

20. Clark, Reginald. Family Life and School Achievement: Why Poor
    Black Children Succeed or Fail. Chicago: University of Chicago
    Press, 1983. 249 pp.

    The author discusses interaction, home activities, and psychologi-
    cal orientations of ten Black families whose children are either
    high or low school achievers. Clark states that a student's family
    and home environment has some effect on his/her scholastic achieve-
    ment. The researcher surmises that higher achievers' parents have
    high expectations from their children. They expect (1) their child-
    ren to pursue postsecondary education, (2) provide clear role boun-
    daries among family members, (3) maintain a harmonious environment,
    (4) encourage them to participate actively in family discussions,
    (5) monitor their school work and homework, (6) structure achieve-
    ment training activities, and (7) share family responsibilities
    with their children. The low school achievers' parents expected

Clark:

little scholastic achievement from their children. The author concludes, in part: "...the forms and substance of the family psychosocial patterns are the most significant components for understanding the educational effects of high achievers' families and low
achievers' families - not their race or social class background per
se....Learning must first take place in the home and the family,
and then in the school."

21. Clarke, Robert L., Editor. Afro-American History: Sources For
     Research. Washington, DC: Howard University Press, 1981, pp. 123-
     161.

     Chapter 5 deals with the Black family and is called "Afro-American
     Social History Based on Federal Archives: The Family". The fol-
     lowing essays are included: "The Other Side of Slavery", by Andrew
     Billingsley and Marilyn Cynthia Green; Herbert G. Gutman wrote
     "Familial Values of Freedmen and Women"; and Alex Haley essayed
     "Genealogy of Afro-Americans."

22. Coles, Robert. Children of Crisis: A Study of Courage and Fear.
     New York: Dell Publishing Co., 1967, pp. ix, 16, 74-75, 86-90, 98-
     100, 139-146, 321-329, 366-370.

     This book explores the attitudes of people caught up in the tense
     and often violent process of racial strife. The author, a psychia-
     trist, has one section on the Black family, as well as making refe-
     rence to it throughout the book. The Moynihan Report, meaningful-
     ness of children in the family, and absence of father in the family
     are also discussed in this work.

23. _____. The South Goes North. Boston: Little, Brown, and
     Co., 1967, pp. 29, 33-34, 97-98, 121-124, 131-141, 230, 296, 318,
     434, 484-486, 594.

     The author discusses the Black children in the Black family as they
     move from the South to urban Northern cities. The writer suggests
     that many Black children from the South follow the same life style
     of their parents when they grow up and become adult-uneducated,
     jobless and poor.

24. Comer, James P. Beyond Black and White. New York: Quadrangle
     Books, 1972, pp. 22-23, 45-47, 149-150, 163, 169, 173-174, 180-
     181, 226.

     Various references on the Black family are seen throughout the
     book: Man-woman relationships, children, Comer family, momism,
     family planning, mothers, Stoner family. There are footnotes,
     bibliography and index.

25. _____. The Black Family: An Adaptive Perspective. New Haven, CT: Child Study Center, Yale University, 1970. 10 pp.

The author argues that a full description of the task of the Black family and the related adaptive efforts should suggest a family effectiveness assessment that goes beyond levels of illegitimacy, unemployment, crime, etc. In addition, Black family practices, from strict child-rearing approaches to the absent father, might represent adaptive rather than pathological efforts when viewed from this different perspective, states Dr. Comer. According to the writer, at least four major Black family orientations and resultant adaptive efforts emerged after slavery in America: (1) Some Black families turned toward the mainstream and took a total culture orientation with little Black sub-culture or Black church reference. (2) Some Black families maintained a strong Black church tie as well as a total society orientation. (3) A group found their social frame of reference in the Black church or Black sub-culture and operated beyond it only to earn a living. Combined with this group was a non-church going Black sub-culture too complex to describe in detail here. Its organizing force was the "Black world" which emerged from the Black church roots but turned away from the church and the total society. (4) The fourth group was the persistence of a rootless, referenceless, traumatized group with inadequate adaptive capacities....

26. _____ and Alvin F. Poussaint. Black Child Care: How to Bring Up a Healthy Black Child in America: A Guide to Emotional and Psychological Development. New York: Simon and Schuster, 1975. 408 pp.

The title tells what this book is about. These two Black psychiatrists argue that the responsibility of all parents is to help their children develop in a way that will equip them to function well as individuals, family members, and citizens. Parents are most able and willing to do this when they have a sense of belonging that can only be felt when the rights of parents are protected and obstacles to earning a living and respect are not placed in their way. This book was designed to serve as a practical reference guide for parents. The bulk of it is devoted to a stage-by-stage study of the Black child's development from infancy through adolescence, with special emphasis on the role of parents and teachers of school-age children. The authors conclude: "Social problems of poverty and racism continue to affect a great bulk of the black community. But, today blacks are attempting to look beyond the basic struggle for survival and want to participate fully in the dreams and opportunities shared by all citizens. Building strong Black children will help these dreams to come true."

27. Cottle, Thomas J. Black Children, White Dreams. Boston: Houghton Mifflin Co., 1974, 187 pp.

The author studied a number of Black families and individuals in the poor Black section of Boston called Roxbury. These Black individuals express themselves on a variety of topics: school

Cottle:

desegregation, the dangers faced by families, the changes in the North and the South, and in their own city. The writer attempts to describe Blacks' sensitivities to political issues and the ways these issues touch the lives of children and their families in the course of living one day at a time....

28. Crawford, Charles O., Editor. Health and the Family: A Medical-Sociological Analysis. New York: MacMillan Co., 1971, pp. 35-60.

Chapter 3, "The Matrifocal Family in the Black Ghetto: Sign of Pathology or Pattern of Survival," discusses the Black family and was written by Helen I. Safa. The writer points out that the matrifocal family in the Black Ghetto is the PRODUCT of the cycle of poverty and deprivation, rather than its source. Dr. Safa focused on the marginal role of the man in the ghetto and points out at least three principal factors weakening his authority in the family and in the community, resulting from lack of leadership roles and his inability to serve as spokesman for his family in dealing with the outside world; and the threats posed to his domestic role absence of a close tie to children and kin. The author concludes: "If we wish to bring about change in the form of family structure in the Black ghetto, we must attack in the larger society those socio-economic forces that have served to maintain matrifocality: namely, unemployment, low income, poorly paid unskilled jobs, an archaic welfare system, and a limited public role for Black men in their own communities."

29. _____. Health and the Family: A Medical-Sociological Analysis. New York: MacMillan Co., 1971, pp. 175-200.

Chapter 9, "The Black Family Experience and Health Behavior," discusses the Black family and was written by Ira E. Harrison and Diana S. Harrison. The authors surmise that it is most important that health practitioners, administrators, and any other persons responsible for decisions in the organization and provision of health care learn to understand the Black family experience, look for strengths in the Black community, and not view the life of Black persons as a complex of pathologies which must be treated as such. The writers conclude: "Once health officials and the Black community bridge this mental barrier, they will have achieved an important and most necessary and urgent breakthrough in providing Black families with quality health care."

30. David, Paul A., et al. Reckoning with Slavery: A Critical Study in the Quantitative History of American Negro Slavery. New York: Oxford University Press, 1976, pp. 94-133.

Herbert Gutman and Richard Sutch penned "The Slave Family: Protected Agent of Capitalist Masters or Victim of the Slave Trade?" This essay basically discusses Robert W. Fogel and Stanley L. Engerman's Time on the Cross. Gutman and Sutch conclude: "...

David, et al.

to deny that the condition of bondage (slavery) could have totally
transformed the social and psychological meaning of family separation for the blacks who experienced them, giving the legendary geo-
graphical mobility of nineteenth-century Americans a profoundly
different significance for Afro-American people than it had for
other members of our society."

31. Davis, Allison and John Dollard. Children of Bondage: The Personality Development of Negro Youth in the Urban South. Washington,
DC: American Council of Education, 1940. 299 pp.

The researchers attempt to recreate the personalities and to describe the socialization of Black children who lived in New Orleans,
Louisiana, and in Natchez, Mississippi. The authors point out the
importance of the family, the life histories of the families of the
children, the middle and lower-class patriarchal, etc. The writers
believe that in order to change an individual's familial, sexual,
economic, or educational relationships, the social engineers must
first know what his present class-typed habits are and how they are
being reinforced. They will then be in a position to use this
knowledge for the establishment of new modes of behavior. But,
conclue the authors, there can be no new learning with regard to
war, economic relations, education, or family life, unless old habits are first broken and old rewards and punishments withdrawn....

32. _____ and Burleigh B. Gardner. Deep South: A Social Anthropological Study of Caste and Class. Chicago: University of Chicago Press, 1965. (Originally published in 1914), pp. 21, 24, 33-42,
243-247, 388, 409-413, 451-452.

Various references are made throughout the book to the Black family:
color preferences within the family, as an economic unit, free family, family during slavery, immediate family, matriarchal, middle-
class, old upper-class families, patriarchal, family and plantation
controls, weakness of the family as a class sanction, and miscege-
nation. This book deals mainly with the State of Mississippi and
with the various classes of white society and social mobility within the upper caste, as well as the social cliques and the class
system within the Black society....

33. Douglass, Joseph H. The Negro Family's Search for Economic Security.
Washington, DC: United States Department of Health, Education, and
Welfare, 1956. 200 pp.

It was stated that the continued high level of national economic
activity and growth in production should see continued improvement
in the Negro family's economic status, particularly as discriminatory hiring policies are relaxed and the progress being made toward
the improved climate of human relations is accelerated. Dr. Douglas concludes, in part: "...To the extent that the group becomes
organized, vocal and acclimated to urban life, its new-found

Douglas:

political potential should result to a greater degree than at present in its socio-economic self-determination and its overall improved social status...."

34.   Drake, St. Clair, and Horace R. Cayton. Black Metropolis: A Study
      of Negro Life in a Northern City. New York: Harcourt, Brace and
      World, Inc., 1945, pp. 139-143, 557-563, 582-595.

      This study is a comprehensive description of the Chicago Black
      ghetto, its physical characteristics, social organizations and pro-
      cesses. The authors discuss the relationship that those variables
      have on Black family life in Chicago. This work, unlike others,
      combines the discipline of both sociology and anthropology.

35.   DuBois, William E. B. The Negro American Family. Atlanta: Atlan-
      ta University Press, 1908. 156 pp.

      The author attempts to study the family among Black Americans --
      its formation, its home, its economic organization and its daily
      life. This book also attempts to connect present conditions in
      America with the African past. Dr. DuBois sees a distinct nexus
      between Africa and America and it should not be neglected by the
      careful student. The author concludes: "If there be a further
      transition from ignorance, poverty and moral darkness, to enlighten-
      ment, thrift, industry, and improvement of the individual and the
      Negro family, the Church and the Home must unite in a more vigorous
      warfare to reduce to a minimum the prevailing evil of divorce...."

36.   _____. The Philadelphia Negro: A Social Study. Philadel-
      phia: University of Pennsylvania Press, 1899, pp. 164-196.

      Chapter II deals specifically with the Black family: the size of
      the family, incomes, property, and family life. Dr. DuBois points
      out that the mass of Black people must be taught sacredly to guard
      the home (and family), to make it the center of social life and
      moral guardianship. The writer continues, such emphasis undoubted-
      ly means the decreased influence of the Black church, and that is
      a desirable thing. The author concludes that the home was destroy-
      ed by slavery, struggled up after emancipation, and is again not
      exactly threatened, but neglected in the life of city Blacks....

37.   Dunbar, Leslie W., Editor. Minority Report: What Has Happened to
      Blacks, Hispanics, American Indians, and Other Minorities in the
      Eighties. New York: Pantheon Books, 1984, pp. 41-46, 61, 76-81,
      86-88, 108-109.

      The editor suggests that the critical issue is how to diagnose the
      persistence of Black and Hispanic poverty and deprivation. The
      Black situation is better known but not unlike other urban minori-
      ties. One thesis, relying on the cessation of overt practices of

Dunbar:

racial discrimination and the success that many Black people have
had in gaining access to opportunity, holds that the plight of the
underclass is now determined largely by socioeconomic factors such
as the lack of education and skills, rather than by racial factors.
The writer concludes that this theory is wrong at least in part, it
seems, because it fails to take into account two important facts:
first, that a disproportionate number of black people are still in
poverty as a direct result of the caste system and the barriers it
imposes, whose effects are both heritable and real even if the system itself has ended; and second, that people still suffer from racial discrimination which, if less blatant than before, is no less
damaging.

38.   Edwards, E. Franklin, Editor. E. Franklin On Race Relations:
       Selected Writings. Chicago: University of Chicago Press, 1968,
       pp. 119-237.

       Several articles in this collection deal with the Black Family and
       annotations on them have appeared elsewhere in this book: "The
       Negro Family in Chicago"; "The Impact of Urban Civilization upon
       Negro Family Life"; "The Negro Family in America"; "Certain Aspects
       of Conflicts in the Negro Family" and "Problems and Needs of Negro
       Children and Youth Resulting from Family Disorganization."

39.   Fanshel, David. A Study of Negro Adoption. New York: Child Wel-
       fare League of America, Inc., 1957. 108 pp.

       This book was based on a five year study between 1951-55 of the
       outcome of contacts initiated by 224 Black couples interested in
       adoption through the Family and Children Service. The author
       studied the characteristics of Black couples who succeeded in adopt-
       ing children as compared to those who withdrew their applications
       or who were rejected by the agency. A similar analysis was also
       made of 183 white couples for comparative purposes.

40.   Fantini, Mario D. and Renee Cardenas, Editors. Parenting in a
       Multicultural Society. New York: Longman, Inc., 1980, pp. 43-53,
       120-137.

       There are two essays in this volume on Black families. The first
       one is by James F. Comer and is entitled "The Black Family: An
       Adaptive Perspective". This essay is a revision of an earlier pu-
       blication and is mentioned elsewhere in this work. The second es-
       say was written by Magdalene Carney and Elizabeth Bowen and they
       deal with "Implications for National Policy Decisions: The Black
       Family Perspective". The writers examine some of the realities af-
       fecting Black family life in the United States and on the basis of
       that examination suggest recommendations to guide and influence po-
       licy-making at the national level. They conclude that the single
       greatest impediment to the establishment of a national family policy
       that deals with Black equitably is injustice....

41. Farley, Reynolds. <u>Growth of the Black Population</u>. Chicago:
     Markham Publishing Co., 1970, pp. 166-191.

     There is one chapter that deals specifically with the Black family,
     "The Process of Family Formation." The author came to several con-
     clusions in this book. First, there is considerable agreement that
     Black women desire to have stable marriages and reasonably sized
     families. In general, there seemed to be no desire for very large
     families; rather, Blacks apparently want to have approximately the
     same sized families as whites. Second, the characteristics of
     higher socioeconomic status undoubtedly engender greater marital sta-
     bility; elevated socioeconomic standing is obviously not a necessary
     and sufficient condition for stable marriages and small families.
     Third, among Black women in the early stages of family building,
     their fertility depended chiefly upon their age at marriage, al-
     though among these young women education did have a small signifi-
     cant effect, suggesting that even early in marriage educational at-
     tainment led to control of fertility.

42. Ferman, Louis, A., et al. <u>Poverty in America: A Book of Readings</u>.
     Ann Arbor: University of Michigan Press, 1986, pp. 394-442.

     Various references are made throughout the book to Black men, wo-
     men, children, and the family: description of population and gene-
     ral data, education, employment and unemployment, income, residence
     and communities, fatherless, and to mothers. There are also seve-
     ral specific articles in this book of readings on the Black family,
     as well as a Selected Bibliography at the end of each chapter.

43. Frazier, E. Franklin. <u>The Negro Family in the United States</u>.
     Chicago: University of Chicago Press, 1939, 372 pp.

     This book was the classic work on the Black family until recently.
     Many of the theories are outdated. This book has "Selected:
     Family-History Documents," "Supplementary Statistical Tables,"
     "A Classified Bibliography," and an Index.

44. _____. <u>The Free Negro Family</u>. New York: Arno Press and The
     New York Times, 1968. 75 pp.

     This is a study of Black family origins before and after the Civil
     War. Measurements of the changes in Black family resulting from
     urbanization in relation to the economic social and organization
     of the Black community in the city are also discussed....

45. _____. <u>The Negro Family in Chicago</u>. Chicago: University of
     Chicago Press, 1932. 294 pp.

     The author concludes that Black families became disorganized and
     unstable as they moved to the city. Frazier also believed that the
     disorganization of the Black family was part of the process of se-
     lection and segregation of those elements in the Black population

Frazier:

which have become emancipated from the traditional status of the masses. Moreover, he surmises that the disorganization of the Black family in Chicago was closely tied up with the economic and social structure of the Black community....

46. _____. Black Bourgeoisie. New York: Free Press, 1957. 264 pp.

The essence of this work is that the Black middle-class as well as the Black middle-class family exhibits most strikingly the inferiority complex of those who would escape their racial identification. Dr. Frazier concludes that this element, the Black middle-class, has striven more than any other element among Blacks to make itself over in the image of whites....

47. _____. Negro Youth at the Crossways. Washington, DC: American Council on Education, 1940, pp. 5, 20, 41-55, 56-69, 278-279.

There are many references to the Black family throughout this book. Chapter I, "The Negro Community," has some discussion of the Black community in terms of its character; urbanization in North and South; migration patterns, social stratification and the relation of the Black community to the white world. Chapter II, "The Role of the Family," focuses on the influence of the Black woman and family upon the personal responses of Black youths to their minority status. Dr. Frazier makes several conclusions: In lower-class families the parents undertake to pass on to their children their attitudes of accommodation to an inferior status; their children, however, reject this notion and rebel. In middle-class families the parents are less inclined to teach their children to eschew the ways of lower-class Blacks and win the respect of whites by acting according to conventional standards. In upper-class families the parents undertake to shield their children against the more subtle as well as the cruder forms of discrimination; they conceal racial identity from the child.

48. Gary, Lawrence E., Editor. Black Men. Beverly Hills, CA: Sage Publications, 1981, pp. 73-138.

Part Two is called "Black Men and Their Families" and includes the following articles: "Black Male and Female Relationships: An Afrocentric Context" was written by Molefi K. Asante; Ronald L. Braithwaite penned "Interpersonal Relations Between Black Males and Black Females". "Moms, Dads, and Boys: Race and Sex Differences in the Socialization of Male Children" was essayed by Walter R. Allen; John L. McAdoo contributed "Black Father and Child Interactions"; "Black Unwed Adolescent Fathers" was written by Leo E. Hendricks.

49. Gary, Lawrence E., Editor. Mental Health: A Challenge to The
     Black Community. Philadelphia: Dorrance and Co., 1978, pp. 18, 60-
     62, 73-94, 97-99, 104-111, 130, 172, 193, 324-326, 350.

     Various references are made to the Black family throughout this
     book, including the extended family, female headed household, nu-
     clear family, family life, family structure and adolescence.
     There is also a specific chapter in this collection written by
     Robert Staples, entitled, "Black Family Life and Development."
     Prof. Staples states that the Black family is dialectically linked
     to the functioning of internal colonialism. The relationship be-
     tween changes in the economic order and Black family functioning
     is quite clear. What is not understood is that culture is a two-
     edged sword: it can act as a mechanism for survival or as an ap-
     paratus of control, argues Dr. Staples. To the extent that Blacks
     forsake the family and the role they must play in it, the greater
     will be their vulnerability to the racial colonialism. Diffused
     groups of peoples who are detached from their cultural roots are
     powerless to resist the forces of oppression that they must eventu-
     ally encounter in a society which is based on race and class ex-
     ploitation. The family represents the basic collectivization of
     the Black community and contains within it the potential for Black
     survival in a world composed of the colonizers and the colonized,
     concludes the author.

50. _____. Editor. Social Research and the Black Community:
     Selected Issues and Priorities. Washington, DC: Institute for
     Urban Affairs and Research, Howard University, 1973, pp. 39-87.

     Part II is called "Socialization and Black Family Life" and in-
     cludes the following essays: "Beyond Pathology: Research and
     Theoretical Perspectives on Black Families", by Richard English;
     Brin Hawkins and Inabel Lindsey discuss "Research Issues Relating
     to the Black Age"; "The Socialization of Black Children: Priorities
     for Research" was penned by Harriette McAdoo; the final essay deals
     with "Socialization of the Black Male: Research Implications" by
     Gwendolyn Cooke.

51. Geismar, Ludawig. 555: A Social-Psychological Study of Young
     Families in Transition. New Brunswick, NJ: Transaction Books,
     1973. 267 pp.

     This work was a study of 555 families in Newark, New Jersey. The
     research population was 61 percent Black, 35 percent White and 4
     percent Spanish-speaking, mostly Puerto Rican. The author suggests
     that many of these families were well functioning entities. Prof.
     Geismar surmises that intergenerational continuity was clearly
     demonstrated through a comparison of the young families unity with
     their respective families of origin....

52. Gibson, William. <u>Family Life and Morality: Studies in Black and White</u>. Washington, DC: University Press of America, 1980. 109 pp.

The author deals with the concept of the American family, with emphasis on the Black family, addressing the customary issues of illegitimacy, views and attitudes, pathological weakness in Black family structure and disorganization in simple language. Many of the issues-problems discussed are increasingly being publicized and the general public is more aware of them than in the past. But, dealing with them under one cover is important for a total picture and a total understanding, believes Dr. Gibson. The approach is from a historical perspective, dealing with the scholarly output of the past as well as the more current scholarly output on the Black family. The first chapter is an attempt to deal with the historical background from the slave experience through the 1920s. The intent is to take the numerous variables that Black Americans had to contend with historically in their efforts to maintain a family kinship and, more importantly, even to survive. This meant that the various issues-problems faced had to be picked up and taken to some kind of a conclusion. Therefore, this approach might appear to be disjointed in many parts, but it is necessary, he believes, in order to lay the foundation of the Black experience. Chapters two through five deal more with the specific issues mentioned above, with the concluding chapter going into the origin of the family concept and the definition of family. The last chapter also emphasizes that Black Americans are the oldest continuous immigrant group, growing-expanding with the country, without dual loyalties.

53. Giddings, Paula. <u>When and Where I Enter ... The Impact of Black Women on Race and Sex in America</u>. New York: William Morrow, 1984, pp. 24, 42, 57, 79, 148-151, 252-256, 314, 324-335.

The author discusses the Black family and its relationship to a variety of topics: the Black family being abandoned by fathers, Black family and lodgers, Black family and slavery, Black family under stress - then and now. Chapter 18 deals specifically with the Black family and is entitled "Strong Women and Strutting Men: The Moynihan Report." She states that the Moynihan Report perpetuated the misconception that the success of Black women, not racism, was responsible for the problems of Blacks....

54. Ginzberg, Eli, et. al. <u>The Middle-Class Negro in the White Man's World</u>. New York: Columbia University Press, 1967. pp. 1-18, 96-126.

The authors interviewed 40 high school seniors, college sophomores, and college seniors living in Atlanta and New York City to examine the reactions of a group of middle-class Black college youths to the reality they confront. Using actual excerpts from the interviews, the authors describe the family backgrounds of the youths, with special emphasis on the educational level of their parents and of their families; their choices of college, fields of study, and plans for graduate work; their attitudes toward marriage and children and the roles they expect to play in the community; and their

Ginzberg, et al.:

feelings about the race question and the Civil Rights movement.
The authors conclude that the goals of middle-class Black youths
are conditioned by their background and education, not bv the sole
factor of race.

55.   Gordon, Michael, Editor. The American Family in Social-Historical
Perspective. New York: St. Martin's Press, 1978, pp. 441-489.

There are two articles in this collection that deal with the Black
family: "The Beginnings of the Afro-American Family in Maryland"
by Allan Kulikoff and "Persistent Myths About the Afro-American
Family". Prof. Kulikoff states that the beginning of the Afro-
American family in Maryland started sometime in 1728 when Harry, a
slave, escaped from his master in southern Prince George's County....

56.   Grier, William H. and Price M. Cobbs.   Black Rage.   New York:
Basic Books, Inc., 1968, pp. 75-101.

Various references are made to Black men, women and children
throu5hout the book. Chapter V, "Marriage and Love," deals specifically with the Black family. The authors point out that all
Black families in the United States face the task of establishing a
family in a nation that is institutionally opposed to this fundamental function of the Black family. Moreover, continue the writers, a program for strengthening Black families would have to include a change in the fabric of the nation so that a Black man
could extend physical protection to his family everywhere, throughout the country. The doctors conclude that in spite of the problems facing them, Black couples continue to marry, establish families, try to make a worthwhile contribution to the stream of life,
etc.

57.   Gutman, Herbert G.   The Black Family in Slavery and Freedom, 1750-
1925. New York: Pantheon Books, 1976.   664 pp.

A study of the Black family based around the study of six plantations in Virginia, North Carolina, Alabama, Louisiana, and South
Carolina. The writer used quantitative records, from the United
States Census, slave plantation journals, books, letters of slaves
who wrote each other, testimony given to Government commissions
and observations of foreign travelers, and the mythology of the
Black family. The author spends more time showing what the Black
family was not and little what it was. The slave family and kinship system, he argues, was so wide-spread, so sturdy, so reasona-
ble, and so close at hand that it offered an alternative to the
planter's ideology. Gutman shows how slaves strove to maintain
and pass down kin names, how individuals forced together created
appellations of "aunt", "uncle", and "cousin", for each other, and
how these preserved or created tissues of family identity formed a
basis for defining obligations between people in the larger slave
community. The Black Family in Slavery and Freedom, 1750-1925,
is one of the major "definitive" works on the subject. The author,

Gutman:

however, attempted to cover too much material in this 664 page
book and left many unanswered questions on the Black family.

58. _____. Slavery and the Numbers Game: A Critique of Time on
the Cross. Urbana: University of Illinois Press, 1975, pp. 84-164.

Section 4 discusses "The Slave Family, Slave Sexual Behavior, and
Slave Sales." The author contends that the writers of Time on the
Cross whole argument about the stable family rests entirely on du-
bious quantitive data meant to show a low incidence of familial
and marital breakup by owners. Gutman also argues that Time on the
Cross barely begins to examine seriously the development of an adaptive family and kinship system among enslaved Afro-Americans. The
author concludes that a number of variables and pertinent questions
were not dealt with by Time on the Cross and that is why it is so
inadequate an analysis of "the slave family."

59. Guttentag, Marcia and Paul F. Secord. Too Many Women? The Sex
Ratio Question. Beverly Hills, CA: Sage Publications, 1983,
pp. 199-230.

According to the researchers, the majority of Black marriages will
endure until the death of one of the spouses. It is easy to lose
sight of this when looking at indices of family disruption. Despite this state of affairs, the low sex ratios for the Black population prevailing for several decades and becoming worse in the
1970s appear to have had profound effects on the relationships between men and women. The form that these have taken is, of course,
partially shaped by a number of other social/economic factors that
characterize the Black population, argues the author. Given the
depressed incomes of Black people, the lower educational levels
achieved, and the restricted opportunities, the shortages of Black
men reflected in the low sex ratios have made an appreciable number
of them reluctant to commit themselves to relationships with Black
women, especially marital ones, just as they are reluctant to support children. The large oversupply of Black women makes such com-
mitments unnecessary. They concluded: "The only important sense
in which being Black contributes to this social complex is that
Black people have been objects of racial prejudice in our society,
which in turn has created many of the unfavorable social/economic
conditions under which they live. These have aggravated the social
consequences of the long-time low sex ratios in the Black population."

60. Hale, Janice E. Black Children: Their Roots, Culture, and
Learning Styles. Provo, Utah: Brigham Young University, 1982,
pp. 10, 46, 48-54, 109-113, 121, 134, 138, 149.

The writer argues that Black parents have always stressed to their
children the importance of their exceeding white children's

Hale:

behavior and performance because falling short would reflect unfa-
vorably upon the group. It was also pointed out that a strong
achievement orientation is a strength of Black families. Black
families place a strong emphasis on work and ambition. Black
child-rearing has a strong religious orientation, concludes the
author.

61. Haley, Alex. Roots: The Saga of an American Family. New York:
     Doubleday, 1976. 688 pp.

     The author traces his ancestral roots from Gambia, Africa to a
     Virginia plantation. Along with discussing his family history, he
     shares the history of this country, including slavery, that was be-
     ing made and the various interactions of Black-White relations.
     This book takes us through the Civil War and into the Reconstruc-
     tion era, when a wagon train took about twenty ex-slave families
     to establish new and improved free lives for themselves in the
     small town of Henning, Tennessee....

62. Harrison-Ross, Phyllis and Barbara Wyden. The Black Child--A
     Parent's Guide. New York: Peter H. Wyden, Inc., Publisher, 1973,
     360 pp.

     This is a collection of cases drawn almost wholly from their cli-
     nic practice and work with both Black and white underprivileged
     children in Headstart and daycare programs in the ghetto areas of
     New York City. The authors, one Black and one white, discuss why
     Black parents have very special problems in raising their children
     and what Black parents want for their children. Other suggested
     readings, related films, and Index are also included in this work.

63. Heiss, Jerold. The Case of the Black Family: A Sociological In-
     quiry. New York: Columbia University Press, 1975. 246 pp.

     The author attempts to resolve the controversy over the extent of
     which the Black family structure has influenced the place of Blacks
     in this country. This work was based on a broad survey of northern
     metropolitan Black families.

64. Herzog, Elizabeth, Cecilia Sudia, Jane Harwood, and Carol Newcomb.
     Families for Black Children: The Search for Adoptive Parents.
     Washington, DC: A cooperative report of the Division of Research
     and Evaluation, The George Washington University, 1969. 85 pp.

     This was a survey that was part of the effort by the Office of
     Child Development to increase the number of adoptive families avail-
     able for Black children in need of placement.

65. Hill, Robert B. The Strengths of Black Families. New York: Emerson Hall Publishers, Inc., 1972. 76 pp.

The author analyzed and interpreted data relating to the manner in which Black families have been able to survive in a hostile environment. Dr. Hill deals mainly with five traits as Black family strengths. The writer contends that strength and stability, not weakness and instability are the model patterns for both low-income and middle-income Black families. The author also disagrees with many social scientists on the strengths of the Black family. Hill concludes that the great majority of Black families are not characterized by criminality, delinquency, drug addiction or desertion....

66. _____. Black Families in the 1974-75 Depression: Special Policy Report. New York: National Urban League, 1975. 76 pp.

This report examined the cumulative effects of the recessions of 1969-71 and 1974-75 on the economic status of Black families. The author contends that the proportion of multiple-earner Black families continued to decline during 1974, while the proportion of multiple-earner white families increased. Thus, whites now have a higher proportion of families with two or more earners than Blacks. He concludes that while the rest of the nation was experiencing an acute recession, the Black community was being racked by a "depression" of profound dimensions.

67. Horten, James O. and Lois E. Horten. Black Bostonian: Family Life and Community Struggle in the Ante-Bellum North. New York: Holmes and Meier Publishers, 1979. 175 pp.

The author pointed out for most Black Bostonians, families and households were central to social relations and community life. Poverty and discrimination did not force disorganization, but often actually encouraged organization. It was also suggested that twentieth-century Blacks worked through extensive survival networks, cooperation and mutual aid. A variety of strategies was occasioned by the necessity to cope with a hostile social and economic environment. Family and household arrangements provided many of these strategies. Where possible, Blacks established institutions to serve their needs, supplementing the family's role and Black people into a community of shared disadvantage, conclude the researchers.

68. Howard, Victor B. Black Liberation in Kentucky: Emancipation and Freedom, 1862-1884. Lexington, KY: University Press of Kentucky, 1983, pp. 108-129.

There is a chapter called "Families in Transition". It was pointed out that with the end of slavery the Black family was able to exercise its freedom of choice for the first time without interference and without having others impose decisions concerning the most intimate affairs of daily life. This new freedom was reflected in many changes in the relationship of husband and wife. The male quickly assumed the role of the head of the house; his wife usually worked

Howard:

within the home or at other domestic pursuits, states Dr. Howard.
The gang system of labor was discontinued, and the family became
tenant farmers, working a plot of land separated from those of
other tenants. A cabin was built or was moved to the plot from the
communal rows that had composed the slave community. Thus, the
family withdrew into privacy, and family life replaced communal
life. At the same time, Black families moved swiftly to develop
autonomous religious bodies by separating from the white churches,
concludes the author.

69.   Jeffers, Camille. Living Poor: A Participant Observer Study of
       Priorities and Choices. Ann Arbor, MI: Ann Arbor Publishers,
       1967. 123 pp.

During the 1960's the author lived in a public-housing project in
Washington, DC so that she might observe the project families.
Mrs. Jeffers was a staff member of the Child Rearing Study of the
Health and Welfare Council of the National Capitol Area. The staff
member carried out the aim of the council by observing how various
kinds of low-income families cope with the problems of child rearing and to discover what kinds of improvement programs were prac-
ticable....

70.   Johnson, Charles S. Crowing Up in the Black Belt. New York:
       Schocken Books, 1967. (Originally written in 1941), pp. 2, 6-9,
       12-15, 23-24, 58-63, 80, 193-196, 206-208, 220-223.

Various references to the Black family seen throughout this book:
family income and educational opportunity, founding a cropper family, family links, home setting, family training, family pattern,
family organization and status, home maladjustment and socio-
economic levels, female domination in family, problems of adolescents in family, women heads of family. This book deepens our understanding of Black people, and especially the Black family in the
rural South.   There are a number of Tables, Charts and Appendices
included in this book.

71.   _____. Shadow of the Plantation. Chicago: University of
       Chicago Press, 1934, pp. 1-102.

Chapter I makes various references to the Black family: types of
family structure, stable old families with strong affectional ties
and a family tradition, families with strong maternal dominance and
with specific moral codes, quasi-families, female heads of assembled
families, male heads of transient family with shifting family members, stable non-legal unions, non-agricultural families, stable
legal unions, disorganized legal unions, stable families with ad-
vanced standards. Chapter II is devoted entirely to the Black family: courtship and marriage, the children, separation and divorce,
what is respectable, shelter and food.

72. Johnson, Daniel M. and Rex R. Campbell. Black Migration in Ameri-
     ca: A Social Demographic History. Durham, NC: Duke University
     Press, 1981, pp. 13, 19-21, 31-37, 47, 65, 78-84, 95, 105, 110,
     119, 121-122, 137-138, 140-148, 169.

     The authors discuss the Black family from Africa through the 1960s.
     They suggest that economic factors were the major reason why Blacks
     migrated.... The researchers state that the revolution of rising
     expectations, associated in large part with migration to urban
     areas, also has been destructive of Black families....

73. Johnson, Willa D. and Thomas L. Green, Editors. Perspectives on
     Afro-American Women. Washington, DC: ECC Associates, Inc., 1975.
     197 pp.

     Various references are made to the Black woman and her role in the
     Black family throughout this collection. Two essays deal specifi-
     cally with the Black family: "The Status of Black Women: Sex,
     Marriage and the Family", by Robert Staples; and "The Role of Black
     Women in Black Families: Teaching About Black Families on a Predo-
     minantly White Campus", by Priscilla White and Patricia Scott.

74. Jones, Jacqueline. Labor of Love, Labor of Sorrow: Black Women,
     Work, and the Family From Slavery to the Present. New York:
     Basic Books, 1985. 432 pp.

     The writer argues that the greatest problems facing poor Black wo-
     men in 1984 are embedded in the nation's social and economic struc-
     ture, and thus do not lend themselves to locally initiated, or
     piecemeal, solutions. The stop-gap measures of the welfare state
     will no longer rescue Black people from the inexorable workings of
     the economy. Labor unions act on behalf of those who already have
     jobs, not those altogether dispossessed by the labor market. Resi-
     dential segregation, a segmented work force, the inequitable fund-
     ing of public education - all these problems call for federal plan-
     ning and federal support. She concludes: "Thus the solutions to
     these problems are by definition radical ones - for instance, a
     massive public works program administered without discrimination
     on the basis of race or sex, institution of a "solidarity wage" to
     narrow the gap between the pay scales of lower- and upper-echelon
     workers, and the migration of blacks out of the inner cities and
     the migration of working-class as well as young professional whites
     into the cities...."

75. Kardiner, Abram and Lionel Ovesey. The Mark of Oppression: Explo-
     rations in the Personality of the American Negro. New York: Nor-
     ton, 1951, pp. 20, 39-59, 64-66, 159, 182, 188, 305, 311, 385-386.

     The researchers discuss "Black Broken Homes", "Constellation", "Dis-
     turbance", "Factors", "Female-centered", "Grandmother-centered",
     "Lower class", "Family under slavery", and "Family of Urban Negro."

76. Kennedy, Theodore R. <u>You Gotta Deal With It: Black Family Rela-
     tionship in a Southern Community</u>. New York: Oxford University
     Press, 1980. 215 pp.

     This book was based upon a year's study in a small southern town.
     The author changed the names of the people to protect them from
     being recognized. Four Black families give most of the dialogue
     in this work. The families discuss many topics: white people, Ku
     Klux Klan, violence, children, elderly, jobs, education, religion,
     marriage, etc.

77. Kephart, William M. <u>The Family, Society, and the Individual</u>.
     Boston: Houghton-Mifflin Co., 1972, pp. 183-212.

     Chapter 8, "Minority Family Types II - Race," discusses the Black
     family from slavery to the future. The author believes that it
     will be many decades before the overall level of Black family-sta-
     bility reaches that of whites. In the meantime, concludes Professor
     Kephart, the sooner the magnitude of the problem is realized, the
     sooner the necessary steps can be taken--by all thoughtful Ameri-
     cans for amelioration.

78. Kriesberg, Louis. <u>Mothers in Poverty</u>. Chicago: Aldine Publishing
     Co., 1970, 356 pp.

     This book discusses Black mothers and children in poor fatherless
     families in Syracuse, New York. The author attempts to explain the
     life of Black poor people and the possible role their way of life
     plays in the inter-generational transmission of poverty. Professor
     Kriesberg emphasizes the contemporary circumstances that make Black
     families poor, keep them poor, and to which they respond. The
     author concludes that because a child comes from a broken home and
     a poor family does not mean that he and his family will live in
     poverty forever.

79. Kronus, Sidney. <u>The Black Middle Class</u>. Columbus, OH: Charles
     E. Merrill Co., 1970. 182 pp.

     Much of his work focuses on the family life of middle-class Blacks.
     The author did case studies on various middle-class Blacks. Kro-
     nus devoted an entire chapter to one specific middle-class Black
     man. This chapter illustrated the generic development of a Black
     middle-class man, Robert Black, by revealing the factors that have
     molded the life of this individual within his cultural setting.
     This book has questionnaires, indexes, Bibliography and subject
     index.

80. Ladner, Joyce A. <u>Tomorrow's Tomorrow: The Black Woman</u>. Garden
     City, New York: Doubleday & Co., 1971. 296 pp.

     Various references are made throughout the book to the Black fami-
     ly: Africa, as disorganized, extended, importance to Blacks, as

Ladner:

matriarchal effects of slavery on family, family and socialization
of children, female-headed households, parental control, liberation
from family, income, fathers, illegitimacy. Dr. Lander concludes
that in many ways the Black woman is the "carrier of culture" because it has been she who has epitomized what it meant to be Black,
oppressed and yet given some small opportunity to negotiate the
different demands which society placed upon all Black people. The
Black woman, continues the writer, is again emerging as an important figure within the family and community.

81. Lake, Robert W. The New Suburbanites: Race and Housing in the
     Suburbs. New Brunswick, NJ: Rutgers University, Center for Urban
     Policy Research, 1981, pp. 5-11, 14-27, 47-69, 107-136, 240-242.

     It was declared that suburban Blacks are on the average younger and
     live in larger families than their suburban White counterparts, and
     are more likely than Whites to live in female-headed families.
     While about 10 percent of all suburban White families are female-
     headed households, a fourth of Black families in the suburbs of
     small Standard Metropolitan Statistical Areas (SMSA) and nearly
     a third of those in the suburbs of large SMSA's are female-headed,
     concludes the researcher.

82. Lawden, Elizabeth A., Janet L. Hoopes, Roberta G. Andrews,
     Katherine D. Lower and Susan Y. Perry. A Study of Black Adoption
     Families: A Comparison of a Traditional and a Quasi-Adoption
     Program. New York: Child Welfare League of America, 1971. 77 pp.

     This study related to the problems encountered by Black couples
     desiring to adopt Black children. This study was also designed to
     increase the confidence of these families in taking the necessarily
     formal legal steps that are a part of adoption.

83. Lawrence, Margaret Morgan. Young Inner City Families: Development
     of Ego Strength Under Stress. New York: Behavioral Publications,
     Inc., 1975. 139 pp.

     Most of the families discussed in this work are Black and Hispanic
     and live in Harlem, New York. The author, a Black female medical
     doctor, narrates some of the hazards of early child development in
     New York. She recalls the struggles of an interdisciplinary mental
     health team as it attempts to assess the damage to these families,
     their infants and young children. Dr. Lawrence states that persons
     trained in the mental health disciplines are bound to work to some
     extent on two fronts: the one for which their disciplines have
     specifically prepared them, and the other to be shared with larger
     segments of the community, a front that is dedicated to fundamental
     social change. She concludes: "Respect and dynamic understanding
     of individuals, their strengths and needs, informs social approach-
     es. Awareness of community needs enriches our support of the
     strength of individuals. Will the strengths of young Harlem

Lawrence:

families survive until significant changes in hazardous social patterns and institutions occur? We are committed to this faith, and
from it derive our hope."

84. Leigh, James W. and James W. Green. Cultural Awareness in the
Human Services: A Training Manual. Seattle, WA: Center for Social Welfare Research, School of Social Work, University of Washington, 1979, pp. 119-169.

The authors discuss "The Black Family and Social Work". The writers state that social workers have a professional responsibility
to become familiar with the Black press, literature, and music,
where expression of the main currents of Black life are reflected.
This background is essential for the social worker in gaining an
understanding of the real problems affecting the client. They conclude: "But social workers especially need to understand that
there is a great need to develop the intervention techniques that
will be helpful with Black clients. Cultural sensitivity is simply the first step in that direction. Beyond that the sensitive
worker will want to know how to mobilize a particular client, a
family, or an entire family network for work on resolving a problem.
Some problems may be treated best by individual therapy, some by
group action. When are these options important and how does the
worker utilize them in dealing with critical issues? Cultural
sensitivity is a beginning in devising more effective helping techniques for resolving the problems of people in a pluralistic society."

85. Lewis, Hylan. Blackways of Kent. Chapel Hill, University of North
Carolina Press, 1955. 337 pp.

This is an account of Black life in the South "from the inside."
Kent, a pseudonym, was chosen by the author because it seems to
embody most of the cultural aspects, characteristics of a "typical"
community in the Piedmont area of the South. There is one section,
"Courtship, Marriage, and the Family", that deals specifically with
Black family life. In this area of the South, the family assumes
a number of forms or features: the extended family, the multiple
family, the family with a skipped generation, the family with half-
brothers and half-sisters or adopted children, boarding out, and
dual family names. Professor Lewis concludes that the Kent Black
family tends to have the child seek satisfactions and goals within
the framework of the local situation. The typical family is no
organ of frontal attack on discrimination, the imparting of resent-
ment and bitterness is indirect and incidental, and it is not a
part of child-rearing doctrine and practice.

86. Lewis, Jerry M. and John G. Looney. The Long Struggle: Well-
Functioning Working-Class Black Families. New York: Brunner/
Mazel, 1983. 193 pp.

Lewis and Looney:

The authors identified and interviewed Black families with adolescent children in Texas. The psychiatrist-writers stressed that Black families are not homogeneous and they should not be studied as such. It was suggested that there were many differences between the well-functioning and dysfunctional Black families. Black working-class families were compared to white working-class families and it was found that both exhibited patterns of interaction similar to upper and middle-class white families. They argue that despite adverse socio-economic conditions, the well-functioning Black families managed to employ coping strategies that are used to strengthen the family structure....

87.   Liebow, Elliot. Tally's Corner: A Study of Negro Streetcorner Men. Boston: Little, Brown and Co., 1967, pp. 72-137.

The writer discusses the personal and family lives of about two dozen Black men who shared a corner in Washington, DC's Second Precinct between 1962 and 1963. Dr. Liebow collected much of this data when he was a fieldworker for the research project "Child Rearing Practices Among Low Income Families in the District of Columbia."

88.   Litwack, Leon F. Been in the Storm So Long: The Aftermath of Slavery. New York: Alfred A. Knopf, 1979, pp. 7-8, 33, 54, 204, 230-240, 244-247, 305-307.

The writer points out that after slavery many former slaves attempted to locate their family members. Prof. Litwack declares: "No matter how they manifested their freedom, black men and women found themselves in a better position (after slavery) to defend their marital fidelity, to maintain their family ties, and to control their own children. That in itself ensured an enhanced dignity and pride as a family that slavery had so often compromised...."

89.   Lopata, Helena Z., Editor. Marriage and Families. New York: D. Van Nostrand Co., 1973, pp. 113-120, 275-324.

Five essays in this collection deal with Black families: Ulf Hannerz, "Roots of Black Manhood"; Gerald D. Suttles, "Anatomy of a Chicago Slum"; Paul Leman, "Child Convicts"; Harris Chaiklin, et al., "Violence and Inner City Families"; and Frances Fox Piven, "The Relief of Welfare".

90.   McAdoo, Harriette Pipes, Editor. Black Families. Beverly Hills, CA: Sage Publications, 1981. 303 pp.

The following articles are included in this collection: "Conceptualization of Black Families", was contributed by Jualynne Dodson; "Interpreting the African Heritage in Afro-American Family Organization", was penned by Niara Sudarkasa; "Old-Time Religion: Benches

Pipes:

Can't Say "Amen", was essayed by William Harrison Pipes; "Afro-
American Family Life: An Instrument of Culture," was written by
Wade W. Nobles; "Perspectives on Black Family Empirical Research:
1965-1978" was detailed by Leanor Boulin Johnson; Paul Glick in-
cluded "A Demographic Picture of Black Families"; Frank G. Davis
added "Economics and Mobility: A Theoretical Rationale For Urban
Black Family Well-Being." John U. Ogbu essayed "Black Education:
A Cultural-Ecological Perspective." Harriette Pipes McAdoo offered
"Patterns of Upward Mobility in Black Families." Robert Staples
did "Race and Marital Status: An Overview"; "Black Men in America:
The Quest for 'Manhood'", was written by Noel A. Cazenave; "Women's
Values Regarding Marriage and the Family" was essayed by Jerold
Heiss; Algea Harrison contributed "Attitudes Toward Procreation
Among Black Adults"; Marie F. Peters penned "Parenting in Black
Families with Young Children: A Historical Perspective"; "Involve-
ment of Fathers in the Socialization of Black Children" was penned
by John L. McAdoo; Wilhelmina Manns wrote "Support Systems of Sig-
nificant Others in Black Families"; "Group Identity Development
Within Black Families" was contributed by James S. Jackson, Wayne
R. McCullough, and Gerald Gurin; Robert B. Hill wrote "Multiple
Public Benefits and Poor Black Families"; "Policies Affecting the
Status of Black Children and Families" was penned by Evelyn K.
Moore; Marian Wright Edelman added "An Advocacy Agenda for Black
Families and Children." The editor suggests that this book addres-
ses some unresolved issues regarding Black families.... A careful
reading of the chapters will reveal fundamental unresolved-and
some probably unresolved-differences in frames of reference to
Black families represented by the authors, states Dr. McAdoo.

91. McCord, William, et al. Life Styles in the Black Ghetto. New
     York: W.W. Norton and Company, Inc., 1969, pp. 21-32, 200-204.

Many references are made to the Black family throughout this book:
family structure of urban Blacks, the family and crime, instability
in the family, interpersonal distrust of the family, matrifocal
structure of the family, sources of stability in the family. This
work has notes at the end of the thirteen chapters, Questionnaires,
an Annotated Bibliography, and Index.

92. McLaughlin, Clara J., et al. The Black Parents' Handbook: A
     Guide to Healthy Pregnancy, Birth, and Child Care. New York: Har-
     court, Brace, Jovanovich, 1976. 220 pp.

The authors discuss the role of the father and mother in the family. They point out that a father should teach his child not only
how to live, but also how to make a living. The child will love
and respect his father regardless of his financial status. The researchers believe that it is the mother's responsibility to point
out her child's strengths and teach him (or her) the art of surviv-
ing. It was also suggested that parents are teachers and they
should instill positive ideas into their children....

93.   Miller, Kent S. and Ralph M. Dreger, Editors. Comparative Studies of Blacks and Whites in the United States. New York: Seminar Press, 1973, pp. 408-445.

There is one long section in this work by Jacquelyn Johnson Jackson, entitled, "Family Organization and Technology," that deals with the Black family. Dr. Jackson surmises that the single most important general conclusion about a comparison of family organization and ideology among Blacks and whites is that much of the research undertaken over the past few decades merely confirms many of the observations made long ago by E. Franklin Frazier and John Dollard. What is most exciting about the recent research is its search for greater specification of the kinds of families exhibiting respectively functional and dysfunctional tendencies. The author concludes: "Apparently, most families reach for the stars for their children; if lower socio-economic position or other adverse factors hamper them, few of them make it, so they lower their reach, but their children reach out again, as far as they can, for their children, and so it goes."

94.   Miller, Randall M., Editor. "Dear Master": Letters of a Slave Family. Ithaca, NY: Cornell University Press, 1978. 281 pp.

This is a collection of letters of a Black slave family living in two worlds. Liberia (Africa) and Alabama (America). Dating from 1834 to 1865, the letters give a rare glimpse into the inner lives of both slaves and freedmen. The letters fall into two groups. The first group was written by Peyton Skipworth and his children from Liberia, where they had settled following their emancipation by Harwell Cocke in 1833. The second, larger series of letters was written by George Skipworth (Peyton's brother) and his daughter Lucy, who worked, respectively, as the slave driver and house-servant-schoolteacher at Cocke's plantation....

95.   Milwaukee County Welfare Rights Organization. Welfare Mothers Speak Out: We Ain't Gonna Shuffle Anymore. New York: W.W. Norton and Co., 1972. 190 pp.

Various references are made throughout this book to welfare families, who are mostly Black, and what can and should be done to help the poor. Unlike some works, this book states the welfare mother's point of view: How it feels to be subjected to the indignities and dehumanization of the welfare system, how welfare mothers prefer not to be on welfare, and how the "Family Assistance Plan" is not reform at all, but a step backward.

96.   Minuchin, Salvador, et al. Families of the Slums: An Exploration of their Structure and Treatment. New York: Basic Books, Inc., 1967. 460 pp.

Many references are made throughout the book to Black slum families. The Black family is compared to a number of other ethnic groups living in the slums. This work also deals with the Black

Minuchin:

family in a number of other ways: unstable, stable, and matriarchy. The book has a reference section at the end of each section.

97. Moore, William, Jr. The Vertical Ghetto: Everyday Life in An
Urban Project. New York: Random House, 1969, pp. 56-69, 75-80,
81-111, 113-118, 127-132.

The following topics are discussed as they relate to the families
in this housing project in a midwestern city in the United States:
"Activities of Families," "Disorganization of Families," "Protection Provided by Families," "Security Provided by Families," "Un-
certainties in Families," etc.

98. Moynihan, Daniel Patrick. The Negro Family: The Case for National
Action. Washington, DC: United States Government Printing Office,
1965, 258 pp.

The Black family instability viewpoint made it debut in this report,
commonly known as the "Moynihan Report." Dr. Moynihan is the person most responsible for developing the Black family instability
thesis. Moreover, he vigorously defended his findings. He traces
the plight of the Black family from slavery to freedom and Black's
migration to the North. Moynihan argues the expanding unstable
family life pattern inhibits Black's adjustments to American society. Much of Moynihan's conclusions were based on the earlier
works of E. Franklin Frazier. Many Black and white scholars dis-
agree with both Moynihan and Frazier's points of view. Several
criticisms of the two author's works are discussed throughout this
book....

99. Myers, Lena Wright. Black Women: Do They Cope Better? Englewood
Cliffs, NJ: Prentice-Hall, 1980. 113 pp.

Many references are made throughout this book to the role played
by Black women in the Black family structure. Dr. Myers states
that the women she interviewed for this book reported the most
admired man in their lives was the father/father substitute. They
also looked to other immediate family members for emotional support. Strong family ties have always been a source of support and
source of strength for Black women, but also the church and the
clergy. Since slavery, the church has been a viable institution
in the lives of Black people. The views of the Black women in
the author's sample support this contention. The majority of the
women felt that the church and religion helped to prepare them for
getting ahead in life. Stable families seem to be important in
the development of self-esteem, although not all people are affected in the same way by a broken home, suggests the writer.

100. Myrdal, Gunnar. An American Dilemma: The Negro Problem and Mo-
      dern Democracy. New York: Harper and Row, 1944, pp. 361-370,
      695-702, 930-935, 964, 1270, 1283-1288.

      References are made throughout the book to the Black family.
      There is one section, however, devoted to the Black family. Much
      of this information was taken from E. Franklin Frazier's book,
      The Negro Family in the United States. Dr. Myrdal points out that
      while the Black masses undoubtedly have much more of all those
      characteristics which define family disorganization in the tradi-
      tional American sense, they have certain other cultural traits
      which tend to reduce the disorganizing effect of those characteris-
      tics. The author declares that although the census would not
      bring out that fact, since there is a confusion over common-law
      marriages and temporary marriage, there are probably significantly
      fewer unattached Black adults than unattached white adults. The
      writer concludes: "The important thing is that Blacks, especially
      in the South, have built up a type of family organization conducive
      to social health, even though the practices are outside the Ameri-
      can tradition...."

101. Noble, Jeanne. Beautiful, Also, Are the Souls of My Black Sisters:
      A History of the Black Woman in America. Englewood Cliffs, NJ:
      Prentice-Hall, 1978, pp. 23-28, 39-41, 63, 68-69, 90-107.

      It was stated that there simply are not enough Black men available
      for marriage. Many Black women have to make the choice of either
      getting pregnant and rearing a child alone, or remaining unmarried
      and childless. But for many Black women, rearing children alone
      is not a choice. It is a consequence of many economic and social
      factors that prevent them from realizing the traditional intact
      nuclear family model. The writer concludes: "...It may well be
      that the Black family can more readily adapt itself to a shared
      equalitarian relationship which would be more humanistic than
      current paternalistic models seem to suggest...."

102. Nye, Francis I. and Felix M. Berardo. The Family: Its Structure
      and Interaction. New York: Macmillan Co., 1973, pp. 88-105, 154-
      166, 440-441, 445-446.

      There is one section that deals with Black American Families. It
      was suggested that although children are desired, the acculturated
      Black couple has developed some commitment to an ideology of plan-
      ned parenthood and therefore tends to restrict the size of the
      family. Unlike the situation observed among matricentric families,
      the socialization of children is a joint responsibility shared by
      the husband and wife. If both parents are working-and they often
      have to in order to maintain a middle-class status and life-style-
      they are more likely to use baby sitters or day-care facilities
      than parents to look after the children. Parents attempt to en-
      courage and inculcate high levels of educational and occupational
      aspirations in their children and are willing to plan and make
      sacrifices in order that such aspirations may achieve reality.
      Evident among these families then is a "joint dedication of husband

Nye and Berardo:

and wife to establish a stable family, to prosper economically,
and to bring forth a succeeding generation of children who will
suffer fewer of the disadvantages experienced by their parents."
The writers conclude: "Acculturated middle majority blacks have
demonstrated that given adequate resources and opportunities they
develop and sustain a highly stable family system as well as a
warm and satisfying home life. The black infant born in the
seventies is apt to experience less difficulty in becoming a middle-class Negro American than his parental ancestors, but the extent to which he will be able to maintain that status will be determined largely by the willingness of members of the white majority, whose institutions he increasingly comes into contact
with, to provide supportive and integrative roles."

103.   Obudho, Constance E., Editor. Black Marriage and Family. Westport, CT: Greenwood Press, 1983. 269 pp.

The editor states that it is the aim of this book to carry forth
the research on Black marriages, to provide some new insights into
the various issues that have continued to be studied within the
area, and to present some new views which may spark further research. The following essays are included in this collection:
Constance E. Obudho penned "Introduction-Black Marriages and
Family Therapy: A Perspective"; "The Loving Relationship: Impetus for Black Marriage" was written by Ruth E. G. King and Jean T.
Griffin; Castellano B. Turner and Barbara F. Turner wrote "Black
Families, Social Evaluations, and Future Marital Relations";
"Husband and Wife Relationships of Black Men and Women" was essay-
ed by Essie Manuel Rutledge; Annie S. Barnes contributed "Black
Husbands and Wives: An Assessment of Marital Roles in a Middle-
Class Neighborhood"; "Race Differences in Husband-Wife Interper-
sonal Relationships During the Middle Years of Marriage" was writ-
ten by Walter R. Allen; Donald P. Addison included "Black Wives:
Perspective About Their Husbands and Themselves"; Cheryl B. Leggon
wrote "Career, Marriage, and Motherhood: 'Coping Out' or Copping?";
John L. McAdoo penned "Parenting Styles: Mother-Child Interactions
and Self-Esteem in Young Black Children"; Castellano B. Turner and
William A. Darity contributed "Black Family Design"; "Marriage and
Family Therapy with Black Clients: Methods and Structure" was essayed by Lorraine Brannon; Adriaan T. Halfhide penned "We Are Our
Parents' Children"; Johnnie McFaddley wrote "Stylistic Counseling
of the Black Family"; "Can A White Therapist Deal with Black Families?" was penned by Vincent D. Foley; Constance E. Obudho added
"Some Final Comments." The title of these essays tells what each
of them is about.

104.   Ogden, Mary Elaine. The Chicago Negro Community: A Statistical
Description. Chicago: Work Projects Administration, 1939, pp. 42-
73, 116-167, 171, 186-188.

The writer mentions the Negro families in Chicago as they relate
to the following areas: "Negro Families By Census Tracts";

Ogden:

"Doubled-Up Negro Families"; "Negro Families by Length of Residence"; "Negro Families By Number of Sub-Heads"; "Quasi-Negro
Families."

105. Parenthood in a Changing Society: Papers From a Symposium At
      Memphis State University, Spring, 1979, Fall 1979, and Spring,
      1980. Washington, DC: National Institute of Education, 1980,
      pp. 27-41.

      One essay in this collection was called "Black Beginnings: A
      Longitudinal, Videotaped Observational Study of the Rearing and
      Development of Infants in the Black Families", by Jean V. Carew.
      The main purpose of this essay was to delineate some new methods
      of data collection and coding currently being used in a longitudi-
      nal observational study of Black toddlers in Oakland, California.
      The emphasis was on methodological innovations using videotaping
      methods, because she found this procedure to be an amazingly va-
      luable research tool. The longitudinal nature of the project,
      confidentiality agreements with participants, and the sheer volume
      of routine data collection procedures prevent her reporting any-
      thing more than tantalizing impressions of her substantive find-
      ings at this time. In less than one year, however, she expects
      to have a story about the Black experience that has never before
      been objectively documented or publicized.

106. Parker, Seymour and Robert J. Kleiner. Mental Illness in the
      Urban Negro Community. New York: Free Press, 1965. 408 pp.

      Various references are made to the Black family throughout the
      book. The authors point out that Black people do not receive
      adequate mental health care because of their social, political,
      and educational conditions. This book was based on interviews
      of Blacks living in Philadelphia.

107. Parsons, Talcott and Kenneth B. Clark, Editors. The Negro Ameri-
      can. Boston: Houghton-Mifflin Co., 1966, pp. 77-79, 90-91, 136,
      147-151, 166-170, 196-199, 209, 216, 286-291, 298, 463, 467, 674,
      738.

      A large number of references are made throughout the book to the
      Black family: Instability of crisis in broken homes, autonomy,
      history of employment opportunities, size preferences, size of,
      measures needed to change size of, per cent with both spouses
      present, ghetto life, educational level of head of, effects of
      migration on, public assistance of, development of from 1865-1915,
      family planning, breakdown and high fertility of Blacks, Black
      response to, Black awareness of "normal" etc. There are also
      three sections devoted specifically to the Black family.

108.   Perkins, Eugene. Home Is a Dirty Street: The Social Oppression
       of Black Culture. Chicago: Third World Press, 1975. 193 pp.

       The author suggests that there is no widespread disruption among
       Black people in general or Black families in particular. He ar-
       gues to some extent, the Black family has had to function like a
       jazz combo which improvises its music according to the skills of
       each member. This improvisational quality of the Black family has
       enabled it to adapt to different situations without being bound to
       a fixed pattern like members of a symphony orchestra. He con-
       cludes: "But the central theme to this type of human orchestration
       has always been one of survival...."

109.   Pinkney, Alphonso. Black Americans. Englewood Cliffs, NJ: Pren-
       tice-Hall, Inc., 1975, pp. 32, 57, 92-109, 132, 140.

       Various references are made throughout the book to the Black fami-
       ly: Child-rearing practices of the family, disorganization, di-
       vorce, separation, and desertion, family among ex-slaves, home
       ownership of the family, illegitimacy, income matricentric pat-
       terns, pattern of family life, regional variations of the family,
       and family life during slavery. There is also one section in
       Chapter V devoted to the family. The author concludes: "From the
       breakup of the African family during slavery to the overwhelming
       urbanization of Black people in the 1960's, family life has been
       in a constant process of change adapting to economic and social
       forces emanating from the larger society...."

110.   Pleck, Elizabeth H. Black Migration and Poverty: Boston 1865-
       1900. New York: Academic Press, 1979, pp. 161-196.

       Chapter 6 discusses various Black families. The author argues
       that the effect of Black urbanization in the North was to dimi-
       nish the powerful regulatory mechanisms in Black life and substi-
       tute an extended family system based on obligations between fos-
       ter parents, other kin, and friends. The mistake of many obser-
       vers has been to label such family arrangement "disorganized."
       In fact, kin and friends residing in several different households
       became the basis of family organization, concludes Prof. Pleck.

111.   Poussaint, Alvin F. Why Blacks Kill Blacks. New York: Emerson
       Hall Publishers, Inc., 1972, pp. 69-111.

       Various references are made throughout the book to Black men, wo-
       men, and children. Section 4 in Part II deals specifically with
       Black parents and their children. Dr. Poussaint believes that
       Black parents' superhuman task is raising an emotionally healthy
       child in a fundamentally unhealthy racist society. No Black-pride
       program in the world can repair the damage should we neglect our
       task of being good parents. The author also surmises that all
       children develop positive self-image mainly from the consistent
       love and care of their environment. This is especially true for
       the children of minority groups, contends the Black psychiatrist,

Poussaint:

since parental nurturing must offset the effects of an antagonistic society. Professor Poussaint concludes: "Black parents have given their children this kind of support in the past, as the events of the last decade have proved. They must continue today to provide the proper love and guidance for their children or the rhetoric of racial dignity will be self-defeating."

112. Proceedings of the Fifth Annual Conference of the National Association of Black Social Workers Held April 18-21, 1973 in New York City. Detroit: Multi Tech Publishers, 1974, pp. 77-141.

The following essays on the Black Family are included in these proceedings: Andrew Billingsley contributed "None Shall Part Us From Each Other"; "African Family Life Styles", was penned by Yosef ben-Jochannon; Victor B. Reid wrote "Traces of African Origins within the American Black Family"; "The Statistics Game-Myths and Realities" was essayed by Harold A. Burton; The final essay, "Black Men, Women, and Children-Their Strengths and Struggles", was discussed by John Henrik Clarke.

113. Proceedings of the Seventh Annual Conference of the National Association of Black Social Workers Held April 2-5, 1975 in Detroit, Michigan. Chicago: C.C.T. Press, 1976, pp. 89-129.

Three articles on or related to the Black Family are included in this collection: "Black Family Therapy" was essayed by Ivor J. Echols; Emily Palmer discusses "A Service Model for Working With the Black Single Parent"; and Thomas F. Waters concludes with "Black Male-Black Female Relationships."

114. Proceedings of the 13th Annual Convention of the Association of Black Psychologists. Washington, DC: Association of Black Psychologists, August 13-17, 1980, pp. 54, 110-111, 114-117.

A summary of the following proceedings of this convention includes the following papers: Joyce Dukes, et al., "Single Parent Family Functioning: Normative and Dysfunctional Patterns"; Noel A. Cazenave, "Middle-Income Black Fathers: Family Interaction, Transaction, and Development"; Frederick Phillips, "Community Psychology and the Black Community: A Marriage of Survival"; Marilyn Johnson and Marilyn Huffman, "The Family Nobody Wants: A Mandate for Nontraditional Practice"; and Nancy Boyd, "Family Therapy with Black People."

115. Queen, Stuart A. and Robert W. Habenstein. The Family in Various Cultures. New York: J. B. Lippincott Co., 1974, pp. 345-375.

Chapter 15 deals with "The Contemporary Black American Family." This chapter deals with the varying forms or profiles of the Black American family, seen first historically and then currently. The

Queen and Habenstein:

writers argue that the adaptive family draws from, and is immersed
in, an expressive church, club, cabaret, and more recently, pro-
test mass Black culture. The elements do not combine into an institutionalized family type; rather, they hang together in a dyna-
mic state of quasi-organization, continually subject to the play
of economic and social forces. The adaptive, nonacculturative elements of family organization, in the last analysis, are likely to
persist just to the extent that prejudice, discrimination, and economic disadvantage remain the lot of the central-city Black families, conclude the authors.

116. Rainwater, Lee. Behind the Ghetto Walls: Black Families in a
      Federal Slum. Chicago: Aldine Publishing Co., 1970. 446 pp.

      Dr. Rainwater discusses the intimate personal lives of some 10,000
      Black men, women, and children who lived in the all-Black public
      Housing project in St. Louis known as the Pruitt-Igoe Project.
      This work does not analyze the larger institutional, social struc-
      tural, and ideological forces that provide the social, economic,
      and political context in which so-called lower-class Black life
      is lived. The author, however, does point out that at the center
      of Black institutional life there is the family. It is the family
      that individuals are trained for participation in the culture and
      find their personal and group identity and continuity, states the
      writer.

117. _____ and William L. Yancey. The Moynihan Report and
      the Politics of Controversy. Cambridge: Massachusetts Institute
      of Technology Press, 1967. 493 pp.

      Much of the information is based on articles that responded to
      the Moynihan Report. There are also several articles analyzing
      the Black family in great detail. A number of reactions by civil
      rights leaders, and intellectuals are also included in this work.

118. Reiss, David, and Howard A. Hoffman, Editors. The American Family:
      Dying or Developing. New York: Plenum Press, 1979, pp. 79-102.

      "The Adaptations of Urban Black Families: Trends, Problems, and
      Issues," by Albert J. McQueen, was written for this collection.
      The author analyzes some of the complex dynamics of Black family
      life with three broad aims in view. First, McQueen summarizes
      the dominant social science images and interpretations of Black
      families. Second, he discusses certain major characteristics and
      trends evident among Black families in recent years and some of
      the underlying reasons for them. Thirdly, he analyzes family
      functioning among inner-city poor and near-poor people, with par-
      ticular reference to the strategies by which they cope with the
      material deprivations and dangers inherent in their environment,
      seek to maintain viable and satisfactory family life, and endeavor
      to raise their children for a better future.

119. Reissman, Frank, Editor. Strategies Against Poverty. New York:
      Random House, 1969. 669 pp.

      Various references are made throughout the book to the Black fami-
      ly. Chapter IV, "The Moynihan Report and the Compensatory Ap-
      proach," however, deals directly with the Black family. The author
      points out that Black families in large numbers believe that edu-
      cation is what "they had missed most in life and what they would
      like their children to have." Reissman concludes that if one
      wants to improve the educability of Blacks, it would seem much
      more relevant to stress changes in school practices and to develop
      these practices so that it is more attuned to the style and
      strengths of the population in question, rather than to emphasize
      the reorganization of the family.

120. Roberts, J. Deotis. Roots of a Black Future: Family and Church.
      Philadelphia: Westminster Press, 1980. 152 pp.

      The author showed how the Black church's theological self-under-
      standing can lay a foundation for ministry to Black families.
      Roberts points out that the extended family has been employed as
      a way of imaging the Black church. Since Black families are the
      source of the Black church's life and growth, the measure of its
      ministry to Black families will determine the quality of its own
      mission, according to the author. The relation of Black families
      and churches is mutual. He concludes: "...Failure of the Black
      church to minister appropriately and urgently to Black families
      will hasten its own death...."

121. Rodgers-Rose, La Frances, Editor. The Black Woman. Beverly
      Hills, CA: Sage Publications, 1980, pp. 67-174.

      Part 2 is entitled "The Black Woman and Her Family" and includes
      the following articles: Carrie Allen McCray, "The Black Woman and
      Family Roles"; Janice Hale, "The Black Woman and Child Rearing";
      Gloria Wade-Gayles, "She Who is Black and Mother: In Sociology
      and Fiction, 1940-1970"; Bonnie Thorton Dill; "Child-Rearing Goals
      and Strategies Among Black Female Domestic Servants"; Harriette
      Pipes McAdoo, "Black Mothers and the Extended Family Support Net-
      work"; Essie Manuel Rutledge, "Marital Interaction Goals of Black
      Women: Strengths and Effects." Lena Wright Myers, "On Marital
      Relations: Perceptions of Black Women."

122. Rohrer, John H., et al. The Eighth Generation Grows Up: Cultures
      and Personalities of New Orleans Negroes. New York: Harper and
      Row, 1960. 346 pp.

      The authors make references throughout the book to the Black fami-
      ly: identification with the family, impact of the family, life and
      class, lower-class family, lower middle-class family, matriarchal,
      middle-class family, structure of the family, systems and types of
      family, values and transmission of family, absence of father fi-
      gure. Chapter 7 deals directly with the Black family. The authors

Rohrer, et al.:

concluded: "In many cases life itself appears to revolve primarily or even exclusively around the family...."

123. Ross, Heather and Isabel Sawhill. Time of Transition: The Growth
of Families Headed by Women. Washington, DC: The Urban Institute,
1975, pp. 67-92.

Chapter Four discusses "Race and Family Structure." The authors
argue that to date, other researchers have not been able to demonstrate convincingly that all of the differences in marital instability are related to differences in current socioeconomic status. However, in our analysis of separation we found no differences by race in recent rates of family dissolution, after we controlled for economic variables, especially the less stable job
market faced by Black men, state the writers. This is not sur-
prising since much of the previous literature has emphasized the
employment prospects of males as a critical determinant of family
stability, but it is the first time that this variable has been
unambiguously identified as a major factor affecting separation
rates in a carefully controlled analysis of the marital behavior
of individual families, conclude the researchers.

124. Rowan Carl T. Just Between Us Blacks. New York: Random House,
1974, pp. 101-190.

The longest section in this book, Part IV, "Black Perspectives on
Black Families," discusses the past, present and future role of
Black families. The author surmises that trauma, conflict, dis-
location, and lack of tradition are still overriding factors in
too many Black families. Mr. Rowan believes that a lot of illegitimacy, promiscuity, venereal disease, flow directly from poverty,
poor housing, lack of privacy. The writer concludes that one of
these days we will stop cursing unwed mothers and thumbing our
noses at welfare recipients long enough to do something about the
problems of poverty, pigsty housing, childhood trauma, and we just
might find the key to a lot of our social woes.

125. Rubin, Roger Harvey. Matricentric Family Structure and the Self-
Attitudes of Negro Children. San Francisco, CA: R & E Research
Associates, 1976. 77 pp.

This book was based on a study of fifth and sixth grade Black
children in Philadelphia, Pennsylvania. The age range was from 9
to 11 years old. The author declares that the formation of a cur-
vilinear relationship between family interaction and self-concept
ratings may be accounted for in the following manner. As interaction in the form of relying upon and talking to one's family increases so does self-concept. However, there seems to be a point
where the possibility of too much interaction due to too many family members results in a competition and comparisons with siblings which can damage self-concept, states Prof. Rubin.

Rubin:

He concludes: "Again, however, only vague support is found for the
hypothesis which states the more the family interaction the more
positive the self-attitudes."

126. Ryan, William. Blaming the Victim. New York: Vintage Books,
      1976, pp. 63-88.

      Chapter 3 is entitles "Mammy Observed: Fixing the Negro Family."
      The writer points out that it is clear that the controversy between
      the family pathologists and those who see such an emphasis as dan-
      gerous and diverting, goes far beyond the scope of academic quib-
      bling about the interpretation of statistics. The controversy is
      more ideological than scientific. We have, after all, no compara-
      tive information on what happens to American Negroes and their fa-
      milies in a racist compared with a non-racist society, the experi-
      mental data are available in huge quantities, but the control data
      are yet to be gathered, states Ryan. He concludes: "It is not
      that Negro inequality cannot be eliminated until the Negro family
      is strengthened, but rather that the achievement of equality will
      strengthen the family, the community and the nation, black and
      white together."

127. Sager, Clifford J., et al. Black Ghetto Family in Therapy: A
      Laboratory Experience. New York: Grove Press, Inc., 1970. 245 pp.

      This book is divided into four parts. The first section, the ver-
      batim transcript of the four sessions that the families attended
      are presented in dialogue form. The second section of the book
      contains the transcript of the two and a half hours of discourse
      that followed the series of family interviews at the American
      Group Psychotherapy Association meeting of February 8, 1969. The
      third part, based on tape-recorded individual conversation with
      family members held six to eight weeks after the demonstration,
      presents their further reflections on the laboratory experience.
      The final section summarizes what the editors learned about engag-
      ing Black impoverished families in the Family Treatment Unit's six
      years of work. This section offers a number of suggestions appli-
      cable in therapy with patients who are poor, minimally educated,
      and burdened with the urgencies of survival. Some of the proce-
      dures outlined are not unique to the treatment of this segment of
      our population, but they take on added dimension when applied to
      patients whose ethnicity, social class, value systems, and style
      of life are different from those of the therapists, conclude the
      researchers.

128. Sanders, Wiley Britton. Negro Child Welfare in North Carolina.
      Chapel Hill: University of North Carolina Press, 1933, pp. 160,
      217-221, 228-249, 252-255, 269-275.

      Various references are made throughout the book to the Black fami-
      ly, children, mothers, and fathers. There are, however, many case

Sanders:

studies of individual families in this work. The primary purpose
of this study was to secure and to present such information as
would enable the public welfare system in all its branches to
function more successfully in extending its services to the Black
population of the state. This is one of the earliest studies on
Black child welfare in the South.

129. Scanzoni, John H. The Black Family in Modern Society. Boston:
Allyn and Bacon, Inc., 1971. 353 pp.

Dr. Scanzoni examines the inextricable link between economic resources and the Black family structure. Most of the information
in this work was gathered by Black interviewers from a sample of
400 Black households, husband-wife present, in the City of Indianapolis during the winter months of 1968. The book also tried to
grapple with the theoretical issues linking stratification, socialization, husband-wife interaction, marital stability, the opportunity system, along with acceptance, persistence, and change
of family structures within modern society....

130. Schneller, Donald P. The Prisoner's Family: A Study of the Effects of Imprisonment on the Families of Prisoners. San Francisco:
R & E Research Associates, 1976. 102 pp.

The researcher discusses the effects of the imprisonment on the
families of 93 men who were in a Washington, DC prison. The author surmises that the families experienced little, if any, extreme hardship in the realm of social acceptance. Most Black families saw imprisonment as part of the overall system of racism
in society. Prof. Schneller suggests that change in social acceptance of the families was not a problem of significance for a
majority of the families, but financial status and sexual-emotion-
al frustration were significantly altered and presented real problems for most wives....

131. Schultz, David A. Coming Up Black: Patterns of Ghetto Socialization. Englewood Cliffs, NJ: Prentice-Hall, Inc., 1969. 209 pp.

Many references are made to the Black family: "illegitimate" in-
terlocking of illegitimate children, kinship large family, rural
origins, socio-economic characteristics, unrelated persons, children, complete families, incomplete families, interpersonal relations, family planning, family structure and poverty, legitimizing
authority, male role model, desertion, surrogate fathers, male
marginality, quasi-father, child-bearing experience, income, in-
dulge children, birth control, father, mother, children.

132. Shimkin, Detmilri B., et al., Editors. The Extended Family in
Black Societies. The Hague: Mounton Publishers, 1978. 526 pp.

Shimkin:

This is a collection of essays on the Black extended family in the southern part of the United States, particularly in Holmes County, Mississippi and its outliers. There is also some material on Black families in Chicago, New Orleans, Los Angeles, Dallas, and Houston, Texas. It was stated that the Black extended family need...to be comprised within, and to contribute to, the humanization of modern societies through ethically valid "social engineering."

133.   Sims, Naomi. All About Success For the Black Woman. Garden City, NY: Doubleday and Co., 1982, pp. 126-127, 136, 142, 182-229.

Chapter 9 in this book is entitled "Managing Marriages and Motherhood." The essence of this chapter is that it is possible for Black women to have a meaningful and successful career and be good wives and mothers. She concludes: "If we are to create a legacy of which our daughters and sons can be justifiably proud, we have to take care of the Whole Black woman!"

134.   Smith, William David, et al., Editors. Reflections on Black Psychology. Washington, DC: University Press of America, 1979, pp. 89-104, 105-148, 311-358.

Various references are made throughout this collection on Black children and Black women and their role in the Black family structure. One specific essay, "Liberation and Struggle: Concepts for the African Family", by Nsenge Warfield-Coppock, deals with the Black American family. The author argues that a strong, healthy Black family is synonymous with a liberated, powerful people who have achieved their freedom. It was also pointed out that the basis of our family, as is our struggle, is love; the love of our children, the love of our ancestors; the love of our land, the love of living Afrikans....

135.   Spencer, Margaret, et al., Editors. Beginnings: The Social and Affective Development of Black Children. Hillsdale, NJ: Lawrence Erlbaum Associates, Publishers, 1985, pp. 3-18, 29-44, 237-292.

Several essays in this collection deal specifically with the Black family: Diana T. Slaughter and Gerald A. McWorter essayed "Social Origins and Early Features of the Scientific Study of Black American Families and Children": "Household, Kinship, and the Life Course: Perspectives on Black Families and Children", was written by Glen H. Elder, Jr.; Velma LaPoint, et al., contributed "Enforced Family Separations: A Descriptive Analysis of Some Experience of Children of Black Imprisoned Mothers"; "Black Children's Sex-Role Ideologies and Occupational Choices in Families of Employed Mothers" was contributed by Geraldine K. Brookins; the final essay "Race, Income and Family Dynamics: A Study of Adolescent Male Socialization Processes and Outcome", was written by Walter R. Allen. A thirty-five page Bibliography is also included in this book.

136. Stack, Carol B. <u>All Our Kin: Strategies for Survival in a Black
      Community</u>. New York: Harper & Row, 1974. 175 pp.

      This is a study of Black family life in a mid-western city. The
      author contends that the Black urban family, embedded in coopera-
      tive domestic exchange, proves to be an organized, tenacious, ac-
      tive, lifelong network. The author concludes that her study shows
      that the strategies that the poor have evolved to cope with pover-
      ty do not compensate for poverty in themselves, nor do they perpe-
      tuate the poverty cycle. But when mainstream values fail the poor,
      the harsh economic conditions of poverty force people to return to
      proven strategies for survival, concludes Dr. Stack.

137. Staples, Robert. <u>Black Masculinity: The Black Male's Role in
      American Society</u>. San Francisco, CA: Black Scholar Press, 1982.
      182 pp.

      The scholar suggests that the conflict between men and women may
      be more apparent than real. The real problem may be largely a de-
      mographic one with strong class overtones. There simply are not
      enough Black men to go around and the ones available are not re-
      garded as viable mates. Regardless of the source of the problem,
      the high number of unmarried and divorced Blacks signals that all
      is not well between Black men and women. The unbalanced ratio of
      men to women and the greater degree of "power" given to men is a
      combustible combination that creates a potential problem, argues
      Dr. Staples. In men this power is often manifested as arrogance
      and insensitivity to women's needs. For women, feelings of insult
      and injury can add up to outrage. White racism may have been the
      force which shaped Black relationships and its spectre may remain
      with us for the foreseeable future. He concludes: "However, the
      future of the Black family may rest upon those Blacks who resist
      the notion that racism will determine their personal relation-
      ships. Otherwise, it seems clear that racism may have decisively
      determined the nature of the most intimate association between men
      and women. Then, their capacity to resist racism itself may be
      brought into question. A house divided against itself cannot
      stand."

138. _____. <u>Introduction to Black Sociology</u>. New York: Mc-
      Graw-Hill Co., 1976, pp. 113-149.

      Chapter 5 is devoted to the Black family. This study demonstrates
      how the Black family is organized to meet the functional prerequi-
      sites of the Black Community. Dr. Staples discusses the forces
      that Black families encounter, which create the existence of large
      numbers of "problem" families, must be carefully examined. This
      book is well-documented and has Notes and a Suggested Reading List.

139. _____. <u>The Black Family: Essays and Studies</u>. Belmont,
      CA: Wadsworth Publishing Company, 1978. 228 pp.

      This work discusses: family organization, bi-parental, matriarchal,

Staples:

female-headed households. Dr. Staples believes that the myth of
the Black Matriarchy was cultivated by America's image makers, and
is part of the divide-and-conquer strategy that ruling classes
have used throughout history. The author sheds new light on such
topics as common-law marriage, power relationships within the marital arrangement, child rearing practices and divorce. This work
has an extensive Bibliography and is indexed.

140. _____. The Black Woman in America: Sex, Marriage, and the
Family. Chicago: Nelson-Hall Publishers, 1973. 269 pp.

This book is more about the Black woman than the Black family.
Yet the two cannot be separated because the Black woman plays a
major role in the family. Dr. Staples surmises that the primary
problems Black women have faced with their men is that there are
not enough of them and that the ones available have not been per-
mitted to provide adequate support for their families. Professor
Staples concludes that once we gain insight into the reality of
the lives of Black women, we shall know what white racism has
wrought and what Black womanhood has overcome. He continues:
"But, in the past as in the present, Black womanhood represents
the finest of the human spirit in overcoming the obstacles en-
countered in the search for freedom."

140a. _____. The World of Black Singles: Changing Patterns of
Male-Female Relations. Westport, CT: Greenwood Press, 1981.
259 pp.

This book is divided into five parts with two chapters each:
Part I, "Black Men and the Social Systems"; Part II, "Crime and
Violence"; Part III, "Sex and Sexuality"; Part IV, "Male/Female
Relationships"; and Part V, "Masculinity and Sexism." There are
also Notes at the end of the book.

141. Sterling, Dorothy, Editor. We Are Your Sisters: Black Women in
the Nineteenth Century. New York: W.W. Norton and Co., 1984,
pp. 31-43, 72, 87-88, 100-104, 112, 154-155, 220-225, 310-318,
338, 343-344, 365, 415.

Many references are made to the Black family throughout this book.
One section entitled, "Courtship and Family Life," deals specifically with the slave family. The writer points out that no slave
marriage was secure. Every family lived with the possibility of
separation....

142. Sterner, Richard, et al. The Negro's Share: A Study of Income,
Consumption, Housing and Public Assistance. New York: Harper &
Row, Publishers, 1943, pp. 47-102.

Various references to the Black family including its composition,

Sterner:

income, expenditures, consumption, types, and definition. The authors compare the Black family with the white family during the 1930's and early 1940's and conclude that the Black family is discriminated against in all phases of American society. The writers used more than seventy charts and tables to prove their points.

143.   Swan, L. Alex. <u>Families of Black Prisoners</u>. Boston: G. K. Hall and Co., 1980. 163 pp.

This book described and identified a composite of Black prisoners' families and determined the nature and extent of the problems these families faced, before, during, and after the imprisonment of a family member. The study was done at the main Tennessee State Prison in Nashville. Prof. Swan argues that the wives of the prisoners considered their families to be strong in spite of the men's imprisonment. Given the employment record and economic status of these families, and the exploitive capitalist nature of the social order, especially as it affects the Black community, it will be difficult for them to recover upon the release and return of the prisoners. Dr. Swan concludes: "There is a crisis situation in the Black community. It suffers from an unjust and oppressive racist system and lacks the resources to help its members gain the opportunities and skills that will enable them to recover, and not only survive but also advance and progress."

144.   Thomas, George B. <u>Young Black Adults: Liberation and Family Attitudes</u>. New York: Friendship Press, 1974. 95 pp.

This work was published for the Committee on Ministries with Black families of the Black Christian Education Project of the National Council of Churches. The Chapters in this work are: "Emerging Perspectives of Familial Values in Black Consciousness," "Black Consciousness and a New Value System," "Social Attitudes in Black Male-Female Relationships," "The Churches' Ministry Through the Black Family of the Community and Larger Society." There are also Appendices, Notes and Bibliography, as well as "A Guide for Group Study and Discussion of Young Black Adults: Liberation and Family Attitudes."

145.   Twombly, Robert C. <u>Blacks in White America Since 1865: Issues and Interpretations</u>. New York: David McKay, 1971, pp. 438-494.

Chapter 11 is entitled "The Society of Contemporary Black America: The Family." This section includes summaries from three works listed elsewhere in this bibliography. Daniel P. Moynihan, <u>The Negro Family: The Case for National Action</u>; David A. Schulz, <u>Coming Up Black: Patterns of Ghetto Socialization</u> and Andrew Billingsley, <u>Black Families in White America</u>.

146. Wakin, Edward. <u>Portrait of a Middle-Class Negro Family at the</u>
      <u>Edge of Harlem</u>. New York: William Morrow & Co., 1965. 127 pp.

      This book discusses the Creary family of New York City. The Crea-
      rys look upon themselves primarily as Americans, Christians, and
      parents. Unlike the down-trodden Black who has become a well-
      known statistic, the Crearys have an immediate future. Poised at
      the edge of Harlem, both physically and psychologically -- they
      are ready to leave, states the author. The Crearys and other
      Blacks like them are moving closer to white America, hoping that
      white America is ready to accept them. There are also more than
      100 photos of Mr. and Mrs. Creary, their six children, and New
      York City in this book.

147. Wallace, Michele. <u>Black Macho and The Myth of the Superwoman</u>.
      New York: Dial Press, 1979, pp. 11-12, 30-31, 53-54, 109-116.

      Various references are made to the Black family, women, men and
      children-throughout this book. One section is devoted specifical-
      ly to the Daniel P. Moynihan Report. The author argues: "Moyni-
      han, and those who picked up where he left off, were using the
      Black woman as a scapegoat. Rather than carve a piece of pie for
      the Black man out of the white man's lion's share, they preferred
      to take away from the really very little that the Black woman had
      and give the meager slice to him."

148. Wallace, Phyllis A. et al. <u>Black Women in the Labor Force</u>.
      Cambridge, MA: The MIT Press, 1980. 162 pp.

      Many references are made throughout the book to the Black woman
      and her role in the Black family as it relates to her contribution
      to family income, raising children, head of family, etc. It was
      stated that Black women workers as well as all other women will
      benefit greatly from full implementation of laws against sex dis-
      crimination. Once there is equal pay for equal work, no differen-
      tiation between males and females on fringe benefits, a limitation
      on separate lines of progression and seniority systems, appropri-
      ate maternity and pregnancy leave policies, earnings of women will
      be increased. The author said that in 1976 approximately 48 per-
      cent of the 2.1 million Black women who headed families lived in
      the South and almost three-fifths of these women had family in-
      comes below the official poverty level. (For a nonfarm family of
      four persons, the poverty threshold in 1976 was $5,815.) "As this
      region of the country alters and expands its industrial base, it
      is important that both racial and sex barriers in employment be
      eliminated. Also there may be regional solutions found on how to
      improve opportunities in the labor marker for these Black women,"
      conclude the writers.

149. Watkins, Mel and Jay David, Editors. <u>To Be a Black Woman: Por-</u>
      <u>traits in Fact and Fiction</u>. New York: William Morrow and Co.,
      1970. 285 pp.

Watkins and David:

References are made throughout the book to the Black family, not only during modern times, but also during slavery. The role of the Black woman in the Black family is seen throughout the book. This includes poetry, narratives, short stories, essays and plays.

150.   Watts, Lewis G., et al. The Middle-Income Negro Family Faces Urban Renewal. Boston, MA: Department of Commerce and Development, 1965. 112 pp.

This is a study of families during the rehabilitation of a Boston, Massachusetts neighborhood that took place in 1964. The writers conclude that most Black's apprehension and timidity tend to be manifested in statements about their children--concern about the children's social lives, the chances of rejection and the fear they may fail to identify themselves with other Blacks and become lost souls. The authors continued to point out that one must recognize that the individual Black family must and will decide for itself the right or the wrong, the appropriateness or the unsuitability of leaving the ghetto, just as in the same city other minorities must make the same decision....

151.   Weisbord, Robert G. Genocide?: Birth Control and the Black American. Westport, CT and New York: Greenwood Press and The Two Continents Publishing Group, Ltd., 1975. 219 pp.

Prof. Weisbord argues that Black people's qualms about birth control may be partially dissipated by inviting Black people to community involvement in birth control projects, by integrating family planning into comprehensive health care programs, by utilizing Black personnel wherever possible. But until America solves the manifold problems of seething cauldrons which are our Black ghettos, until Blacks cease to be an exploited underclass, until Black Americans obtain the power to shape their own destinies, indeed, until the nightmare of racism and oppression is supplanted for all by the American dream, until then it is unlikely that the genocide rhetoric will be muted, concludes the author.

152.   Westoff, Leslie A. and Charles F. Westhoff. From How to Zero: Fertility, Contraception and Abortion in America. Boston: Little, Brown and Co., 1968, pp. 234-277, 301-305.

Chapter 7 is labeled "Black Fertility and Contraception." The author observes that there is very little difference between all large-city Blacks and whites currently married who have ever used contraception. They state that Blacks are no more uniform in their fertility practices and attitudes than whites. It was pointed out that as Blacks improve their economic situation their fertility declines. The Westoffs conclude: "...Thus it seems clear enough that needs for family planning are not restricted by race or income. But the payoff of family planning for Blacks, given their social and economic deprivations, would be even more dramatic than for whites."

152a. Wilkinson, Doris Y. and Ronald L. Taylor, Editors. The Black Male in America: Perspective on His Status in Contemporary Society. Chicago: Nelson-Hall, 1977. 375 pp.

Several references are made to the Black family and all of these essays are mentioned elsewhere in this book. They are: "Social and Psychological Dimensions of the Family Role Performance of the Negro Male"; by Seymour Parker and Robert J. Kleiner; Robert Staples contributed "The Myth of the Black Matriarchy"; "Jobs and the Negro Family: A Reappraisal," was written by Edwin Harwood and Claire C. Hodge; Prof. Charles V. Willie essayed "The Black Family and Social Class"; and David A. Schulz penned "Variations in the Father Role in Complete Families of the Negro Lower Class." Other references to the Black male and his role in the Black family are also discussed throughout this book.

153.   Willie, Charles V. Race, Ethnicity, and Socioeconomic Status: A Theoretical Analysis of Their Interrelationship. Bayside, NY: General Hall, Inc., 1983, pp. 118-121, 138-139, 144, 146-162.

Chapter 14 is entitled "Dominance in the Family: The Black and White Experience." The author concludes: "Overcoming the fallacy of projecting will encourage social scientists to study all racial populations directly and to learn from them the beneficial and harmful effects of various patterns of adaptation. By examining data that are controlled for race and social class, this analysis not only refuted categorically the myth of the Black matriarchy, but indicated that the equalitarian pattern of decision making appears to be the norm for American households, and that the cultural lag, if any, is found not among Blacks but among middle-class white households that now are struggling toward the equalitarian goal."

154.   _____. Editor. The Family Life of Black People. Columbus, OH: Charles E. Merrill Co., 1970. 341 pp.

This work includes a series of articles prepared by competent social scientists which describe and analyze the many variations and adaptations which characterize the family life of Black people. This work attempts to approach the study of the family life of Black people as an integrative, adaptive, functional system rather than as a social problem or as an illustration of deviance. Twenty-six articles are included and they deal with the issue of stability in family life and the question of whether or not there is a breakdown in the Black family....

155.   Wilson, Amos N. The Developmental Psychology of the Black Child. New York: Africana Research Publications, 1978, pp. 23-23, 131-134, 162-171, 200-202.

The author asserts that in the lower class ghetto family the "broken home" does have considerable adverse effects, however, these effects seem due to the presence of economic deprivation. Thus,

Wilson:

rather than fatherlessness, the major problem of the Black family
is "blocked access to the opportunity structure - rather than family wholeness - is clearly more critical with regard to family
functionality." He concludes: "The major result of fatherlessness in Black families seems not to be a confusion of sex identity
but a critically reduced ability of the children from these families when adults to successfully fulfill their roles as husbands,
fathers, wives and mothers. The lack of good role models which
serve to show the children wholesome husband-child relationships
deprives the children of workable models that can be used to maintain their own family relations as adult marrieds...."

156. Winegarten, Ruthe and Frieda Werden, Editors. I Am Annie Mae:
      An Extraordinary Woman in Her Own Words. Austin, TX: Rosegarden
      Press, 1983. 151 pp.

      This book discusses Annie Mae Hunt, a Black Texas woman, and her
      family. Mrs. Hunt was born Annie Mae McDade in 1909. The edi-
      tors, two white women, taped seven hours of interviews with Mrs.
      Hunt and this book is the end result of those interviews. Mrs.
      Hunt's narrative covers a span of nearly 120 years in the history
      of Black women in Texas.

157. Woods, Sister Frances Jerome. Marginality and Identity: A
      Colored Creole Family Through Ten Generations. Baton Rouge:
      Louisiana State University Press, 1972. 395 pp.

      This entire book discusses a specific Creole family from Louisi-
      ana. The direct descendants of this one family comprised a popu-
      lation of nearly 9,000 persons. Also included in this study are
      1,246 "outsiders", which refers to the nondirect descent popula-
      tion who married members of this one specific Creole family during
      the last 200 years.

158. Woofter, Thomas Jackson, Jr., Editor. Negro Problems in Cities.
      New York: Doubleday, 1928. 284 pp.

      Various references are made throughout the book to the Black fa-
      mily. Part I discusses the "Neighborhoods" and their relationship
      to Blacks. Part II discusses the "Housing" and its relationship
      to Blacks. Part III discusses "Schools" and their relationship
      to Blacks. Part IV discusses "Recreation" and its relationship
      to Blacks. In short, this study attempts to interpret the new
      city Black in terms of certain new factors in his city and family
      environment.

159. Wyne, Marvin D., et al. The Black Self. Englewood Cliffs, NJ:
      Prentice-Hall, Inc., 1974. 114 pp.

      This book brings together theories and research related to the

Wyne:

self-concepts of Black Americans. There are concepts of Black
Americans. There are also concepts references to the Black family
throughout the book: child-rearing practices, father-absence, influence of family, size of family, extended family, children,
Father, Mother, etc. This short book has references at the end
of each of the five chapters and an Index.

160. Yetman, Norman R., Editor. Voices from Slavery. New York: Holt,
      Rinehart and Winston, 1970. 368 pp.

      This is a collection of narratives by Blacks who had been slaves.
      This collection was based on oral interviews. The freedmen dis-
      cussed their family life throughout the book. They also discussed
      their parents, children, plantation life, marriage and miscegena-
      tion.

161. Young, Whitney M., Jr. Beyond Racism: Building an Open Society.
      New York: McGraw-Hill Book Co., 1969, pp. 20-22, 35-40, 59-62, 78-
      83, 169-179.

      The writer makes various references throughout the book to the
      Black family. Young concludes that the Black family has strengths
      which should be recognized. Considering the obstacles placed in
      its way by a hostile society and the persistent American attacks
      on Black manhood, the stability of Black families is extraordina-
      ry. The fact that the majority of all poor Black families could
      manage to hold themselves together and meet every test of middle-
      class American standards for stability is nothing short of re-
      markable. The Black family is not the one-fourth that is broken,
      it is the three-fourths that have held together under pressure
      that would devastate other groups, argues Young.

162. Zollar, Ann C. A Member of The Family: Strategies For Black
      Family Continuity. Chicago: Nelson-Hall Publishers, 1985. 174
      pp.

      This book discusses four Black families in Chicago's Austin Com-
      munity area: The Niles family, Edmond family, Baker family and
      the Jones family. She states that these and other Black families
      in the urban environment transmit from generation to generation
      the knowledge that sharing between and among kin constitutes pro-
      per behavior. Dr. Zollar points out the commonalities and dif-
      ferences between each of the four families. The author argues it
      is necessary to debunk the myth which claims that Black involve-
      ment with the extended kin represents an adaptation to conditions
      of urban poverty. She also asks how it can be true when kin in-
      volvement and mutual aid persist after some degree of prosperity
      has been reached and when recent sociohistorical treatments of
      the development of Afro-American family pattern emphasizes the
      role played by the extended family pattern in insuring that en-
      slaved Africans survived to become Black "Americans."

General Books

.

163. Baughman, E. Earl. <u>Black Americans: A Psychological Analysis</u>.
New York: Academic Press, 1971, pp. 76-90.

Chapter 7, "Socialization and the Family," subchapters discuss
origins of Black families: A Post-Slavery Phenomenon, Family
Structure, Rural-Urban Differences, Size, Extended Families, Fatherless Families, The Concept of Matriarchy and Two types of Families: Respectable and Non-Respectable.

164. Blackwell, James E. <u>The Black Community: Diversity and Unity</u>.
New York: Harper & Row, Publisher, 1975, pp. 35-64.

In Chapter Two, Dr. Blackwell discusses "The Black Family in
American Society." This chapter examines the family as the basic
social unit in the structure of the Black community. The author
argues that both structurally and functionally, the Black family
system further exemplifies the high degree of differentiation
within the Black community. The writer discusses the impact of
slavery on family life, pattern of family life, controversial issues such as illegitimacy, divorce, welfare, urbanization and the
changing Black family.

165. Brightharp, George Lenward. <u>The Damned Ones-Undamned</u>. New York:
Exposition Press, 1973, pp. 107-116.

The writer called chapter 11 "Family Control." Mr. Brightharp
suggests that Blacks and all other minorities must not have large
families. American minorities must fight social damnation through
the use of family control. According to the author, we can fight
the evils and prejudices of our society through family control.
He concludes, in part: "...The family, as an institution, must
be preserved if our society is to prosper. Therefore, we must
become UNDAMNED THROUGH FAMILY CONTROL."

166. Brink, William and Louis Harris. <u>Black and White</u>. New York:
Simon and Schuster, 1966, pp. 143-151.

Brink and Harris:

Chapter 7, "The Negro Family," has some discussion on the institution of slavery and its affects on the Black family structure.
There are some analyses and criticisms of the Moynihan Report, and
a survey done by Newsweek Magazine.

167. Bromley, David G. and Charles F. Longino, Jr., Editors. White
      Racism and Black Americans. Cambridbe, MA: Schenkman Publishing
      Co., 1972, pp. 183-290.

      Four essays are included in this book. All have appeared else-
      where in this bibliography. They are: Daniel P. Moynihan, "The
      Tangle of Pathology"; "Savage Discovery: The Moynihan Report," was
      written by William Ryan; Lee Rainwater contributed "Crucible of
      Identity: The Negro Lower-Class"; and "The Strengths of Black
      Families", was penned by Robert B. Hill.

168. Christensen, Harold T. and Kathryn P. Johnson. Marriage and The
      Family. New York: Ronald Press Co., 1971, pp. 61-65, 215-216,
      307-309, 381-383, 397-400, 518.

      The writers believe that the Black family is subject to the same
      pressures as the white family. At present Blacks are over-repre-
      sented in the working class because of lower education and restric-
      ted opportunity in the economic system. The older family norms
      which still exist are more likely to result in female-dominant fa-
      milies than in the male-dominant ones found in the white working
      class. Since social changes involving the Black American are so
      extensive, speculations about their effect on the Black family
      are extremely hazardous at the present writing. To the extent
      that the Black population becomes integrated into the economic
      system on an equal footing with the whites, we would expect that
      the family structure will resemble that of the white family at the
      same class level, as is already apparently true at the middle and
      upper-middle class levels, argue the authors.

169. Gary, Lawrence E. and Lee P. Brown, Editors. Crime and Its Impact
      on the Black Community. Washington, DC: Institute for Urban
      Affairs and Research, Howard University, 1975, pp. 85-96, 155-164.

      Dr. Robert Staples penned the essay, "Race and Family Violence:
      The Internal Colonialism Perspective." The author showed how
      acts of Black family violence and the machinations of internal co-
      lonialism are inextricably linked. While other forces operate on
      the incidence of family conflict that may transcend race, the cru-
      cial variable in maintaining the practice of the intra-family vio-
      lence among Blacks has been their status as a colonized people.
      There is no reason to believe that the lower-class or Blacks are
      any more prone to violence than the middle class or white popula-
      tion. Yet, they are so over-represented in the official statis-
      tics on crimes of family violence as to preclude any explanation
      other than racial and economic forces as being responsible for

Gary and Brown:

the amount of violence in their family constellation, concludes the author. There is also another essay in this collection by James F. Scott, entitled "Police Authority and the Low-Income Black Family: An Area of Needed Research." This article presented a conceptual analysis of the impact of certain situational factors on the establishment of police authority in encounters where police are required to quell disturbances occurring within low-income Black families. The discussion centers on the premise that how policemen respond to prevent many of these family disturbances from becoming "criminal encounters" is contingent upon the ease or difficulty that policemen have in establishing and exercising their authority to act. Hence, this article examines some of the factors which help to shape social situations where police have the option of assuming either a "crime control" approach to dealing with disturbances in low-income Black families. The objectives of this analysis are three-fold: (1) to underscore the necessity for police to pursue the goal of crime prevention with the same emphasis as the goal of crime control in coping with crime in the Black community; (2) to focus research upon sensitive areas of police-Black relations; and (3) to direct attention to areas of research concerned with better evaluation measures of the service delivery capability of urban police organizations in Black communities, concludes Dr. Scott.

170.   George, Eaton Simpson and J. Milton Yinger. Racial and Cultural Minorities. New York: Harper & Row, 1965, pp. 348-354.

Chapter 16, "Family Patterns of Minorities," briefly discusses the Black family, emphasizing the matriarchal system and socio-economic status of Black people.

171.   Glenn, Norval D. and Charles M. Bonjean, Editors. Blacks in the United States. San Francisco, CA: Chandler Publishing, 1969, pp. 4, 17, 83-84, 130-132, 156, 160-162, 296, 333.

Various references are made throughout the book to the Black family: disorganization of the family, characteristics of the family, background of the family, variety in the family, matriarchal, need for effective functioning of the family, adjustment and socialization of children, stereotypes by children, and fathers. This anthology attempts to give new interpretations to older theories on Blacks in the United States. This book has a Bibliography and an Index.

172.   Goldstein, Rhoda L., Editor. Black Life and Culture in the United States. New York: Thomas Y. Crowell Co., 1971, pp. 4, 17, 83-84, 156, 160-162, 296, 333.

Many references are made to Blacks: men, women, children, and the family. Several important points are brought out concerning the Black family; that the Black family is a survival structure--a

Goldstein:

strong, resilient social institution characterized by an amazing degree of strength and stability, and that even mobility played a survival role within the interpersonal web relations of the Black family.

173.   Green, Dan S. and Edwin D. Driver, Editors. W.E.B. DuBois on Sociology and the Black Community. Chicago: University of Chicago Press, 1978, pp. 199-213.

Section 10 is entitled "The Negro American Family", and was taken from W.E.B. DuBois The Negro American Family, that was published in Atlanta, Georgia in 1909. This book is annotated elsewhere in this bibliography.

174.   Hendin, Herbert. Black Suicide. New York: Basic Books, Inc., 1969, pp. 93-121, 146-147.

In Chapter 5, "Women and Suicide", the author describes frustrations of Black women that have led to suicide. There is also emphasis on maternal abandonment, pregnancy and motherhood.

175.   Iowa State University College of Home Economics. Families of the Future. Ames, Iowa: Iowa State University Press, 1972, pp. 3-15.

There is one chapter in this collection on the Black family entitled "Stability of the Black Family and the Black Community" by Samuel D. Proctor. The writer gives a profile of the Black family beginning with it in Africa and carrying it to present day America. Dr. Proctor surmises that what happens to the Black family will be determined by what happens to Black people. He concludes that there should be a residual moral momentum among various movements of the country to bring us to a new plateau of justice and fairness in America, a climate where the Black family can really prosper.

176.   Jones, Reginald L., Editor. Black Psychology. New York: Harper & Row, 1972, pp. 44-45, 169, 173, 179, 322, 372.

It was pointed out that the Black family represents another area in which the use of traditional white psychological models leads us to an essentially inappropriate and unsound analysis.

177.   Klagsbrun, Francine, Editor. The First Ms. Reader. New York: Warner, 1973, pp. 36-41.

Chapter Three was called "The Black Family and Feminism" and was written by Cellestine Ware. This essay is basically a conversation between the author and Eleanor Holmes Norton. Mrs. Norton was at the time Chairman of the New York City Commission on Human

Klagsbrun:

Rights and Executive Assistant to Mayor John V. Lindsay. Mrs.
Norton concludes that Black family life will be a disaster if it
copies white family life....

178. Larner, Jeremy and Irving Howe, Editors. Poverty: Views from the
      Left. New York: William Morrow and Co., 1968, pp. 196-206.

      Laura Carper discusses "The Negro Family and the Moynihan Report"
      in this collection. The author suggests that the Negro family is
      not the source of the "tangle of pathology" which the Moynihan Re-
      port attributes to the Black community. It is the pathological
      relationship between white social institutions and the Black com-
      munity which has bred the statistics the report cites, states
      Carper. She also points out that people living under oppression
      always develop social formations which appear to be surrounding
      oppressive culture to be excessive or pathological....

179. Leslie, Gerald R. The Family in Social Context. New York: Ox-
      ford University Press, 1976, pp. 284-298.

      There is one chapter on "Black Families." The author contends
      that social scientists have focused far too much upon the problems
      faced by Black families, and have paid too little attention to evi-
      dences of strength and resiliency in the system. The writer con-
      cludes that the strength of kinship bonds is shown in the large
      proportion of intact nuclear families....

180. Levita, Sar A., et al. Still A Dream: The Changing Status of
      Blacks Since 1960. Cambridge, MA: Harvard University Press, 1975,
      pp. 105-127, 195-196, 338-339.

      Chapter 5 discusses "The Black Family." This is a very negative
      assessment on the Black family. The authors suggest that whatever
      the socioeconomic variables, it is clear that the changes in Black
      marital and family status are not positive developments. The
      long-run positive impacts of rising education and income did not
      balance the negative factors, and in the short-run may have con-
      tributed to apparent family problems..., state the writers....

181. Lewis, Hylan. Black Families: A Sociological Profile. Atlanta:
      Atlanta University, 1974. 20 pp.

      The author relates the research and writings of W.E.B. DuBois to
      the sociology of the Black family in the United States; and second,
      presented selected data having to do with the structure and func-
      tioning of contemporary Black families. The writer also discusses
      the issues of knowledge, theory, methodology, and social policy
      raised by the study of family life among Blacks....

182. Low, W. Augustus and Virgil A. Clift. <u>Encyclopedia of Black America</u>. New York: McGraw-Hill Book Co., 1981, pp. 379-383, 459-463, 698, 700, 801.

The writers assert that one of the great advantages of most Black families has been their tremendous adaptive flexibility, that stoical ability to survive. They conclude: "In many ways, with such changes as those noted of the increasingly excessive number of females now found among whites, whites may well benefit by learning more about a Black familial advantage-how do you make it, indeed, with less than one male for every female."

183. Lyman, Stanford M. <u>The Black American in Sociological Thought</u>. New York: G. P. Putnam's Sons, 1972, pp. 55-61, 145 ff.

Various references are made throughout the book to the Black family: family structure, cultural origins of the Black family, ecology of the Black family, family structure as source of frustration, Black matriarchy, mate selection and frustration. This work has notes at the end of each chapter, and there is an index.

184. Millman, Marcia and Rosabeth Moss Kanter, Editors. <u>Another Voice: Feminist Perspectives on Social Life and Social Science</u>. New York: Anchor Press, 1975, pp. 240-250.

Lena Wright Myers wrote "Black Women and Self-esteem" for this collection of essays. She argues that it is time for a new view of the Black woman, one that allows for the possibility of self-esteem and pride. She states that Blacks do not necessarily measure themselves against whites, not Black women against white women. The mother-headed household has assets as well as liabilities, and, in fact, may be a source of strength and pride, concludes Dr. Myers.

185. Pettigrew, Thomas F. <u>A Profile of the Negro American</u>. Princeton, NJ: D. Van Nostrand Co., Inc., 1964, pp. 15-24, 80-82, 113-114, 144-147.

There is one section on the Black family called "Family Disorganization and Personality." The writer concludes that personality development of children in families without fathers may also be related to three recurrent problems among Black Americans: juvenile delinquency, crime against person, and schizophrenia. More research, continues the author, is necessary to link definitely these symptoms of social disorganization to impaired family structure, but present (1964) data are most suggestive. This work has more than 560 references, name and subject index.

186. _____. Editor. <u>Racial Discrimination in the United States</u>. New York: Harper & Row, 1975, pp. 279-281, 283, 314-315, 317, 320-322, 359, 376-382.

Pettigrew:

It was pointed out that the Moynihan Report (1965) documents the many factors related to the decline in family stability among Negroes, such as high rates areas of unemployment, poverty, high rates of mobility from rural areas to city slums and within city slums, etc. Presumably, if these factors were reduced, family stability would increase and the equality index (EI) for marital status would climb, concludes the writer.

187.   Ploski, Harry A. and Ernest Kaiser, Editors. The Negro Almanac. New York: Bellwether Co., 1971, pp. 369-383.

The editors give several points of view on the Black Family: "Analysis of the Moynihan Report," "The Muslim View," "The Black Panther View," "Economic Polarization," "Income and Family Stability," "Reproductivity and Health." They also give some selected facts and selected tables on the Black family....

188.   _____ and James Williams, Editors. The Negro Almanac: A Reference Work on the Afro-American. John Wiley and Sons, 1983, pp. 475-526.

The editors discuss the following topics on the Black family: "Current Status," "Number and Size," "Shortages of Eligible Males," "Income," "Public Assistance," "Effects of Unemployment and Poverty," "Decline of Family Farms," "Housing," "Suburban Living," "Health Care," "Sickle-Cell Disease," "Victims of Crime," "Budget Cuts and The Family," "Family Charts," "Selected Family Facts," and "Family Tables."

189.   Reid, Inez Smith. "Together" Black Women. New York: Emerson Hall Publishers, Inc., 1972, pp. 32-34, 54-78, 88-98, 99-112.

This book was prepared for the Black Women's Community Development Foundation. Various references are made throughout the book to Black women, men, and families. The work has seven chapters and an index.

190.   Riessman, Frank. The Inner-City Child. New York: Harper & Row, 1976, pp. 32-45.

Many references are made to the Black family throughout this book. One section however, is entitled "Family Life." The writer points out that the history of the Black family in America consists of a continued struggle to carve out family roles and structures that could withstand the assaults of slavery, segregation, discrimination, and poverty. Census statistics, which are the basis for most assessments of Black family life, indicate the damaging effects of these encounters. What the statistics fail to reveal, however, states Dr. Riessman, are the nature and pervasiveness of the destructive social and political influences on Black families

Riessman:

in America. Nor do the statistics reveal the mechanism that the Black culture has developed in its attempt to counteract their impact, and the sources of strength that have enabled Blacks to maintain their struggle for a viable family life, concludes the author.

191.   Rosaldo, Michelle Z. and Louise Lamphere, Editors. Woman, Culture, and Society. Stanford: Stanford University Press, 1974, pp. 10, 26, 110-128, 130-134, 150-156.

The writers state that many previous studies of the Black family have taken a male perspective, emphasizing the street-corner life of Black men and viewing men as peripheral to familial concerns. Though correctly stressing the economic difficulties that Black males face in a racist society, these and other studies have fostered a stereotype of Black families as fatherless and subject to a domineering woman's matriarchal rule. From such simplistic accounts it is all too easy to come to blame juvenile delinquency, divorce, illegitimacy, and other social ills on the Black family, while ignoring the oppressive reality of our political and economic system and the adaptive resiliency and strength that Black families have shown, conclude the authors.

192.   Smythe, Mabel M., Editor. The Black American Reference Book. Englewood Cliffs, NJ: Prentice-Hall, 1976, pp. 316-340.

Chapter 8, "The Black Family" was essayed by Joseph H. Douglass and Mabel M. Smythe. They assert: "Due in part to a determination to eliminate racial discrimination and achieve equality on all fronts, and in part to the broadened opportunities for personal development and greater public regard for civil rights, it is likely that in the future fewer and fewer distinctions will be drawn between the great mass of Black families and those of the general population." The majority of differences which exist today between white and Black families are more closely linked with social class than with racial identity; as Black Americans become more widely dispersed along the socioeconomic scale, most of these differences should tend to disappear. It is to this end that the battle against inequality must address itself vigorously until discrimination assumes its rightful place as a dusty relic of the past, conclude Douglass and Smythe.

193.   Solomon, Barbara B. Black Empowerment: Social Work in Oppressed Communities. New York: Columbia University Press, 1976, pp. 170-193.

Chapter Six is entitled "...in Black Families." The writer observes that the most important factor in the role the family has played as carrier of society's negative valuation of Black people has been the strong connection between characteristics more common in Black families and "problem" behavior; i.e., single-parent households, marital instability, even poverty have been identified as primary factors in the etiology of problem behavior. However,

Solomon:

direct, linear relationships between family process and problem behavior have not been clearly demonstrated, states the writer. Finally, sources external to the family but which serve to characterize Black Families have been identified as reinforcers of society's negative valuation of Blacks. These negative images of
Black families can be found in various presentations in the mass
media. However, much of the negative impact comes not so much
from inaccurate portrayals of Black family life but from the tendency to perceive any portrayal as "typical" and therefore more
diverse portrayals are needed to reflect the actual diversity in
the form and content of Black family life, concludes Prof. Solomon.

194. Somerville, Rose M. Introduction to Family Life and Sex Education.
      Prentice-Hall: Englewood Cliffs, NJ: 1972, pp. 29-30, 48-49, 52-
      54, 138-139, 222-226, 377-378.

      It was pointed out that 10 percent of urban Black families are up-
      per class, 40 percent middle class, and 50 percent lower class.
      It was also suggested that the lifestyle of middle class Black
      families is similar to the upper-middle-class white family. The
      author argues that among Northern younger Black families in which
      only the husband worked, family income relative to whites showed
      no gain from 1960 to 1970. She concludes that family income among
      Black families at all economic levels was more apt to include the
      wages of several earners than among white families....

195. Steiner, Gilbert Y. The Futility of Family Policy. Washington,
      DC: Brookings Institution, 1981, pp. 16-17, 21, 37-38, 42.

      The writer points out that if strengthening the family meant na-
      tional action to preclude continued growth of matriarchal Black
      families, the cost to pride and race consciousness would exceed
      the benefits even of economic and education programs....

196. Swan, L. Alex. Survival and Progress: The Afro-American Experi-
      ence. Westport, CT: Greenwood Press, 1981, pp. 109-127.

      Chapter 7 is entitled "Family Relations Therapy, the Black Family."
      This essay delineates some of the many problems in Black family
      relations and the various possible techniques and approaches for
      handling problems and crises in the family. The primary aim of
      Black families is to stay together as families and experience
      growth and development, but they need assistance to understand
      their particular situation and organize their efforts to handle
      diverse forces that affect them, states Dr. Swain. Although most
      families are aware of these forces, they do not always fully under-
      stand their nature and character nor have appropriate and effec-
      tive ways of dealing with them. Once this understanding is achie-
      ved, the employment of adequate, appropriate, and effective means
      of handling these forces becomes the major concern of the families,
      concludes the author.

197. Taylor, Arnold H. Travail and Triumph: Black Life and Culture in the South Since the Civil War. Westport, CT: Greenwood Press, 1976, pp. 161-183.

    In Chapter 8 Dr. Taylor discusses "The Reconstruction of the Family," "The Persistence of the Two-Parent Family," "The Paternal Family," "The Maternal Family," "The Extended Family," "No Motherless Children," "Children Rearing Under Apartheid," and "The Dilemma of Wives and Daughters." The author traces the Black family from reconstruction to present. He contends that the Black family has a history of stability....

198. Webster, Staten W., Editor. The Disadvantaged Leader: Knowing, Understanding, Education. San Francisco: Chandler Publishing Co., 1966, pp. 146-147, 152, 153-158, 164-169.

    Many references are made throughout this book to the Black family. The editor gives the overall theme of the book when he points out that the behavior of disadvantaged groups and the individuals should be seen both as a product of their past social heritage and as an adjustment to present social pressures and problems. Without these insights, continues the editor, the aggressive, hostile physical behaviors of some Black children will be viewed solely as evidence for the group's supposed lack of social and moral standards of conduct. But, concludes Prof. Webster, with knowledge, and understanding of the problems faced by Black families, one can understand the possible necessity of such behaviors.

199. Willhelm, Sidney. Who Needs the Negro? Cambridge, MA: Schenkman Publishing Co., Inc., 1970, pp. 4-11.

    Chapter II is entitled "Family Structure and Social Status," and it discusses the Black family from slavery to present (1970). The author attempts to present both points of view on the stability and instability of the Black family. He declares that we can make one certain general conclusion about the causes and consequences of an unstable family life for the American Black. Black households merely reflect the more fundamental processes that condemn the Black in so many ways, namely, the interrelationship between economic conditions and white racism, concludes the author.

200. Williams, James D., Editor. The State of Black America, 1979. New York: National Urban League, January 17, 1979, pp. 25-40.

    Dr. Robert B. Hill contributed "The Economic Status of Black Families" to this book. The writer argues that contrary to some depictions in the news media, increasing proportions of Black families are not "making it" economically today (1979). The economic gains of many middle and upper-income Black families have eroded in recent years. He concludes that the economic cleavage between Black and white families is widening and not narrowing....

201.   _____. The State of Black America, 1980. New York: National
Urban League, January 22, 1980, pp. 29-58.

"Black Families in the 1970's" was written by Dr. Robert B. Hill.
The researcher points out that the unemployment and income gaps
between Black and white families widened during the 1970's. He
states that the proportion of economically middle-class Black families did not significantly increase during the 1970's, but remained relatively unchanged. Dr. Hill predicted that in the 1980's
that extended families will continue to play influential roles in
providing vital social and economic support to middle-income and
low-income Black families....

202.   Wiseman, Jacqueline P., Editor. People As Partners. San Francisco: Canfield Press, 1977, pp. 365-385.

There is one section from this collection that deals with the
Black family by Robert Staples. This essay was taken from Dr.
Staples' book, Introduction to Black Sociology. Dr. Staples concludes: "Whatever the future of Black families, it is time to put
to rest all the theories about Black family instability and give
recognition to the crucial role of this institution in the Black
struggle for SURVIVAL."

203.   Woods, Frances J. Cultural Values of American Ethnic Groups. New
York: Harper and Brothers, 1956, pp. 151, 183-185, 242-245, 268-
271, 296-298, 318-319, 337-338.

The author asserts that of all ethnic family types the Negro is
perhaps the most unstable. He states that to some extent this
instability was rooted in the history of the American Negro family
when it was under slavery. Prof. Woods based much of his conclusions on the works of E. Franklin Frazier. Hence, he came to
faulty conclusions.

204.   Young, Carlene, Editor. Black Experience: Analysis and Synthesis.
San Rafael, CA: Leswing Press, 1972, pp. 155-172.

Three essays in this collection deal with the Black family and are
annotated elsewhere in this book. They are: "Black Families in
Perspective" by Andrew Billingsley; Robert Staples' "The Myth of
the Black Matriarchy"; and "Culture, Class, and Family Life Among
Low-Income Negroes" by Hylan Lewis.

1. BLACK FAMILY AND SLAVERY

205.   Ashmore, Harry S. The Other Side of Jordan. New York: W. W.
Norton and Company, Inc., 1960, pp. 54-62.

This is a narrative story about the life of a slave family. Chapter 4, "Profile of Poverty," gives account of the Black family and
its struggle in poverty.

206. Blassingame, John W. Black New Orleans, 1860-1880. Chicago: Uni-
      versity of Chicago Press, 1973, pp. 79-106.

      Chapter 4 discusses the "Family Life" of Blacks. The scholar be-
      lieves that considering the Black male's conception of the family
      and of women in conjunction with the statistics on maleheaded
      households, the almost inescapable conclusion is that the Black
      family in New Orleans during Reconstruction was matriarchal in na-
      ture. Dr. Blassingame concludes that relatively open housing,
      memories of the denial of opportunities for stable family during
      slavery, concerted drives to promote family stability, and the
      economic opportunities resulting from weak labor unions led to a
      relatively stable patriarchal Black family in New Orleans during
      Reconstruction.

207. _____. The Slave Community: Plantation Life in the Antebel-
      lum South. New York: Oxford University Press, 1972, pp. 77-163.

      Dr. Blassingame declares that the love the slaves had for their
      parents reveals clearly the importance of the family. Although it
      was weak, although it was frequently broken, the slave family pro-
      vided an important buffer, a refuge from the rigors of slavery.
      While the slave father could rarely protect the members of his
      family from abuse, continues the author, he could often gain their
      love and respect in other ways. The author concludes that in his
      family, the slave not only learned how to avoid the blows of the
      master, but also drew the line on the love and sympathy of its
      members to raise his spirits. The family was, in short, an impor-
      tant survival mechanism....

208. Brawley, Benjamin. A Short History of the American Negro. New
      York: Macmillan Company, 1919, pp. 48-60.

      In Chapter 4, "The Institution of Slavery", Dr. Brawley gives a
      brief discussion on this "peculiar institution" and points to in-
      justices done to the Black family. There are also sections on the
      effects of the treatment of slaves and slave breeding....

209. Censer, Jane Turner. North Carolina Planters and Their Children:
      1800-1860. Baton Rouge, LA: Louisiana State University Press,
      1984, pp. 140-148.

      The author points out that some planters cared little about divi-
      ding slave families. Other planters apparently saw division by
      slave families primarily as a way to equalize their own children's
      legacies, concludes Dr. Censer.

210. Davis, George A. and O. Fred Donaldson. Blacks in the United
      States: A Geographic Perspective. Boston: Houghton Mifflin Co.,
      1975, pp. 4, 11, 113, 127-129, 209-210.

      The writers argue that the fundamental problem of housing for

Davis and Donaldson:

Black families has not only been one of the quantity or quality of dwellings, important as these may be, but also one of whether they should be concentrated in separate areas or be free to seek their housing in the general market. The authors argue that the urban ghetto performs many of the same functions for Blacks, both social and spatial, as the slave plantations. Both the plantation and the ghetto are adaptations in space and time to the racism of the society in which they exist. Until the larger society's definition of the innate groups changes, social institutions will be developed to confine them, conclude the authors.

211. Donald, Henderson H. The Negro Freedman: Life Conditions of the American Negro in the Early Years After Emancipation. New York: Henry Schuman, Inc., 1952, pp. 56-75, 77-92, 184-185.

Chapter 5 is called "Marriage and Family Life of Blacks." The author points out that the great anxiety of many Blacks, after they had been set free, was to unite their scattered families to bring back the mother, child, wife, or husband who had been sold away before, or in some cases had become separated in the hurry and confusion of their flight from slavery. Dr. Donald concludes: "Conditions of slavery were responsible for the development of the odd relations between parents and children. When Blacks became free, these relations were still identified with their family organization. They remained so until Blacks were able to adopt the better ways pertaining to this social institution...."

212. Dormon, James H. and Robert R. Jones. The Afro-American Experience: A Cultural History Throughout Emancipation. New York: John Wiley & Sons, Inc., 1974, pp. 169-226.

There is one chapter entitled "Plantation Slavery II: Psychocultural Dynamics." The authors contend that both slave men and slave women carried out viable familial roles and worked together to accomplish the goals they set for their families. The writers point out that there is little indication from slave sources that the slave family was tenacious and a vital institution because of the strength and energy infused into it by both slave men and women.

213. Elkins, Stanley M. Slavery. Chicago: University of Chicago Press, 1968, pp. 53-54, 73, 130-140.

This work gives a short discussion of the impact of the institution of slavery on Black marriages and the Black family.

214. Escott, Paul D. Slavery Remembered: A Record of Twentieth-Century Slave Narratives. Chapel Hill, NC: University of North Carolina Press, 1979, pp. 46-51, 94, 138-139, 144-149.

The writer states that the slave narratives make clear that

Escott:

families were a vital institution and a towering source of strength
for the slaves. Slaves often went to great lengths to keep their
families intact. One indication of the slave's efforts to maintain their families was their method of choosing surnames. The
former slaves reported that their family names usually followed
their father's...,and his children viewed that name as their own....

215. Feldstein, Stanley. Once a Slave: The Slaves View of Slavery.
New York: William Morrow and Co., 1971, pp. 52-61.

Many references are made throughout the book to the slave and his
family. One section, "Marriage and Family Life," deals directly
with the family life of slaves on the plantation--the arena of dehumanization. The author points out that the Southern slaveholder
feared that real family life among the slaves could undermine the
foundation of slavery itself. Hence, the slaveholder was convin-
ced that family life had to succumb to slavery and slavery must
reign supreme over every right and every other institution, however venerable or sacred. Professor Feldstein surmises that although the threat of separation of the family was always present,
the slaves patiently endured in order to teach the principles of
family life. The author concludes that all their pleasure came
from the family and they spent what free time they had in family
assemblage....

216. Fogel, Robert William and Stanley L. Engerman. Time on the Cross:
The Economics of American Negro Slavery. Boston: Little, Brown &
Co., 1974, Vol. 1, pp. 5, 49, 52, 80-85, 107-109, 127-128, 134-
144, 155-156.

There is one section that discusses "The Family." The authors argue that planters assigned three functions to the slave family.
First, it was the administrative unit for the distribution of food
and clothing and for the provision of shelter. The family was also an important instrument for maintaining labor discipline.
Third, the family was the main instrument for promoting the increase of the slave population. The writers concluded that the
anguish on the auction block as well as the struggle of Blacks to
reunite their severed families, both during and immediately after
slavery, suggests that the love that permeated slave families elu-
ded most white observers -- perhaps because of a veil of racial
and class biases which obscured their vision and prevented them
from seeing the real content of Black family life.

217. Fremantle, Sir Arthur J. Three Months in the Southern States:
April-June, 1863. New York: John Bradburn, 1864, pp. 84-86.

The writer was an English traveler who reported his observations
while traveling through the South. While in Louisiana and Texas,
he observed Blacks from Mississippi who had to leave their family.
Sir Fremantle noted slaves all over the South were separated from
their families because of the Civil War. After the war many ex-
slaves tried to locate their families and many did.

218. Furnas, J. C. Goodbye to Uncle Tom. New York: William Sloane As-
      sociates, 1956, pp. 135-138, 185-188, 192-193, 247-248.

      The author points out that in many cases when slaves escaped and
      went North or to Canada, they frequently returned South to get
      their families and help them to escape to free territory. Some
      were successful and some were not. Many ex-slaves tried to locate
      their families after slavery.

219. Greene, Lorenzo J. The Negro in Colonial New England, 1620-1776.
      New York: Columbia University Press, 1942, pp. 191-217.

      Chapter 8 deals with "The Slave Family." The author suggests that
      forcible mating and the breeding of slaves for market were rare in
      New England. Hence, these things did not demoralize the slave fa-
      mily. It was stated that New England slaves were compelled to
      marry in the manner prescribed for the general population. He
      concluded, in part: "Once married, moreover, they were expected-
      as were free white persons-to observe the sanctity of the nuptial
      tie...."

220. Hepworth, George H. The Whip, Hoe, and Sword: or, The Gulf-
      Department in '63. Boston: Walker, Wise and Co., 1864, pp. 140-
      143.

      The writer suggests that the Union Army tried not to break up
      slave families when they advanced in the Southern states. The
      Army was impressed by the concerns that the slaves showed for
      wanting to locate their families....

221. Herskovits, Melville J. The Myth of the Negro Past. Boston:
      Beacon Press, 1958, pp. 139f, 167-190, 198f.

      The author believes even in the United States, where Africanisms
      persisted with great difficulty, much family organization as
      existed during slave times in terms of relationship between pa-
      rents and children, and between parents themselves, did not lack
      African sanctions. Prof. Herskovits argues that slavery did not
      cause the "maternal" family; but it tended to continue certain
      elements in the cultural endowment brought to the New World by
      Blacks....

222. Huggins, Nathan, et al., Editors. Key Issues in the Afro-American
      Experience. New York: Harcourt Brace Jovanovich, 1971, pp. 26-39.

      Chapter Two in this collection was written by Robert H. Abzug and
      is entitled "The Black Family During Reconstruction." The author
      suggests that the quality of Black family life in the post-Emanci-
      pation years, suggests that many racist accounts of Black mores
      have been allowed to prevail. Dr. Abzug argues that a moral and
      emotional commitment to family not only survived within Blacks
      during slavery, but remained a primary concern in their first
      years of freedom....

223. Magdol, Edward. A Right to The Land: Essays on the Freedman's
      Community. Westport, CT: Greenwood Press, 1977, pp. 23-25, 49,
      56-60, 107, 181-183, 222.

      The author points out that during their enslavement Afro-Americans
      made of their several modes of family structure an instrument for
      survival and for creating community. The writer observes that
      slave fathers provided for their families through hunting, fishing,
      gardening, working to provide extra income, building and furnish-
      ing the interiors of slave cabins to make them more comfortable,
      and giving gifts to wives and children. Slaves also maintained
      elaborate kinship networks....

224. Marshall, Albert O. Army Life: From a Soldier's Journal: Inci-
      dents, Sketches and Records of a Union Soldier's Army Life, in
      Camp and Field, 1861-1864. Joliet, IL: The Author, 1883, pp.
      396-399.

      The author states that when the Union Army liberated the slaves
      in the South, many of them constantly asked if they were free to
      join their wives or husbands. The Union Army tried not to separate
      slave families when they occupied the South....

225. Martinson, Floyd Mansfield. Family in Society. New York: Dodd,
      Mead & Co., 1972, pp. 56-74.

      Chapter 4 discusses "Slavery and the Black Family." The writer
      contends that American slavery destroyed bonds of sympathy and
      affection between men and women of the same household. In order
      to survive, states Martinson, they had to acquire a new language,
      adopt habits consistent with forced agricultural labor, and at-
      tempt to imitate the social systems of the "master" race. Their
      slave children, continues the writer, knew only the plantation
      system of inferior status and developed modes of behavior appro-
      priate to that system. Professor Martinson does point out that
      the majority of present day Black families are bi-parental and
      stable, and this fact is often overlooked....

226. Mullin, Gerald W. Flight and Rebellion: Slave Resistance in
      Eighteenth-Century Virginia. New York: Oxford University Press,
      1974, pp. 26-28, 48, 55, 65-66, 79, 88, 103-106, 109-111, 180n,
      198n.

      Various references are made to the slave family throughout the
      book. Professor Mullin points out that even though many slaves,
      men and women, escaped, they did not forget their families. In
      fact, some of the fugitives took their families with them when
      they ran away. The author surmises that one hundred and forty-
      two women slaves were advertised as runaways from 1737 to 1801.
      This book has extensive notes, Bibliography and Index.

227. Owens, Leslie Howard. This Species of Property: Slave and Cul-
      ture in the Old South. New York: Oxford University Press, 1976,
      pp. 183-213.

      Chapter 8 discusses "A Family Folk" and deals with the slave fami-
      ly. The author argues that whenever the slave family--natural or
      extended--was intact, however, and slave males were reliably per-
      forming their duties, they most likely did symbolize authority
      within the family structure. Some writers disagree with that as-
      sertion.

228. Rawick, George P. The American Slave: A Composite Autobiobiogra-
      phy: From Sundown to Sun-Up: The Making of The Black Community.
      Westport, CT: Greenwood Publishing Co., 1972, pp. 77-94.

      Chapter 5 discusses "The Black Family Under Slavery." Author
      notes that the activity of the slaves in creating patterns of fam-
      ily life that were functionally integrative but did more than mere-
      ly prevent the destruction of personalities. It was part of the so-
      cial process out of which came Black pride, Black culture, Black
      identity, the Black community, and the Black revolution in Ameri-
      ca, argues Prof. Rawick.

229. Scott, Donald M. and Bernard Wishy, Editors. American Families:
      A Documentary History. New York: Harper and Row, 1982, pp. 122,
      310-334, 607.

      There is one essay in this collection entitled "The Black Family
      Under Slavery and After." It states that the family was consi-
      dered a mechanism of control; slaves in the family state, the ar-
      gument went, were less "wild", more content, and thus better wor-
      kers and, because of their ties to their families, less likely to
      run away. The slaves put rather difficult stock in their familial
      order and looked to it as a cushion against the condition of sla-
      very. Several recent studies, in fact, have shown that the slave
      family extended across time and space and incorporated a vast ar-
      ray of real and "fictitious" kin, providing slaves with a suppor-
      tive and protective community, argue the editors. Transition from
      slavery to freedom removed the threat of forced separation from
      most Black families and provided Black marriages with legal stand-
      ing. In the first three years following the close of the Civil
      War, tens of thousands of Black men and women rushed to give sanc-
      tion and protection to the marriages they had made under slavery.
      "But emancipation opened few lasting opportunities to the freedmen,
      and for the rest of the century and after they faced the unrelent-
      ing and largely successful attempt of white society to defeat their
      efforts to secure at least the white level of economic gains and
      civil rights that freedom was supposed to mean. Throughout the
      later parts of the century the vast majority of the Blacks conti-
      nued as agricultural laborers for white planters, comprising a
      kind of Black peasantry made up of tenant farmers and sharecrop-
      pers," conclude the authors.

230.   Smith, Julia Floyd.   Slavery and Plantation Growth in Antebellum
        Florida: 1821-1860. Gainesville: University of Florida Press,
        1973, pp. 6, 7, 77, 79, 91-93, 116, 118, 208-209.

        The author mentions the separation of the slave families. She
        points out that there was a certain amount of personal tragedy in-
        volved in the system of hiring since the place of hire was some-
        times far away from family and friends. It was noted that ex-
        slaves and fugitive slaves showed great concern for their families
        and many tried to rescue them. It was also stated that some plan-
        ters sold slave children because they were their fathers and they
        did not want to be constantly reminded of that fact, especially
        by their wives.

231.   The War of the Rebellion: A Compilation of the Official Records
        of the Union and Confederate Armies. Washington, DC: United
        States Government Printing Office, 1889. Vol. 26, Part 1, p. 775.

        It is apparent from the following letter that the leadership in
        the Union Army during the Civil War had some compassion for Black
        families. Major-General W. B. Franklin sent a letter to Brig.
        General A. L. Lee in October, 1863, requesting men for the cavalry.
        He ordered: "...Negroes without families, able-bodied, who will
        be of use to us as teamsters, should be brought in. No women or
        children, and no Negroes who have families dependeht upon them
        for support, must be taken...."

232.   Thorpe, Earl E.   The Mind of the Negro: An Intellectual Afro-
        American. Baton Rouge, LA: Ortlieb Press, 1961, pp. 136-149.

        Chapter 7 discusses "Ante-Bellum Classes and Family Life Among
        Negroes." The writer argues that a unique characteristic of
        Black family life has been the prevalence of matriarchal tenden-
        cies. This has been a heritage from slavery. During the ante-
        bellum period both tradition and economic necessity were lacking
        to instill in the slave wife subordination to masculine authority.
        After emancipation, since many mothers had to support themselves
        and their children, female independence and self-reliance were
        further strengthened. Dr. Thorpe concludes that it was among
        ante-bellum free persons that family life first became institu-
        tional among Blacks....

233.   _____. The Old South: A Psychohistory. Durham, NC: See-
        man Printery, 1972, pp. 17-18, 146-159, 209-211.

        In the chapter on "Master and Slave," Dr. Thorpe states that the
        majority of slaves lived on family or yeoman farms where intimacy
        between the races was greater than on large plantations. He con-
        cludes, in part: "...Indeed, brutality in the slave system seemed
        to strengthen the slave family. Both male and female slaves loved
        their children dearly and agonized over the prospect of their fu-
        ture in bondage. All slaves tended to view their family as a
        place of refuge...."

234. Weatherford, Willis Duke. The Negro From Africa to America. New
      York: Negro Universities Press, 1969. (Originally published in
      1924), pp. 139-167.

      Chapter VII, "Plantation Life During the Slave Regime," discusses
      the Black family. The author discusses slavery in several states
      in the South. Weatherford surmises that perhaps the greatest
      hardship of slavery lay in the possible separation of families in
      cases of sale of slaves. Not infrequently, one or the other of
      the planters would buy the husband or the wife in order to get
      them together on the same plantation. It should be pointed out
      that this was done not so much for any humanitarian motives, but
      also in the interest of efficiency.

235. Webber, Thomas L. Deep Like the Rivers: Education in the Slave
      Quarter Community, 1831-1865. New York: W.W. Norton and Co.,
      1978, pp. 111-117, 157-179.

      Both Chapters 9 and 13 deal with the slave family. The frequent
      appearance in the narratives of uncles and aunts, particularly the
      mother's brother, caring for, protecting, and educating their sis-
      ters' and brothers' children can perhaps best be explained by the
      familial ties and reciprocal duties which siblings internalized
      during their childhoods and which continued through their adult
      lives. The impression that the children of the quarters had a
      multitude of family members all vying with one another to nurture,
      protect, and educate them is neither intended nor accurate. How-
      ever, the Black sources do depict a common extended pattern of
      family relationships in which most quarter children associated
      closely with many other individuals filling several different
      kinds of educational roles. Although the realities of slavery
      meant that the individual membership of given families sometimes
      changed drastically and suddenly, what stands out is that such
      change over time did not greatly affect the quarter family's abi-
      lity to educate its children. For most quarter families were com-
      posed of a number of individuals who felt a responsibility to step
      in and fill roles that were vacated through a death or sale.
      The author states: "Thus, although many a grandparent, uncle, or
      older sister played an important educational role in the presence
      of mother and father, they were ready to fill the roles of father
      and mother as well. It was this willingness and ability on the
      part of an extended number of family members to play the primary
      educational roles of father and mother that made the family not
      only an effective but a stable educational instrument of the quar-
      ter community."

236. Williamson, Joel. After Slavery: The Negro in South Carolina
      During Reconstruction, 1861-1877. New York: W.W. Norton and Co.,
      1965, pp. 306-312.

      The author observed that many Blacks emerged from slavery with
      orthodox family associations already well defined. In 1865, seve-
      ral Black families on a South Carolina cotton plantation were like
      a number of white families, in ages, sizes and proportions between

Williamson:

male and female in the families. Even at the time of emancipation,
among Blacks the demands of kinship above the immediate family
level were deep and wide. Dr. Williamson concludes, in part:
"The freedman not only recognize the claims of sons, daughters,
and wives, but he also values his ties with cousins, uncles, and
aunts, with ancestors back through the generations, and with his
children's children ad infinitum. This clannishness among Negroes,
if it changed at all, grew richer in Reconstruction when they were
relatively free to express their attitudes by actions...."

237. Williamson, Robert C. Marriage and Family Relations. New York:
John Wiley & Sons, Inc., 1972, pp. 79-95, 407-408, 425, 452-453.

Chapter 4 is devoted to ethnic groups including the four historical developments of the Black family: (1) the slavery period,
(2) emancipation and post-Civil War, (3) urbanization and migration, and (4) the present day liberation movement. The writer
argues that the class and income levels of the Black family have
effects comparable to those found in white society. For this
reason we should be cautious about making "The Negro family a
special target of social action apart from a massive attack upon
socio-economic structure of American society,"concludes the author.

2.   BLACK FAMILY AND ABORTION

238. McCormick, E. Patricia. Attitudes towards Abortion: Experiences
of Selected Black and White Women. Lexington, MA: Lexington
Books, 1975, pp. 40, 44, 49, 51, 54, 59-129.

This book was based on a study done in the Baltimore-Washington
metropolitan area. About 200 women were involved in this study.
The author used more than 50 Tables to show that there is a substantial differential in racial attitudes toward abortion, with
Black women being less receptive to the use of induced abortion
either as a supplement or an an alternative to contraception....

3.   BLACK FAMILY AND ALCOHOLISM

239. Harper, Frederick D., Editor. Alcohol Abuse and Black America.
Alexandria, VA: Douglas Publishers, 1976, pp. 177-185.

Muriel W. Sterne and David J. Pittman wrote an essay for this collection called "Alcohol Abuse and the Black Family." According
to the authors, alcohol abuse, whether defined in terms of addiction to alcohol, impaired role performance due to excessive in-
take, situationally inappropriate drinking, or the committing of
alcohol-related arrestable offenses, has ramifications for the
Black family by contributing to family dissolution and inadequate
parental performance. They conclude: "These adult problems of
the family lead to school failure and delinquency in the next generation, setting into motion a 'vicious circle' of adult heavy

Harper:

drinking and problem drinking, inadequate parenting, and juvenile problems. This chain of problems frustrates family efforts to move out of the world of conflict and hopelessness and into a more stable and gratifying life."

4. BLACK FAMILY AND CHILDREN

240. Baughman, E. Earl and W. Grant Dahlstorm. Negro and White Children: A Psychological Study in the Rural South. New York: Academic Press, 1968, pp. 85-95.

Chapter 5 is entitled "The Relationship of Selected Family Variables to Ability and Academic Achievement." The authors suggest that the mother's birthplace is less definitely related to the child's intellective performance than the father's birthplace. Also, as a variable, the origin of a child's mother has greater significance among the Negro children than among the white children. In general, Negro children with non-nuclear mothers tend to show stronger intellective performances than children with nuclear mothers, state the authors.

241. King, Margaret A. and Alfred L. Karlson. A Non-Racist Framework For the Analysis of Educational Programs For Black Children. Palo Alto, CA: R & E Research Associates, Inc., Publishers, 1982, pp. 25-35.

The writers suggest that the Black family and community are an integral part of the development of Black children and that this relationship between the Black family and the community provides the survival mechanisms that are needed for Black children to cope with the larger society....

242. Ooms, Theodora, Editor. Teenage Pregnancy in a Family Context: Implications For Policy. Philadelphia: Temple University Press, 1981, pp. 307-325.

June Dobbs Butts contributed an essay to this collection entitled "Adolescent Sexuality and Teenage Pregnancy From a Black Perspective." The writer discussed a number of characteristics of the Black experience, that she believes, have relevance to teenage pregnancy: the Black family, Black extended family, a sex-positive view of life, and the historical value of fecundity.

243. Williams, Thomas, Editor. Socialization and Communication in Primary Groups. The Hague: Mouton, 1975, pp. 183-205.

There is one essay in the collection written by Prof. Carol B. Stack, entitled, "Who Raises Black Children: Transaction of Child Givers and Child Receivers." This essay was based on an urban Black community in the Midwest, called the Flats. The

Williams:

The author points out that the Black children move back and forth from the households of their mothers to households of close female kin. The woman who temporarily assumes the kinship obligation to care for a child acquires the major cluster of rights and duties ideally associated with "motherhood", concludes the researcher....

5. BLACK FAMILY AND ECONOMICS

244. Bell, Carolyn Shaw. <u>The Economics of the Ghetto</u>. New York: Pegasus, 1970, pp. 45, 48, 51, 63-64, 86-88, 169-172, 195-203.

Many references are made throughout the book to the Black family: family size, consumption, housing, income, poverty, children, work requirements, education, expenditures, and AFDC (Aid to Families with Dependent Children). This book includes notes, appendix, Bibliography, and Index, as well as various tables, charts and graphs.

245. Schiller, Bradley R. <u>The Economics of Poverty and Discrimination</u>. Englewood Cliffs, NJ: Prentice-Hall, Inc., 1973, pp. 90-101.

One section, "Family Size and Status," refers mainly to Blacks. The author surmises that there exists a strong presumption that family size and status are important causes of poverty, for most of the poor families either grew large or broke up. Moreover, economic insecurity itself may have contributed to the dissolution of the family or to excessive reproduction. Professor Schiller concludes that family breakup and growth, are more likely to extend and deepen a family's poverty than bring it about....

246. Silberman, Charles E. <u>Crisis in Black and White</u>. New York: Vintage Books, 1964, pp. 111-119, 226-231.

Several references to the Black family are discussed throughout the book. The writer does point out that a number of studies have demonstrated that Black parents have surprisingly high aspirations for their children--higher, in fact, than those held by white parents in the same socio-economic class.

247. Vatter, Harold G. and Thomas Palm, Editors. <u>The Economics of Black America</u>. New York: Harcourt Brace Jovanovich, Inc., 1972, pp. 252-265.

Many references to Blacks and the Black family are discussed throughout the book. The authors point out that Black Ghetto families are caught in a vicious economic cycle and the only way they can escape from it is that the Federal Government must have a policy of full employment for all and there must be a meaningful federal "war on poverty."

248. Willie, Charles V. The Caste and Class Controversy. Bayside, NY:
     General Hall, 1979, pp. 80-91.

     James A. Hefner penned "The Economics of The Black Family From
     Four Perspectives" for this book. The four perspectives discussed
     are: income, economic security, self-determination, and economic
     freedom. Prof. Hefner states that racism and economics are the
     societal forces which have the greatest impact on the structure
     and functioning of the Black family in the United States. He con-
     cludes: "But more education must continue to be emphasized in the
     Black community; not only does it increase the well-being of the
     Black family, but it also reduces anti-social behavior and the
     birth-rate as well...."

6. BLACK FAMILY AND EDUCATION

249. Broom, Leonard and Norval D. Glenn. Transformation of Negro Ame-
     rica. New York: Harper & Row, 1965, pp. 81-104.

     The authors believe that the maternal Black family tends to be
     perpetuated by the fact that Black females are, on the average,
     better educated and therefore are more able to find secure employ-
     ment than the male. They continue to surmise that the greater ed-
     ucational attainments of Black females, in turn, result partly
     from the traditions of maternal families. The writers surmise
     that because of primary responsibility for family support has re-
     sided with the mother, it has been more important for females to
     have good occupational qualifications, and Black parents have
     therefore been more willing to sacrifice for the education of
     daughters. The professors conclude: "The changes in Black sex
     and family life will be slow and will depend mainly on growth of
     the middle class. Growth of the middle class, in turn, depends in
     large measure upon removal of discrimination and segregation and,
     especially, upon improved education...."

7. BLACK FAMILY AND HEALTH

250. Goering, John M. and Marvin Cummings. Health Needs of Low-Income
     Families in Urban Areas. St. Louis, MO: Medical Care Research
     Center, 1968, pp. 125-139.

     The authors discuss some systematic survey data comparing Black
     and white attitudes toward urban and rural life. The researchers
     found that among Blacks there was a greater proportion of female-
     headed families among migrants than among non-migrants. They also
     found that the greatest proportion of female-headed families was
     found among urban rather than rural-born heads of households....

251. Jones, Enrico E. and Sheldon J. Korchin, Editors. Minority Mental
     Health. New York: Praeger, 1982, pp. 227-249.

     There is one chapter written by Nancy Boyd devoted to the Black
     family entitled "Family Therapy with Black Families." The author

Jones:

states that therapists who treat Black families must be willing to
expand their concept of "family" beyond the limits of the nuclear
family unit. We must adopt a broader approach to family therapy,
which is based on our understanding of the extended family systems
in Black families. It is critital that we utilize the natural
support systems in order to help families in times of stress. We
must expand our models of family therapy to include the "significant others" who are extremely important in the lives of many
Black families. The author concludes: "Alternative methods of
treatment such as network therapy, short-term treatment, multiple
family groups, and the use of paraprofessional aides, which have
been explored in this chapter, must be expanded in order to meet
the needs of Black families. Finally, there is a need for the ex-
pansion of the training of family therapists of all professional
disciplines to include training in the cultural issues, which must
be acknowledged and utilized if we are to provide viable mental
health services in our Black and other minority communities."

252.   Owens, Charles E. Mental Health and Black Offenders. Lexington,
       MA: D. C. Heath and Co., 1980, pp. 95-109.

In the topic on "Preventing Black Crime," Dr. Owens suggests that
the majority of poor Black families are sincerely interested in
keeping their children out of the clutches of the juvenile system.
They want the same things for their children that other parents
want including equal access to educational and employment opportunities. The author argues that a number of valuable services are
needed in prevention resources. He concludes: "Many of these
services can be performed by mental-health professionals. Child
rearing and communication skills that can strengthen closer relationships through effective communication among family members can
be taught to parents. Programs that reduce the negative influences
in the environment by helping family members to obtain needed medical, educational and employment services are very much needed."

8.   BLACK FAMILY AND ILLEGITIMACY

253.   Roberts, Robert W., Editor. The Unwed Mother. New York: Harper
       and Row, 1966, pp. 133-157.

Andrew Billingsley and Amy Tate Billingsley contributed an essay
called "Illegitimacy and Patterns of Negro Family Life," to this
collection. The authors state that there are essentially three
distinct patterns of Negro family life which have emerged over the
years: matriarchal, equalitarian and patriarchal. Efforts to de-
crease illegitimacy among Negroes might well take these patterns
into account, according to the researchers. They argue that it
may be that the illegitimacy rate would be more effectively attack-
ed by policies designed to build two-parent families involving men
who exercise status, authority, and influence equal to that of
other men outside the home, and equal to that of their wives inside the home. The researchers conclude: "Thus concerted efforts

Roberts:

to raise the levels of education, employment, and adequate housing conditions, would seem to have more effect than public exhortations to stamp out illegitimate children. It may also be that those social welfare policies designed to attack the problem by keeping men away from the homes of unwed mothers might have a more desirable effect if they were completely reversed."

254. Ross, Heather L. and Isabel V. Sawhill. Time of Transition: The Growth of Families Headed by Women. Washington, DC: The Urban Institute, 1975, pp. 67-92.

The authors discuss "Race and Family Structure" in Chapter 4. Ross and Sawhill point out that high illegitimacy among Blacks is due to a higher incidence of premarital intercourse, less utilization of effective contraceptives and abortion, less chance that the pregnancy will be legitimized through marriage, and a lower probability that the child born out of wedlock will be adopted. They conclude: "...The recent higher rate of growth among Blacks is related to the continuing urbanization of the Black population; to increased sexual activity and improved health, combined with a low level of effective contraception, among teenagers; to the bleak employment prospects for Black men with little education, and to the greater availability of income outside of marriage for the poorest group of Black women."

9. BLACK FAMILY AND OCCUPATIONS

255. Edwards, G. Franklin. The Negro Professional Class. Glencoe, IL: The Free Press, 1959, pp. 86-87, 94-95, 121, 127-133, 154-156.

Various references are made throughout the book to the Black family: motivation of Southern respondents, income, influence on career selection, differences in structure of physician and dentist, role in support of physicians, characteristics of respondents, parents, marital status. The author concludes that the family was one of the chief influences for many Blacks entering certain fields....

256. Everett, Faye Philip. The Colored Situation. Boston: Meador Publishing Co., 1936, pp. 299-302.

The author makes many references to the Black family throughout the book. One section, "Character and Family Life," does deal with the Black family. Miss Everett believes that when Blacks choose a vocation they should consider the possible effects that it will have on the family life. Therefore, concludes the writer, this will abate the abnormally high percentage of broken Black homes; and will likewise reduce child delinquency, of which fifty percent is the result of family discord. This book also has a number of short biographies of various individuals.

10. BLACK FAMILY AND POVERTY

257. Allen, Vernon L., Editor. Psychological Factors in Poverty.
Chicago: Markham Publishing Co., 1970, pp. 73-82, 141-166, 167,
229-241, 326-364.

Many references are made throughout the book to the Black family:
childrearing practices, modification of the family, mother's control strategies and teaching style, family size, prenatal damage
of family, motivation parental absence, parent education, interactions with children, etc. The essence of the articles in this
book is that it is the white man who is in the first instance primarily responsible for the inadequacies of Blacks and their way of
life....

258. Batchelder, Alan B. The Economics of Poverty. New York: John
Wiley and Sons, Inc., 1966, pp. 1-4, 6-15.

Various references are made throughout the book to poor Blacks--
men, women, children, and the family. The author believes that
the United States cannot have freedom for Blacks to work on the
basis of ability and, at the same time, have freedom for employers
to discriminate on the basis of race. We cannot, continues Professor Batchelder, have superior (or even equal) schools in non-
poor areas and, at the same time, have kids in schools in poor
neighborhoods catching up. The writer concludes that we cannot
have higher transfers to poor households without leaving non-poor
households with less. We must choose, states Batchelder.

259. Caplovitz, David. The Poor Pay More: Consumer Practices of Low-
Income Families. New York: The Free Press, 1963, pp. 1-4, 6-15,
115-129, 130-136.

The families in this study lived in New York. The main part of
this work deals with various aspects of the consumer behavior of
low-income (Black) families. The author believes that in the final analysis, the consumer problems of low-income families cannot
be divorced from the other problems facing them. Until society
can find other ways of raising their educational level, concludes
Caplovitz, improving their occupational opportunities, increasing
their income, and reducing the discrimination against them--in
short, until poverty itself is eradicated--only limited solutions
to their problems as consumers can be found....

260. Ford, Thomas R., Editor. Rural U.S.A.: Persistence and Change.
Ames, Iowa: Iowa State University Press, 1978, pp. 145-152, 166-
167, 184, 190.

It was observed that the increasing number of female-headed Black
families has been viewed as an important influence perpetuating
Black poverty. To determine whether family instability contributes to rural poverty the percent of female-headed families in
rural and urban areas was compared. The editor concludes that

Ford:

family instability does not explain rural poverty; if anything,
rural families are better off than urban families....

261. Glasser, Paul H., and Lois N. Glasser. Families in Crisis. New
      York: Harper and Row, 1970, pp. 15-89.

      Part II, "Poverty," is devoted to the Black family. The authors
      point out that many Black families are concerned about having
      enough food, clothing, and shelter to maintain themselves, and
      these serve as a constant set of stressors on the Black family.
      The writers conclude that some of the crises of the poor Black
      family may be monthly, weekly, or ever daily affairs, and to ex-
      pect families to maintain themselves indefinitely in this situa-
      tion may be asking too much.

262. Gurin, Patricia and Edgar Epps. Black Consciousness, Identity,
      and Achievement: A Study of Students in Historically Black Col-
      leges. New York: John Wiley and Sons, 1975, pp. 43-44, 105-114,
      117, 120, 125, 129-141, 248-249, 250-255, 260-263, 359.

      Various references are made to Black student's families throughout
      this work. It was pointed out that the proportion of Black stu-
      dents wnose family income was below the poverty line was five
      times ⅃arger than the percentage of white students in white col-
      leges ⱳho came from poverty conditions. Chapter 5 is entitled
      "Precollege Family Background and Student's Aspirations, Motiva-
      tion, and Performance."

263. Keniston, Kenneth and The Carnegie Council on Children. All Our
      Children: The American Family Under Pressure. New York: Harcourt
      Brace Jovanovich, 1977, pp 27-28, 33-35, 92, 138, 148.

      Various references are made to the Black family and their children.
      It was pointed out that in 1974, 41 percent of all Black children
      lived in poverty. In 1976, 39 percent of teenage Blacks living in
      the inner cities were unemployed.

264. Klebanow, Diana, et al. Urban Legacy: The Story of America's
      Cities. New York: New American Library, 1977, pp. 96-98, 211-
      216, 320-324, 367.

      The authors assert that faced with the hardships of broken home
      and scarcity of employment, many Black families have sought public
      assistance. While the problem of poverty has been mitigated to a
      certain extent by welfare payments, food stamp programs and aid to
      families with dependent children--which represent the kind of con-
      tinuing assistance that was not available to immigrants or disad-
      vantaged groups in the past--it remains one of the more pressing
      of all urban problems, conclude the writers.

265. Liston, Robert A. The American Poor: A Report on Poverty in the
      United States. New York: Delacorte Press, 1970, pp. 57-69.

      There is one chapter entitled "A Visit to a Poor Harlem (New York)
      Family." The author discusses the "Smith" family and relates his
      observations of it. In this family both father and mother are to-
      gether as a family. Mr. Smith had a high-school education and was
      able to enter a training program. The family had several children
      and had no serious health problems. Mr. Liston concludes that at-
      tempting to lift this family out of poverty will surely be a dis-
      couraging task.

266. Stein, Bruno. On Relief: The Economics of Poverty and Public
      Welfare. New York: Basic Books, Inc., 1971, pp. 3-26, 165, 191-
      194.

      Various references are made throughout the book to the Black fami-
      ly: female-headed poor fragmentation of family, in lowest fifth
      of income distribution with all families, FAA (Family Assistance
      Act), FAP (Family Assistance Plan). The writer surmises that per-
      haps the rising concern with environment will again direct the
      public's attention toward poverty. In any case, concludes the
      author, the public may place a higher value on the benefits deri-
      ved from a substantial alleviation of poverty.

267. Winter, Jerry Alan, Editor. The Poor: A Culture of Poverty, or
      A Poverty of Culture? Grand Rapids, MI: William B. Eerdmans,
      Publishers, 1971, pp. 55-68.

      Chapter 2, "Family Structure, Poverty, and Race," was written by
      Charles V. Willie and deals specifically with the Black family.
      The writer concludes that the task for sociologists is not to dis-
      cover ways of overhauling the Black family so that it may be fash-
      ioned in the image of whites. More important is the task of un-
      derstanding the unique strengths in the Black family in America
      that have enabled it to accomplish in one century a kind of sta-
      bility similar to the stability that the white family in America
      has required almost three centuries to develop, continued the
      author.

11. BLACK FAMILY AND RELIGION

268. Wiseman, Jacqueline P., Editor. People as Partners: Individual
      and Family Relationships in Today's World. San Francisco: Can-
      field Press, 1971, pp. 168-182.

      There is one section in this work dealing with the Black family:
      "Black Muslim and Negro Christian Family Relationships." This
      article is a revised presentation of Harry Edwards' Master's The-
      sis, "The Black Muslim Family: A Comparative Study." In this at-
      ticle Dr. Edwards contrasts Christian and Muslim Blacks to illus-
      trate how their varying family behavior patterns, the roles of
      husband or wife in the family, child-rearing practices, relation-
      ships with in-laws, and general outlook on family life-- can be

Wiseman:

traced to the values and belief system of each religion....

12.   BLACK FAMILY AND SEX

269.   Reuter, Edward Byron. The American Race Problem. New York: Thomas Y. Crowell Co., 1970, pp. 197-224.

There is one chapter entitled "Negro Sex and Family Life." The writer surmises that the review of Negro sex standards, family life, and home conditions shows a remarkable assimilation all along the line. For the mass of the Black population, he continues, an independent and self-responsible family life is a matter of only two generations. In view of the relatively short period of freedom and the general economic and social conditions of Black life, the degree of conformity to the white standards is surprisingly complete. The author concludes that in every respect the trends in Black family life parallel those going on in the white families....

270.   Watson, Peter, Editor. Psychology and Race. Chicago: Aldine Publishing Co., 1973, pp. 176-212.

There is one chapter in this work that deals with the Black family. The section was essayed by Harold Proshansky and Peggy Newton entitled "Colour: The Nature and Meaning of Negro Self-Identity." The writers surmise that the matriarchal character of the lower-class Black family and its associated disorganized home life have important implications for the child's learning of sex attitudes and his attitudes toward marriage and child-rearing. They concluded that parents who have had few experiences with family stability and adequacy are unlikely to be able to provide these experiences for their child. Proshansky and Newton do admit, however, that their research was concerned almost exclusively with lower-class family life, and therefore some of their conclusions may not be valid for other social classes.

13.   BLACK FAMILY AND THE AGING

271.   Lichtman, Allan J. and Joan R. Challinor, Editors. Kin and Communities: Families in America. Washington, DC: Smithsonial Institution Press, 1979, pp. 145-154.

Dr. Jacquelyn J. Jackson and Dr. Bertram E. Walls contributed the article "Aging Patterns in Black Families" to this volume. In an effort to counteract the trend of spurious generalizations about aging patterns of the later years in Black kinship networks, as well as their inappropriate comparisons with white kinship networks, this article provides an overview of available data about aged patterns in Black kinship networks in the South, and, to the extent possible, comparisons of those patterns with non-Southern Black kinship networks and with white kinship networks. Finally,

Lichtman and Challinor:

they suggest several types of studies which may be crucial in furthering our sociological and anthropological knowledge and understanding kinship patterns for aged Blacks, the results of
which, we believe, could be applied readily to continuing social
programs for the aged involving, but not restricted to, Blacks....
conclude the authors.

272. Manuel, Ron C., Editor. Minority Aging: Sociological and Social
      Psychological Issues. Westport, CT: Greenwood Press, 1982, pp.
      39, 41-43, 109-114.

      Dr. Manuel makes a number of references to the Black aged through-
      out this book. One particular essay by Gari Lesnoff-Caravaglia,
      entitled "The Black Granny' and Soviet 'Babushka': Commonalities
      and Contrasts," deals specifically with the role of the Black aged
      in the Black family. The author points out that the Black granny
      was often regarded as the economic mainstay, with family members
      treating her as the focal point of the family assistance scheme.
      It was also noted that the significance of the granny is probably
      felt most in the area of childrearing....

14. BLACK LOWER-CLASS FAMILY

273. Banks, James A. and Jean Dresden Grambs, Editors. Black Self-
      Concept. New York: McGraw-Hill, 1972, pp. 55-70, 117-140.

      Various references are made throughout the book to the Black fami-
      ly. The overall theme of this book as it relates to the Black fa-
      mily is that the lower-class Black families (in common with all
      Blacks) that have to overcome deprivations of poverty plus those
      of racism, do have the momentous task of aiding the child to esta-
      blish a positive and healthy self-identity. There are extensive
      notes and Bibliography at the end of each article in the book.

274. Barash, Meyer and Alice Scourby, Editors. Marriage and the Family:
      A Comparative Analysis of Contemporary Problems. New York: Ran-
      dom House, 1970, pp. 215-259.

      "Crucible of Identity: The Negro Lower-Class Family," discusses
      slum Black family patterns as these reflect and sustain Blacks'
      adaptations to the economic, social, and personal situations into
      which they are born and in which they must live. The writer, Lee
      Rainwater, concludes: "The 'me' of personal identity and the
      multiple 'we' of family, Black and American identity are all in-
      extricably linked and a healthier experience of identity in any
      one sector with repercussions on all the others...."

275. Meier, August and Elliot Rudwick, Editors. The Making of Black
      America: Essays in Negro Life and History, Volume II. New York:
      Atheneum, 1976, pp. 455-480.

Meir and Rudwick:

There is one essay in this collection on the Black family by Lee Rainwater. She penned "Crucible of Identity: The Negro Lower-Class Family." This article has appeared elsewhere in this book.

276. Miller, Roger R. Race, Research and Reason. New York: National Association of Social Workers, 1969, pp. 145-164.

Elizabeth Herzog and Cecellia E. Sudia essayed "Family Structure and Composition: Research Considerations" for this collection of articles. The writers conclude, in part: "It is only fair to admit also a belief that improved education, job training, jobs, income maintenance and family planning are likely ultimately to reduce the frequency of fatherless homes among low-income Negroes, and that this would be a good thing."

277. Ross, Arthur M., and Herbert Hill, Editors. Employment, Race, and Poverty. New York: Harcourt, Brace & World, Inc., 1967, pp. 149-174.

Many references are made throughout the book to Black men, women and children. Chapter 6, "Culture, Class, and Family Life Among Low-Income Urban Negroes," deals specifically with the Black family and was written by Hylan Lewis. The author focuses on two issues: first, he illustrates some of the faulty ways in which the term "culture" and "class" are used to describe and explain family behavior of low-income urban Blacks; and second, to present some findings and illustrative materials from a study of low-income families in the District of Columbia. Professor Lewis concludes that these findings and materials accent further the belief that family forms and functions among Blacks in today's cities are understood best, and dealt with best, as products of contemporary urban life.

278. Shostak, Arthur B. and William Gomberg, Editors. Blue-Collar World: Studies of the American Worker. Englewood Cliffs, NJ: Prentice-Hall, 1964, pp. 282-297, 579-583.

Various references are made to Black families, Black workers and Black children throughout this book. Rose Stamler wrote "Acculturation and Negro Blue-Collar Workers" for this volume. "The Lower Classes and the Negroes: Implications for Intellectuals" was contributed by Hyman Rodman.

15. BLACK MIDDLE-CLASS FAMILY

279. Burgess, Ernest, et al., Editors. The Family. New York: Van Nostrand Rineholt Co., 1971, pp. 99-129.

There is one chapter in this collection on the Black family. The authors discuss the Black family in four parts: (1) the transition

Burgess, et al.:

from slavery to present; (2) the changing Black family; (3) mobility and urbanization; and (4) forms of the family. Three forms are discussed: (a) the matricentric family; (b) the small-patriarchal family; and (c) the equalitarian family. The writers conclude that historically the mother in the family has had power and authority, but this is changing, particularly in middle and upper-income Black families.

280. Davis, Lenwood G. I Have A Dream: The Life and Times of Martin Luther King, Jr. Westport, CT: Negro Universities Press, 1973, pp. 12-18.

The author emphasizes the influence and impact that the King family had on the early life of Martin Luther King, Jr. and his brother and sister. Davis argues that it was the guidance and strength of the King family that made it possible for the younger King to maintain his vision of life.

281. Leslie, Gerald R. The Family in Social Context. New York: Oxford University Press, 1973, pp. 284-309.

Chapter 10, "Racial, Ethnic, and Class Variations," has one section on "American Black Families." The writer surmises that there are no Black families, only families whose members are Black, and which families differ markedly among themselves. The author contends that the most significant generalization that can be made about middle-class Black families, however, probably is that the factor of race is not of great significance and, even in a minor race, is of only temporary significance. Professor Leslie concludes: "Many Black families already are caught up in the success-seeking patterns that more fully characterize whites, and to a steadily increasing degree, middle-class Black family patterns approach those of the middle-class model."

16.   BLACK RURAL FAMILY

282. Dabbs, James McBride. The Southern Heritage. New York: Alfred A. Knopf, 1959, pp. 1-15.

Chapter I entitled, "Southern Heritage," gives a narrative of the life of a Black family in the South, and attention is focused on the role of mother and grandmother in the family....

283. Dollard, John. Caste and Class in Southern Town. Garden City, NY: Doubleday & Co., 1957, pp. 14, 52, 57, 138, 153, 189-190, 275-278, 414, 434-441, 451-453.

Various references are made throughout the book to the Black family: patriarchal, symbolism between castes, ties in the Negro family, attitudes. In this work the author attempts to see the

Dollard:

social situation as a means of patterning the effects of white and
Negro people, as a mold for love, hatred, jealousy, deference, sub-
missiveness, and fear. Dr. Dollard concludes that only in the
individual life can one see the emotional forces surging against
the barriers and outlets of the governing social order....

284. Dunbar, Tony. Our Land Too. New York: Pantheon Books, 1971,
      pp. 6-56.

This book describes what life is like in rural Mississippi and
Appalachia. Part One is devoted to poor Blacks in Louise, Mid-
night and Humphreys County, Mississippi. The author interviewed
ninety-seven poor Black families. In the study the writer argues
that for the poor man survival implies above all else, obtaining
food, and the poorer he is, the more he is involved in trying to
provide food for his family. Robert Coles wrote the Introduction
to this book.

285. Epps, Edgar, Editor. Race Relations: Current Perspective. Cam-
      bridge, MA: Winthrop Publishers, 1973, pp. 163-258.

Section 3 is devoted to perspectives on the Black family. Topics
include: The Myth of the Black Matriarchy, Jobs and the Negro
Family and Family and Childhood in a Southern Negro Community.

286. Powdermaker, Hortense. After Freedom: A Cultural Study in the
      Deep South. New York: Viking Press, 1939, pp. 5, 56, 63, 143-147,
      198-199, 209, 219, 246-247.

Section II of this book is devoted to the Black family. This
study was done in the state of Mississippi during the mid-1930's.
The author believes that in any society, children contribute to
the cohesion of the family group. In Mississippi, continues
Powdermaker, where the Black family is so loosely held together,
their role as an integrating force is more potent than that of the
white children. If the cohesive power of the children is not
strong enough to keep the family from breaking up, there is no
other force that will; then they are given away and absorbed into
some other household. For they, continues the author, are the
chief effective nucleus of family life.

17. BLACK URBAN FAMILY

287. Abrahams, Roger D. Positively Black. Englewood Cliffs, NJ:
      Prentice-Hall, Inc., 1970, pp. 107-130.

This book centers around a discussion of the folklore of urban and
rural Blacks. There is some discussion of the Moynihan Report but
only in passing. Discussion of folklore in Chapter 5 relates to
the Black man and Black woman.

288.   Bullock, Paul, Editor. <u>Watts: The Aftermath, An Inside View of</u>
        <u>the Ghetto by the People of Watts</u>. New York: Grove Press, 1969,
        pp. 197-216.

        Various Black individuals talk about their lives and those of
        their family in Watts. Some families discussed in this work were
        on welfare. Others were from the middle-class. Primarily, this
        book is an account of how people feel, and why they feel that way,
        in an area in which a major riot has occurred.

289.   Clark, Kenneth B. <u>Dark Ghetto: Dilemmas of Social Power</u>. New
        York: Harper and Row, 1965, pp. 63-86.

        The author discusses what it means to be a resident of a ghetto
        and the social, psychological, and economic effects it has on the
        personality of individuals, especially Blacks. Dr. Clark also
        discusses "The Negro Matriarchy and the Distorted Masculine Image."
        He points out that among Black teenagers the cult of going steady
        has never had the vogue it seems to have among white teenagers;
        security for Blacks is found not in a relationship modeled after
        a stable family--for they have seen little of this in their own
        lives--but, upon the unstable and temporary liaisons. The margi-
        nal young Black male tends to identify his masculinity with the
        number of girls he can attract. The high incidence of illegiti-
        macy among Black young people reflects this pervasive fact. Dr.
        Clark concludes that in this compensatory distortion of the male
        image, masculinity is, therefore, equated with alleged sexual
        prowess....

290.   Davis, John P. <u>The American Negro: Reference Book</u>. Englewood
        Cliffs, NJ: Prentice-Hall, 1966, pp. 337-359.

        Joseph H.Douglass contributed the essay "The Urban Negro Family"
        for this volume. The author argues that the many trends affect-
        ing the American family generally, such as rising levels of health,
        increasing levels of educational attainment, improved occupational
        distribution, improved housing conditions and increased security
        through participation in public programs, are all having their
        beneficial effects on the Negro family. In part as a result of
        their determination to eliminate racial discrimination and achieve
        equality on all fronts, it is to be expected that in the future
        fewer and fewer distinctions may be drawn between the great mass
        of Negro families and those of the general population, concludes
        the author.

291.   Duncan, Otis Dudley, and Beverly Duncan. <u>The Negro Population of</u>
        <u>Chicago: A Study of Residential Succession</u>. Chicago: University
        of Chicago Press, 1957, pp. 9, 19, 37, 49, 52-54, 56, 79-84, 276-
        277, 291.

        Many references are made throughout the book to the Black family:
        characteristics of Black families, disorganization of Black fami-
        lies, doubling-up of Black families, selective mobility of Black

Duncan and Duncan:

families, tradition with respect to Black family, Black families as units of migration, zonal variation in characteristics of Black families, marital status, household relationship, income, education, regression of non-white characteristics of families, fertility of non-whites, divorce.

292. Etzkowitz, Henry and Gerald M. Schaflander. Ghetto Crisis. Boston: Little, Brown and Company, 1969, pp. 14-18, 63-74, 124-142.

Chapter 3, "The Negro Ghetto Nonfamily," has a short discussion of the causes of the "breakdown" of the Black family. Chapter 9, "Infants and Toddlers," has a discussion on the problems faced by Black mothers in relation to child health and child health care centers.

293. Foley, Eugene P. The Achieving Ghetto. Washington, DC: The National Press, Inc., 1968, pp. 46-48, 55-65.

Some criticism of the Moynihan Report in terms of the analysis of the Black family. There is also a discussion of matriarchal structure of the Black family.

294. Forman, Robert E. Black Ghettos, White Ghettos, and Slums. Englewood Cliffs, NJ: Prentice Hall, Inc., 1971, pp. 103-139.

Various references are made throughout this book to Blacks: men, women, children, and the family. The author concludes that given the changed status of Blacks, the changed attitudes on the part of many whites, the outlawing finally of residential racial segregation (with means available for combatting segregation), it is difficult to believe that the 1970's will see a continuation of the same old ghetto pattern and the involuntary segregation that have been characteristic of the past half-century.

295. Gordon, Michael, Editor. The American Family in Social-Historical Perspective. New York: St. Martin's Press, 1978, pp. 152-178.

There is one chapter in this work on the Black family. Chapter 8, "The Two-Parent Household: Black Family Structure in Late Nineteenth Century Boston," was written by Elizabeth N. Pleck. The author discusses three aspects of the population, the depressing occupational position of Black heads of households and the physical circumstance of life--which severely constrained family survival. Ms. Pleck concludes that the evidence suggests a family pattern of nuclear, two-parent households which prevailed among migrants and rural Black heads of households. Moreover, Black families included husband, wife, and children.

296.   Kiser, Clyde Vernon. Sea Island in the City. New York: Atheneum, 1969, pp. 201-206, 214, 220-222, 235-238, 253-254.

A study of St. Helena Islanders, and their adaptation to life in Harlem and other major urban centers. There is, however, a short section on domestic life, that gives an interesting discussion of the family and to the problems they have to face in this adjustment.

297.   Kornweibel, Theodore, Jr., Editor. In Search of the Promised Land: Essays in Black Urban History. Port Washington, NY: Kennikat Press, 1981, pp. 114-132.

There is one essay by Elizabeth H. Pleck, called "The Two-Parent Household: Black Family Structure in Late Nineteenth-Century Boston," that has appeared elsewhere in this work.

298.   Lindsey, Paul and Ouida Lindsey. Breaking the Bonds of Racism. Homewood, IL: ETC Publication, 1974, pp. 35-43, 47, 78.

The authors describe the lifestyle of Blacks in the United States--including the problems of housing, economics, stereotypes--and the perspective of both Blacks and whites regarding education and learning. There are also references to Black families in this work, of special interest is the section, "Ghetto Families." The authors point out that the ghetto is characterized by a number of types of families. Moreover, surmised the writers, it is particularly important that school teachers and administrators realize that students in ghetto schools are likely to reflect the entire range of family types existing in the general society. The authors gave nine examples of kinds of family types existing in the general society, including the ghetto....

299.   Ovington, Mary White. Half A Man: The Status of the Negro in New York. New York: Longmans, Green and Co., 1911, pp. 138-169.

Chapter III, "The Colored Woman as a Bread Winner," deals with the role the Black woman played in the Black family. The author also compares the role of the Black woman with that of white women. The writer points out that family life can be studied in the census table: while 59 percent of unmarried white women at work live at home, only 25 percent of Black women, however, live at home. In other words, 75 percent of all unmarried Black women working, live with their employer or board....

300.   Reed, Ruth. Negro Illegitimacy in New York City. New York: Columbia University Press, 1926, pp. 12, 15, 19-23, 38, 41, 86, 95, 98, 111-113.

The author surmises that the traits of family life existing among Blacks at the present (1926) time show some variation from the family life characteristic of the remainder of the community;

Reed:

marriages take place earlier, a large number of women widowed, and
fewer married women at the child-bearing ages. There are also
higher illegitimacy rates among Blacks than among any other population class. There is no conclusive evidence that Black women
are meeting their problems of family life in any way which may be
regarded as characteristically racial, concludes the writer.

301. Schuchter, Arnold. White Power/Black Freedom Planning the Future
      of Urban America. Boston: Beacon Press, 1968, pp. 417-450.

      Chapter 8, "Black Peasant to Black Proletariat," makes specific
      references to the Black family. The author points out that Black
      women who head families, in many respects, bear the heaviest bur-
      dens in all Big City ghettos: the longest periods of unemployment;
      the lowest pay when and if employed; the largest number of depen-
      dents; the lowest-skilled jobs; the fewest opportunities for train-
      ing; the least coverage by unemployment insurance; the most serious
      health problems; the greatest emotional burdens of family life.
      The writer concludes: "Despite the prevalence in the ghetto of
      what outsider-experts call "family disorganization," employed and
      underemployed Blacks themselves do not give this factor much
      weight. Lack of job skills, education, and money were seen by
      many Blacks in the ghettos as the main barriers to their two main
      goals: economic security and a better home to live in."

302. Sherman, Richard, Editor. The Negro and the City. Englewood
      Cliffs, NJ: Prentice-Hall, Inc., 1970, pp. 109-119.

      Two chapters deal directly with the Black family: "Urbanization
      and the Negro Family," and "The Moynihan Report." In the section
      on urbanization it is pointed out that urban life was having ad-
      verse effects on the Black family. The Moynihan Report states
      that at the heart is the deterioration of fabric of Black family
      and it (the family) is the fundamental source of the weakness of
      the Black community at the present (1965) time....

303. Simon, Arthur. Stuyvesant Town U.S.A.: Pattern for Two Americans.
      New York: New York University Press, 1970, pp. 73-120.

      This work discusses in detail one neighborhood of one city -- New
      York City's Stuyvesant Town, and the people, mainly Blacks, who
      live in it. Various references are made to the family life of the
      residents. Black families in this area of New York City are caught
      up in a vicious social and economic dilemma....

304. Spear, Allan H. Black Chicago: The Making of a Ghetto, 1890-1920.
      Chicago: University of Chicago Press, 1967, pp. 3, 91-111, 167-
      177.

      Various references are made throughout the book to the family.

Spear:

Much attention is given to Chicago's "Black Elite," "The New Leadership," "The Institutional Ghetto," "The Impact of the Migration," and "Black Community Life." There are a number of plates,
maps, tables, and photos included in this work.

305. Suttles, Gerald D. The Social Order of the Slum: Ethnicity and
Territory in the Inner City. Chicago: University of Chicago
Press, 1968, pp. 9, 18, 22-27, 36-37, 84-85, 99, 119-120, 132-135,
223-225.

Various references are made throughout the book to Blacks: men,
women, children, and the Black family. A great deal of attention
is devoted to young Blacks living in the inner city and their relations with other ethnic groups living in the same area. This
book focuses on the Addams area--a slum area of Chicago.

306. Taeuber, Karl E. and Alma F. Taeuber. Negroes in Cities. Chicago: Aldine Publishing Co., 1965, pp. 105-114, 126-149.

This work deals specifically with residential segregation and
neighborhood change as it affects Blacks in various cities. The
authors do, however, analyze the characteristics of Black families
that migrated from the South between 1940-1960, and point out the
socio-economic effects that this migration had on them. The writers conclude that the continuing changes in patterns of Black
population distribution have profoundly altered the character of
race relations in the United States....

307. Thompson, Daniel C. Sociology of the Black Experience. Westport, CT: Greenwood Press, 1974, pp. 64-87.

"The Black Ghetto: The Family," discusses the nature and extent
to which the family and the school cooperated in the process of
socializing the child in New Orleans in 1968-1969. The writer
concludes: "The Black family in New Orleans, because of its long
history in dealing with social crisis stemming from racism, and
its unique flexibility, is the most effective instrument Blacks
have had in their precarious struggle to survive in American
society...."

308. Warner, William Lloyd, et al. Color and Human Nature: Negro Personality Development in a Northern City. Washington, DC: American Council on Education, 1941, pp. 15-16, 22, 54, 79, 91-93, 104,
122, 133, 136-138, 141, 154, 185, 205, 208, 217, 235, 249, 269,
279.

Many references are made throughout the book to the Black family:
conditioning of color attitudes, domination by father, examples
of family, matriarchy in lower classes, occupation, pathology.
The authors conclude that color becomes more acute and painful in

Warner, et al.:

its consequences the closer the individual approximates those behavior traits and general standards of the larger society for lack
of which the race is usually reproached. The book attempts a systematic study in which the effects of color discrimination upon
personality are examined for every shade of Blackness and for every type of social position within Black society.

309. Whitten, Norman E., Jr. and John F. Szwed, Editors. Afro-American
Anthropology. New York: Free Press, 1970, pp. 303-312.

Carol B. Stack wrote "The Kindred of Viola Jackson: Residence and
Family Organization of an Urban Black American Family," for this
volume. The writer suggests that domestic functions are carried
out for urban Blacks by cluster of kin who may or may not reside
together. Individuals who are members of households and domestic
units of cooperation align to provide the basic functions often
attributed to nuclear family. She concludes, in part: "...it is
suggested that these households and domestic units provide the
assurance that all the children will be cared for."

18.   COMPARATIVE FAMILIES

310. Allport, Gordon W. The Nature of Prejudice. Reading, MA: Addi-
son-Wesley Publishing Co., 1954, pp. 190-198, 307-308, 320-326,
344, 467-470.

Various references are made throughout the book to the Black family and to Blacks in general. The author has extensive notes at
the end of each chapter. Even though this book is outdated, it
still brings out interesting points concerning Blacks and other
ethnic groups.

311. Bane, Mary Jo. Here to Stay: American Families in the Twentieth
Century. New York: Basic Books, 1976, pp. 9, 66, 119-120, 136-
137, 161n.

The writer said the risk of divorce and separation is not, however,
distributed randomly. Low-income people are somewhat more likely
to divorce and separate than better-off people. Blacks are somewhat more likely to divorce than whites, although the differences
in rates seem to be accounted for by differences in income. Nothing is known about separation rates, but at any given time a
much larger proportion of Blacks than whites report themselves as
separated. Moreover, the proportion of Black children living in
single-parent families is much higher than the proportion of white
children. In March 1974, for example, 35.5 percent of Black
children and 10.4 percent of white children lived in families
headed by their mother without their father. The Black-white differential in the proportion of children living in female-headed
families has narrowed somewhat in recent years, but the change has
been very small. These high Black-white differentials may have

Bane:

contributed to a public perception that the single-parent problem
is a problem of "theirs"--the poor Blacks in the central cities--
and not of "ours", declares the author.

312. Brinkerhoff, Merlin B., Editor. Family and Work: Comparative
and Convergences. Westport, CT: Greenwood Press, 1984, pp. 141-
174.

Chapter 6 was written by Ronald Angel and Marta Tienda and called
"Household Composition and Income-Generation Strategies Among Non-
Hispanic Whites, Blacks, and Hispanic-Origin Groups in the United
States." The authors state that non-Hispanic whites are the least
likely to form extended households, whereas Blacks are most likely
to do so. For the latter, the propensity to extend is not altered
when we control for income adequacy, headship, and education, in-
dicating that race has a pronounced independent effect on the propensity to extend. Considering the pervasive economic deprivation
suffered by the Black population, extension probably represents a
long-term adaption to poverty, according to the researchers. Female headship and education seem to be major determinants of household structure. Indeed, next to race, female headship exerts the
largest independent impact, greatly increasing the probability of
extension. Education, on the other hand, has a significant impact
on extension. They argued that higher levels of education may be
associated with tastes for more private family living arrangements, but they also observed that various racial and ethnic groups
differ in the impact education has on their propensity to extend.
"Insofar as education is associated with higher income, the economic argument would predict that higher levels of education would
be associated with the possibility of maintaining more private family living arrangements. This phenomenon may be at work for
Blacks and to some extent for Mexicans," conclude Angel and Tienda.

312a. Carter, Hugh and Paul C. Glick. Marriage and Divorce: A Social
and Economic Study. Cambridge, MA: Harvard University Press,
1970, pp. 386, 400-410, 413-415, 428, 436-437.

Various references are made throughout the book to Black men, women, children, marriages, and the family: Black-Black marriages,
White-Black marriages, migration of Blacks, Blacks in mixed marriages, Black subfamilies, employment rate among women, divorce
rate among women, separation rate among Blacks, widowed among
Blacks, widowed head of households among Blacks, income changes in
rate of illegitimacy.

313. Day, Beth. Sexual Life Between Blacks and Whites. New York:
World, 1972, pp. 153-170.

Chapter Ten is called "Or Is She a Matriarch?" The writer points
out that incest is universally taboo among Black families. Sexual
child abuse is also rare in Black families. Black families are
more likely than white families to contain ill and aging members.

Day:

Dr. Day suggests that there is a strong work-orientation in Black families. There is also a strong religious orientation among many Black families, deriving chiefly from the mother, concludes the author....

314.   Farley, Reynolds. Blacks and Whites: Narrowing the Gap? Cambridge, MA: Harvard University Press, 1984, pp. 142-171, 181-188, 199-220n.

The writer compares the education, employment and occupation of Black families with those of White families. The author argues that the economic, educational and social gap between Black families and white families will shrink in the year 2010 or 2020....

315.   Goldschmidt, Marcel L., Editor. Black Americans and White Racism. New York: Holt, Rinehart and Winston, Inc., 1970, pp. 75-114.

Chapter 8 was written by Robert Harrison and Edward H. Kass. They discuss the differences between Black and white pregnant women on the MMPI. Section 3, however, is devoted entirely to "The Black Family and Child Development." Chapter 9, "Characteristics of Negro Mothers in Single-Headed Households," was written by Seymour Parker and Robert J. Kleiner. Chapter 10, "Effects of Paternal Absence on Sex-typed Behaviors in Negro and White Preadolescent Males," was written by E. Mavis Hetherington. Chapter 11, "Child Rearing Practices Among Low-Income Families in the District of Columbia," was written by Hylan Lewis. Chapter 12, "Exposure to Child-Rearing Experts: A Structurel Interpretation of Class-Colored Differences," was written by Zena Smith Blau.

316.   Halpern, Florence. Survival: Black/White. New York: Pergamon Press, 1973, pp. 49-66, 206-208.

Chapter 3, titled "Child-Rearing Practices," gives a discussion of child-rearing practices of Black and white families. Chapter 4, "Adolescence and Adulthood," gives a discussion of the growth of adolescents to adulthood from the standpoint of environmental factors, Black and white. Chapter 5, "Intelligence," tries to establish a relationship between environments of Black and white children and intelligence quotients....

317.   Stuart, Irving, et al. Interracial Marriage: Expectations and Realities. New York: Grossman Publishers, 1973, pp. 51-61.

Vladimir Piskacek and Marlene Golub wrote the chapter on "Children of Interracial Marriages." The authors conclude: "The black-white child's struggle with himself, his parents, society, and with his past and present elicits our respect, admiration, and compassion. The interracial family is a microcosm of race relations, and should be intensively studied in order to understand

Stuart:

many variables -- social conflicts in general and identity formation in early childhood in particular. These families' successes
are our hopes -- the failures our warnings."

318.   Thomas, Alexander and Samuel Sillen. <u>Racism and Psychiatry</u>. New
York: Brunner/Mazel, pp. 83-100.

In Chapter 6, "Family and Fantasy," the authors compare the Black
family with the white family. The authors conclude that in the
absence of detailed, scientifically controlled studies, it is nothing less than racist to generalize about the "pathologic" Black
family and the "castrating" Black mother. Moreover, the tendency
to parrot such stereotypes can only encourage the superstition of
white supremacy, state the researchers.

319.   Wireman, Perry. <u>Urban Neighborhoods, Networks, and Family</u>. Lexington, MA: Lexington Books, 1984, pp. 23-25, 103-108, 120-123,
153-154.

The author points out that a number of studies have noted the
importance of extended kin support among Black Families. It was
also stated that many white families living in integrated neighborhoods do not want to become personal friends with Black families....

Articles

1. BLACK FAMILY AND SLAVERY

320. Billingsley, Andrew and Marilyn Greene, "Family Life Among the
Free Black Population in the 18th Century," Journal of Social
and Behavioral Sciences, Vol. 20, No. 2, Spring 1974, pp. 1-18.

When the first census of the United States was taken in 1790, there
were approximately 750,000 persons of African descent enumerated
in the returns for the 17 states and territories which comprised
the continental United States at that time. Of that number,
roughly 59,000 had legally free status. Despite the fact that the
original census manuscript schedules for almost one-third of the
states were destroyed in the War of 1812, the authors' research in
the remaining 12 states identifies almost 27,000 free Blacks living in family units in 1790. This article focuses on the existence of family life among free Blacks. It is our view that the
18th century represents a critical period for the study of Blacks
in America, for it was during this time that the basic structure
of Black family life was developed, the broad outlines of which
continue to the present time, conclude the researchers.

321. _____. "None Shall Part Us From Each Other: Reflection on
Black Family Life During Slavery and Beyond," Proceedings of the
Fifth Annual Conference of the National Association of Black So-
cial Workers. April 18-21, 1973, pp. 78-88.

The writer contends that the Black family structure was not destroyed during slavery. He attempts to prove this point by giving
numerous examples of family life from slave narratives and autobiographical studies. Dr. Billingsley emphasizes the nuclear and
extended family as examples of patterns of intact Black slave families.

322. Blackburn, George and Sherman L. Ricards, "The Mother-Headed Family Among Free Negroes in Charleston, South Carolina, 1850-1860,"
Phylon, Vol. 42, No. 1, March, 1981, pp. 11-25.

Blackburn and Ricards:

The authors suggest that the free Negro women in Charleston lived
under severe handicaps in the antebellum period. Not only were
they, along with free males, subject to legal restrictions, but
the census manuscripts show that the free female had limited occupation opportunities; not surprisingly, free family were less
successful in accumulating wealth than were males. In addition,
there were substantially larger numbers of free Negro females than
males in the adult years. They conclude: "One result was that
female-headed families among free Negroes were more common than
male-headed families. The census manuscripts also provide data
which suggest that the female-headed families were stable. Thus
stable, female-headed families among free Negroes, despite difficulties, were a norm in antebellum Charleston, South Carolina."

323. Brouwer, Merle G. "Marriage and Family Life Among Blacks in
      Colonial Pennsylvania," Pennsylvania Magazine of History and
      Biography, Vol. 99, No. 3, July, 1975, pp. 368-372.

The author points out that slaves changed hands frequently in
eighteenth-century Pennsylvania, finding themselves in many different situations during their lifetimes, with whatever family
ties they were able to form sundered several times in the process.
The writer states that the materials available for an assessment
of Black family life in colonial Pennsylvania are rather limited.
That material which is available, however, in the legal statutes,
church records, and newspaper advertisements suggests that Blacks
could form only tenuous marital relationships which were not recognized by law. The unofficial marriages of Blacks could be
severed by fiat if a master decided to sell one or both partners,
and the ties binding children and parents could be severed in the
same arbitrary manner, concludes Prof. Brouwer.

324. Brown, Steven E. "Sexuality and the Slave Community," Phylon,
      Vol. 42, No. 1, March, 1981, pp. 1-10.

Prof. Brown states that although the environment of slavery was
not conducive to strengthening traditional family ties, Blacks
were insistent upon forming familial relationships. Slaves may
not have conducted themselves according to white standards of
behavior, but their statements eloquently express a code of behavior to which they adhered. He concludes: "Most slaves emphasized family relationships which formed an integral aspect of
their existence. This family pride reflects the strong sense of
community which slaves developed. Although other aspects of community development may or may not have occurred, slaves clearly
formed community values to guide sexual relationships."

325. Clarke, John Henrik. "The History of the Black Family," Journal
      of Afro-American Issues, Vol. 3, Nos. 3 & 4, Summer/Fall, 1975,
      pp. 336-342.

Clarke:

The author traces the history of the Black family from earliest
times in Africa to the United States in the 1970's. Prof. Clarke
argues that it is now known mankind, the family as a functioning
unit and as the first organized society, started in Africa. He
concludes: "...The greatest achievement of the first Black families was, in a different time and setting, the same as the greatest achievement of Black people today - their survival...."

326. Cody, Cheryll Ann. "Naming, Kinship, and Estate Dispersal: Notes
      on Slave Family Life on a South Carolina Plantation, 1786 to 1833,"
      William and Mary Quarterly, Vol. 39, No. 1, January 1982, pp. 192-
      211.

      To slaves, separation from kin was an ever-present threat. The
      names they selected for their children reveal both the importance
      and the fragility of kinship bonds. The Gaillard plantation
      slaves frequently named children for both paternal and maternal
      kin, indicating recognition of bilateral descent. At the same
      time, the priorities of naming suggest that slaves were more con-
      cerned to preserve paternal and fraternal ties, which they per-
      ceived as most vulnerable to separation, states the author. After
      the estate division had demonstrated the durability of paternal
      ties, this practice was modified as parents attempted to mend bro-
      ken bonds symbolically. Naming patterns also suggest that the
      bonds between siblings of the same sex were highly valued and that
      the reciprocity of naming may have represented a functional reci-
      procity as well, according to Prof. Cody.

327. Davis, Angela. "Reflection on Black Woman's Role in the Community
      of Slaves," Black Scholar, Vol. 3, No. 10, December, 1971, pp.
      2-15.

      The author attempts to sketch the Black woman as an antislavery
      rebel. There is no systematic study on the role of Black women in
      resisting slavery. The vast majority of incidents she relates are
      either tactically unsuccessful assaults or eventually thwarted at-
      tempts at defence. The status of Black women within the community
      of slaves was definitely a barometer indicating the overall poten-
      tial for resistance, concludes the author.

328. Frazier, E. Franklin. "The Negro Slave Family," Journal of Negro
      History, Vol. 15, No. 4, April, 1930, pp. 198-259.

      Dr. Frazier examined printed documents and from biographies and
      autobiographies of slaves showed that a wide range of differences
      in status of the Black family under slavery existed. One impor-
      tant aspect of stabilization within their social world was a dis-
      tinction of status and social function. They had their own reli-
      gious and moral leaders. Even under most favorable conditions of
      slavery, the family was insecure in spite of the internal charac-
      ter of the family, concludes the sociologist.

329.   Genovese, Eugene D. "The Slavery Family, Women - A Reassessment
        of Matriarchy, Emasculation, Weakness," Southern Voices, Vol. 1,
        No. 3, August/September, 1974, pp. 9-12.

        The writer argues that slave families and rural Southern Black fa-
        milies were remarkably stable after slavery. He also states that
        Black women supported their men during and after slavery. Dr.
        Genovese suggests that the Black man and his wife were close to
        today's (1974) ideal of individual strengths and development....

330.   Gutman, Herbert G. "Family and Kinship Grouping Among the Ensla-
        ved Afro-Americans on the South Carolina Good Hope Plantation:
        1760-1860," Annals of New York Academy of Science, Vol. 292,
        June, 1977, pp. 242-258.

        This article was abstracted from Gutman's book, The Black Family
        in Slavery and Freedom, 1750-1925 (1977). The data for this essay
        was taken from the Good Hope Plantation Birth Register.

331.   Hill, Robert B. "Black Families in the 1970's," Urban League
        Review, Vol. 5, No. 1, Summer, 1980, pp. 42-53.

        This article was excerpted from The State of Black America, 1980,
        that was published by the National Urban League. Dr. Hill argues
        that there is strong evidence to support the view that the number
        of low-income or "underclass" Black families has increased over
        the past decade, while the proportion of low-income Black families
        has remained relatively unchanged. However, since the proportion
        of middle-income Black families remained virtually unchanged during
        the 70s, there does not appear to be strong evidence for the no-
        tion of a widening economic cleavage in the Black community,
        states the author. Blacks are still slaves to the system.

332.   Jones, Jacqueline, "My Mother Was Much of a Woman: Black Women,
        Work, and the Family Under Slavery," Feminist Studies, Vol. 8,
        No. 2, Summer, 1982, pp. 235-270.

        The purpose of this article is to suggest that the burdens shoul-
        dered by slave women actually represented in extreme form the dual
        nature of all women's labor within a patriarchal, capitalist soci-
        ety: the production of goods and services and the reproduction
        and care of members of a future work force. The antebellum plan-
        tation brought into focus the interaction between notions of women
        qua "equal" workers and women qua unequal reproducers; hence a
        slaveowner just as "naturally" put his bondwomen to work chopping
        cotton as washing, ironing, or cooking. "Furthermore, in seeking
        to maximize the productivity of his entire labor force while re-
        serving certain domestic tasks for women exclusively, the master
        demonstrated how patriarchal and capitalist assumptions concerning
        women's work could reinforce one another. The "peculiar institu-
        tion" thus involved forms of oppression against women that were
        unique manifestations of a more universal condition," concludes
        the researcher.

333. King, Charles E. "The Negro Maternal Family: A Product of an Eco-
      mic and a Culture System," Social Forces, Vol. 24, No. 1, October,
      1945, pp. 100-104.

      Dr. King believes that the maternal family pattern is a heritage
      from slave society wherein the Negro family was centered around
      the woman and the woman was the dominant figure even in dealing
      with the master class. An attitude among both white and Black was
      created relative to the Negro as being different and not required
      to conform to the same norms of family relations as the master
      class, according to the sociologist. He concludes: "The economic
      system of buying and selling slaves aided in rationalizing this
      attitude. One could more easily sell a male slave than a male and
      his whole family, and a woman and her children were more valuable
      than the man and father...."

334. King, James R. "African Survivals in The Black American Family
      Key Factors in Stability," Journal of Afro-American Issues, Vol.
      4, No. 2, Spring, 1976, pp. 153-167.

      The author declares that it is very likely that he (the Black man)
      was conditioned to being adaptable in West Africa where members
      of a tribe might be captured many times and forced to learn the
      customs of the conquering tribe or tribes. He concludes: "Thus
      the American Negro's survival in America can be summed up by stat-
      ing that he survived because he had the ability to adapt; and this
      ability had come down through the generations of Blacks in America
      from the first slaves brought from West Africa where adaptability
      is one of the prime requirements of life."

335. Lantz, Herman R. and Lewellyn Hendrix. "The Free Black Family at
      the Time of the U.S. Census: Some Implications," International
      Journal of Sociology and The Family, Vol. 7, No. 1, January-June,
      1977, pp. 37-44.

      This article reports on an examination of Black family size in the
      federal census of 1790. The data reveal that Black family size re-
      ported is smaller than the White. Those racial differences are
      found consistently in every category and in all regions, state the
      authors. Explanations for such findings are discussed. These in-
      clude the possibility of an undercount for Blacks, higher infant
      mortality for Black children, and higher rates of Black illegiti-
      macy which were not reported. None of these reasons appears to
      provide a satisfactory reason for differences in family size. The
      hypothesis that voluntary constraints on Black fertility were pre-
      sented in the eighteenth century is introduced as a possible expla-
      nation. This hypothesis is supported with evidence from Puritan
      influences present in the north, and the hypothesis is further
      supported by evidence of the existence of stable Black communities
      in the south. Several limitations inherent in this analysis are
      presented. These include problems with early census data especi-
      ally in the areas of Black infant mortality and Black fertility.
      The possibility that several different types of Black family
      structures may have existed in the past is suggested.

336. _____. "Black Fertility and the Black Family in the Nineteenth Century: A Re-Examination of the Past," Journal of Family
History, Vol. 3, No. 3, Fall, 1978, pp. 251-261.

The researchers state that we can no longer continue to assume that
it is only the contemporary Black family which is not well understood; the same may apply to the Black family of the past. Since
the drop in fertility began prior to large scale urbanization and
industrialization of the Black populace, it is necessary to re-exa-
mine and redefine the relationship of these macroscopic processes
to the apparent drop in Black fertility which commenced certainly
as early as 1850. This information could enhance our understanding of Black fertility and the Black family, and could provide us
with an understanding of the role of different social variables
that affected the Black community, assert the writers. They conclude: "Finally, the lessons we may learn from a re-examination of
Black families may provide us with an understanding of how social
relationships and social structures such as the family maintain
themselves under the most adverse conditions."

337. Lewis, Ronald L. "Slave Families at Early Chesapeake-Ironworks,"
Virginia Magazine of Historical Biography, Vol. 86, No. 2, April,
1978. pp. 169-179.

Prof. Lewis argues that an ironworks where a skilled and semiskil-
led Black labor force existed, was a stable slave family structure;
most ironmasters desire to preserve stability in the production
process. Incentive systems, such as overwork, helped to strengthen
the foundations of the slave family by enabling the male slave to
play an important role in maintaining his wife and children, if
not altering the status of bondage itself. That a large number of
slave ironworkers took advantage of the opportunity indicated that
Black slave ironworkers did not live up to the lazy, shiftless,
Sambo stereotype developed by whites to rationalize the most pecu-
liar of American institutions. More significantly, the lives of
slave ironworkers refuted the notion that slavery killed the vital
core of the male slave's manhood, and thus, a major component in
the modern matrifocal family thesis, concludes Dr. Lewis.

338. Manfra, Jo Ann and Robert R. Dykstra. "Serial Marriage and the
Origins of The Black Stepfamily: The Rowanty Evidence," Journal
of American History, Vol. 72, No. 1, June, 1985, pp. 18-44.

The researchers observed that while the Rowanty evidence adds support to the existence of strong demographic continuities between
the Black family in slavery and the Black family in freedom, it
does indeed call into question the implication that the main continuity was the existence of the "conventional" family. They conclude: "Gutman vanquished the myth that the Black female-headed
household of the twentieth century had its roots in slavery, but
that ought not blind historians to the possibility that the antebellum period gave rise to other important and long-lasting influences on Black family composition, of which a lengthy tradition of
serial marriages and step-family formation is one. There are, in
short, persistent continuities in the history of the Afro-American
family other than just a preference for the simple nuclear household."

339.   Painter, Diann Holland.   "The Black Woman in American Society,"
       Current History, Vol. 70, No. 416, May, 1976, pp. 224-227, 234.

       The author declares that racism, with its historical roots in the
       slave system, accounts for the differences in roles between White
       and Black women in the home and in the labor market.   Over the
       centuries, the American system has denied Black men the opportuni-
       ty to provide protection and economic security for their families.
       She concludes: "For this reason, Black women have assumed impor-
       tant functions within the family, which, in most white families,
       are assigned to men...."

340.   Ripley, C. Peter.   "The Black Family in Transition: Louisiana,
       1860-1865," Journal of Southern History, Vol. 41, No. 3, August,
       1975, pp. 369-380.

       The writer points out that slave marriages with strong commitments
       existed in antebellum Louisiana; a significant percentage spanned
       a considerable number of years, buttressed from the outside by
       planter paternalism and organization and from the inside by a
       pragmatic subcultural code.   He concludes, in part: "...it is
       clear that slaves and freedmen had strong commitments to their
       families...."

341.   Schewninger, Loren.   "A Slave Family in The Ante Bellum South,"
       Journal of Negro History, Vol. 60, No. 1, January, 1975, pp. 29-
       44.

       The essay discusses the Thomas-Rapier slavery family in Virginia.
       Prof. Schweninger states that an investigation of one slave fami-
       ly can perhaps shed light on the family experience of many slaves
       in the antebellum South.   Sally, the slave mother, devoted her
       life to freeing her slave children.   The author concludes: "For
       Sally, her children, and her grandchildren, the slave family was
       indeed "a refuge from the rigors of slavery."

342.   Steckel, Richard H.   "Slave Marriage and The Family," Journal of
       Family History, Vol. 5, No. 4, Winter, 1980, pp. 406-421.

       The article is based mainly on plantation records and Civil War
       pension files.   It was stated that slave marriage and the family
       were viable institutions.   The writer believes that analysis of
       the seasonal patterns of marriage and first birth indicates that
       reproduction was influenced by marriage.   An important group of
       slave couples made family formation decisions in the context of
       marriage or in anticipation of marriage.   Study of birth lists
       which also enumerate the father indicates that slave unions were
       highly stable, particularly those that survived the first one or
       two years, concludes Prof. Steckel.

343.   White, Deborah G.   "Female Slaves: Sex Roles and Status in the
       Antebellum Plantation South," Journal of Family History, Vol. 8,
       No. 3, Fall, 1983, pp. 248-261.

       Dr. White analyzes female slave life in the context of female
       slave interaction and familial roles.   The author discusses the
       bonded woman's work, her control of particular resources, her
       contribution to slave households, and her ability to cooperate
       with other women on a daily basis.   Prof. White argues that the
       female slave made significant "economic" contributions to the
       slave family, that the slave's world was sex stratified so that
       the female slave world existed quite independently of the male
       slave world, and that slave families were matrifocal, concludes
       the author.

344.   White, John.   "Whatever Happened to the Slave Family in the Old
       South?" Journal of American Studies, Vol. 8, No. 3, December,
       1974, pp. 383-390.

       The writer asserts that while it would be ingenious-or perverse-
       to deny harmful effects of slavery on the Black family in the Old
       South, one can allow that from a mixture of motives, masters of-
       ten chose to respect and encourage the family life of their
       slaves.   More importantly, one can choose to be impressed by the
       resilience and resourcefulness displayed by Blacks themselves,
       according to White.   That the Afro-American family now appears to
       have both survived under and adapted to enslavement, is not simp-
       ly a testimony to the "mildness" of American Negro slavery.   He
       concludes: "Rather, it is a tribute to the sense of individual
       and collective identity which Blacks retained during their 'time
       on the cross'.   Ironically, the 'deterioration' of the Afro-
       American family was not, it now appears, the legacy of slavery,
       but of discrimination, racism, poverty and 'benign neglect' which
       succeeding generations of white Americans have bequeathed to
       their former slaves."

2.   BLACK FAMILY AND ADOPTION

345.   Aldridge, Delores P.   "Problems and Approaches to Black Adopti-
       ons," Family Coordinator, Vol. 23, No. 4, October, 1974, pp. 407-
       410.

       Dr. Aldridge argues that regardless of the literature which sug-
       gests that "Blacks don't adopt," and "Black children are unadopta-
       ble," the real issue is one of devising new ways, and means of be-
       coming more responsive to the needs of Black children.   She con-
       cludes: "And, until white-run agencies can modify their policies
       and practices; reorient their staffs' attitudes toward Blacks and
       the differences in their lifestyles; and provide equal amounts of
       monies and energies in the adoptive process of Black children,
       there will concinue to be a smaller percentage of Black children
       placed with Black families than white children placed with white
       families."

346.   Deasy, Lelia Calhoun, and Olive Westbrooke Quinn. "The Urban Negro and Adoption of Children," Child Welfare, Vol. 41, No. 4,
November, 1962, pp. 400-407.

The authors discuss why Black families do not adopt children.
There are many Black children born under adverse circumstances
who need a home, but adoption agencies find it hard to locate parents. The writers seem to feel that the new value system of
Blacks which sees children as a handicap is the reason couples are
not having or adopting children....

3. BLACK FAMILY AND CHILDREN

347.   Barnes, Jonathan, et al. "Family Characteristics and Intellectual
Growth: Examination By Race," Educational and Psychological
Measurement, Vol. 39, No. 3, August, 1979, pp. 625-636.

The researchers of this article argue that later born children
may have lower IQ scores than their older siblings, homes in
which both parents are present may have more intelligent children
than broken families, and smaller families tend to produce
brighter offspring. Increased chronological spacing of child-
births was also found to be related to higher intelligence in
Black homes, state the authors.

348.   Busse, Thomas V. and Pauline Busse. "Negro Parental Behavior and
Social Class," Journal of Genetic Psychology, Vol. 120, No. 2,
June, 1972, pp. 287-294.

This essay is based on a study of 48 fifth-grade Black boys and
both their mothers and fathers. It was found that the mothers'
education was significantly linked to their autonomy-fostering
behavior, their sufficiency of orientation, and their number of
words. The fathers' education was positively associated with
their amount of expressed love and number of words, and was negatively associated with their smiling behavior. The fathers' occupation was positively related to the mothers' autonomy-fostering behavior, conclude the authors.

349.   Clarke, James W. "Family Structure and Political Socialization
Among Urban Black Children," American Journal of Political
Science, Vol. 17, no. 2, May, 1973, pp. 302-315.

According to the author, the results of this study of 94 urban
Black children suggests that father absence is an important variable in their political socialization. Father-absent children
tend to be more cynical and also express much stronger preferences for a racially segregated environment. Beyond this, the results underscore the importance of intra-familial relationships
in the political socialization process, states the author.

350.   Coles, Robert. "Children and Racial Demonstration," American
Scholar, Vol. 34, No. 2, Winter, 1965, pp. 78-92.

Coles:

The author studies the psychological adjustments of children who participate in racial demonstrations, how it affects their childhood and the emotional ties and straings at play in Black families. He studies how these children came to share in their race's present struggle, what happens to them, and how they react and adjust to the stressful roles they must play. Dr. Coles feels that these children are not willing to accept the prevailing values of a segregated society. They are committed to action, and dedicated to affirming new values....

351. Comer, James P. "Black Education: A Holistic View," Urban Review, Vol. 8, No. 3, Fall, 1975, pp. 162-170.

The author argues that there is little that a greater percentage of Black children will achieve high-level academic or vocational skills unless the relationship factors that turn off children in their early school years are reduced, unless the relationships that turn schools into places of chaos or apathy are changed. He suggests that social change permits more families to be able to better meet the needs of their children is also necessary....

352. Daniel, Jessica H., et al. "Child Abuse and Accidents in Black Families: A Controlled Comparative Study," American Journal of Orthropsychiatric, Vol. 51, No. 4, October, 1983, pp. 645-653.

The researchers declare that Black families who abuse their children appear to suffer from poverty, social isolation, and stressful relationships with and among kin. Maternal depression and poor mobility were noted more frequently in Black families whose children's injuries were seen as having been accidental, yet they had many strengths in comparison to the families whose children were disgnosed as abused, conclude the authors.

353. Diggs, Mary H. "Some Problems and Needs of Negro Children as Revealed by Comparative Delinquency and Crime Statistics," Journal of Negro Education, Vol. 19, No. 3, Summer, 1950, pp. 290-297.

This is a study of Black delinquents in Philadelphia. In the area of the courts, more were placed on probation, fewer were dismissed, more were held for further action, and more were admitted to public rather than private institutions. Some social factors leading to Black delinquency were poor home conditions, inadequate recreational facilities, poor relationship with school and teachers, etc. Solution to the problem seems to be that even though there is abundant knowledge of the child and his predicament, this knowledge is not used to help the child overcome his problems, states the writer.

354.   Douglass, Joseph H.   "The Extent and Characteristics of Juvenile
       Delinquency Among Negroes in the United States," Journal of Ne-
       gro Education, Vol. 28, No. 3, Summer, 1959, pp. 214-219.

       Characteristics of juvenile delinquency among Blacks are found
       largely within their socialized and unsocialized aggressive forms.
       Until further research is done in which factors other than race
       are observed, it cannot be stated definitely that any racial
       group is more prone toward delinquency than another, according
       to the writer.

355.   Edwards, Ozzie L.   "Family Formation Among Black Youth," Journal
       of Negro Education,   Vol. 51, No. 2, Spring, 1982, pp. 111-122.

       The following topics are discussed in this essay: "Trends in
       Young Black Marriage," "Childbearing in Young Black Marriages,"
       "Divorce in Young Black Marriages," and "Socioeconomic Status in
       Young Black Marriages." The writer points out that the early mar-
       riage is likely to lead to larger family size, more divorce, and
       lower socioeconomic status for those involved....

356.   Frazier, E. Franklin.   "Problems and Needs of Negro Children and
       Youth Resulting from Family Disorganization," Journal of Negro
       Education,   Vol. 19, No. 3, Summer, 1950, pp. 260-277.

       This study found that one main problem of family disorganization
       was economic because most children had to depend upon earnings of
       the mother. The family does not provide the emotional needs, dis-
       cipline and habits needed for personality development surmises
       the author. Also the absence of the father did not play a domi-
       nant role in the family was another problem. All of these fac-
       tors and more handicap the child in making a successful adjust-
       ment to society, according to the sociologist.

357.   Furstenburg, Frank F., Jr.   "Attitudes Toward Abortion Among
       Young Blacks," Studies in Family Planning, Vol. 3, No. 4, April,
       1972, pp. 66-69.

       This study shows that many Black women are taking advantage of le-
       galized abortions but suspect that many already had several child-
       ren. The availability of safe, inexpensive and easily assessible
       abortions, plus a well-organized contraceptive program would sig-
       nificantly decrease unwanted pregnancy, concludes the writer.

358.   Harris, Edward E.   "Personal and Parental Influences in College
       Attendance: Some Negro-White Differences," Journal of Negro
       Education, Vol. 39, No. 4, Fall, 1970, pp. 305-313.

       According to the author, highly educated Black parents tended to
       influence children's decision to attend college. Whites also re-
       ported greater parental influence if the parents had college train-
       ing. The extent of parental influence among Whites could be

Harris:

associated with dominant value orientations. This study found
that Black respondents are more likely to attend college on the
basis of personal influences....

359. Hawkins, Mildred. "Negro Adoption-Challenge Accepted," Child
Welfare, Vol. 39, No. 5, December, 1960, pp. 22-27.

The writer tells how one community dealt with the problem of finding adoptive parents for Black children. They formed the Citizen's Committee on Negro Adoptions in 1953 and this agency has
recruited and worked with applicants. They make every effort to
increase community resources through interpretation and stimula-
tion of interest, states the author.

360. Hulbert, Ann. "Children As Parents," New Republic, Vol. 191,
No. 11, September 10, 1984, pp. 15-23.

The author asserts that the rise in female-headed Black families,
along with the much noted austere social and economic measures
of the Reagan Administration, has clearly contributed to increasing poverty in this country. Hulbert states that there were
about 133,700 Black teenage girls that had babies and were unwed
in 1980. She concludes that Black leaders are now calling attention to the disturbing numbers of single Black mothers and fathers -- and particularly to the children (teenagers) with children.

361. Hunton, Addie. "Negro Womanhood Defended," The Voice of the
Negro, Vol. 1, No. 4, July, 1904, pp. 280-282.

The author defends statements made against Black women concerning
their moral character. She notes that Black women have often had
to submit to advances of slave owners and employers while no one
could protect them. Black women, even though they have hardships,
have been a beneficial influence in the home, have worked to edu-
cate their children and are constantly working to uplift their
race and their family, concludes the writer.

362. Kamii, Constance, and Norman Radin. "Class Differences in the
Socialization Practices of Negro Mothers," Journal of Marriage
and the Family, Vol. 29, No. 2, May, 1967, pp. 302-310.

Class differences in the socialization practices Black mothers
are studied in context with their child-rearing goals. Middle
and lower-class Black mothers do not differ fundamentally in
their goals but differ in socialization practices, conclude the
writers.

363.   Kandel, Denise B.   "Race, Maternal Authority, and Adolescent As-
        piration," American Journal of Sociology, Vol. 76, No. 6, May,
        1971, pp. 999-1020.

        The present study provided some objective data from a large sam-
        ple of Black parent-absent families in an urban setting. It was
        found that in order to cope with parent-absence significant role
        adjustments were made by different members of the family. This
        was particularly evident when observing factors influencing pa-
        rent-child relationships and family cohesiveness, states the au-
        thor. In addition, a variety of community-social variables were
        demonstrated to affect the attitudes and behaviors of these fami-
        lies. She concludes, in part: "Finally, perception of the impact
        of these variables differently influenced the parent-absent groups.
        These results will have important implications for psychologists,
        sociologists and other professionals who must deal with the grow-
        ing phenomenon of the Black parent-absent family."

364.   King, Karl, et al.   "Black Adolescents' Views of Maternal Employ-
        ment as a Threat to the Marital Relationship: 1963-1973," Jour-
        nal of Marriage and the Family, Vol. 38, No. 4, November, 1976,
        pp. 733-737.

        This study indicated that adolescents whose mothers are employed
        do not view work as a threat to the marriage although adolescents
        whose mothers are housewives do. This study contributed to an
        understanding of the Black family by confirming that the atti-
        tudes of Black adolescents concerning changes occurring in the
        Black family adds to a perspective for interpreting them, accord-
        ing to the researchers.

365.   _____. "Adolescent Perception of Power Structure in the
        Negro Family," Journal of Marriage and the Family, Vol. 31, No.
        4, November, 1969, pp. 751-755.

        The author asserts that his research indicated males and females
        viewed the power structure in their families to be mainly syncra-
        tic in most of the occupational levels. However, the males re-
        ported stronger father participation than did the females, while
        the females reported stronger mother participation than did the
        males. The writer concludes: "It can be said, for this sample,
        that participation by the Negro father in the decision-making
        process in the family was more frequent than has been historically
        presented."

366.   Medley, Morris L. and Katheryn P. Johnson. "The Economics of
        College Plans Among Black High School Seniors," Journal of Negro
        Education, Vol. 45, No. 2, Spring, 1976, pp. 134-140.

        This essay examines the role of family economics in influencing
        college plans. The authors point out that economic factors are
        important considerations in the college plans of many students,
        especially low income students....

367.   Nolle, David B.   "Changes in Black Sons and Daughters: A Panel
        Analysis of Black Adolescents' Orientations Toward Their Parents,"
        Journal of Marriage and The Family, Vol. 34, No. 3, August, 1972,
        pp. 443-447.

        The author's research produced two basic findings: (1) Black
        sons and daughters showed few differences in perceptions of their
        orientations toward their parents over time; but (2) they reveal-
        ed the greatest number of differences in their perceptions of
        their closeness to their fathers. The author asserts that in the
        final analysis, the importance given to these results and their
        interpretation in terms of role theory depends upon the relation-
        ships among perceptions, attitudes, and behaviors in Black fami-
        lies. He concludes: "Research is needed to determine the condi-
        tions under which differences in perceptions generate differences
        in attitudes and the conditions under which differences in atti-
        tudes generate differences in behaviors....At this point it is
        possible to conjecture that less positive perceptions of the fa-
        ther over time might generate less positive self-images for the
        adolescent which, in turn, might generate less favorable exchan-
        ges between the adolescent and his father...."

368.   Perry, Robert L.   "The Black Matriarchy Controversy and Black
        Male Delinquency," Journal of Afro-American Issues, Vol. 4, Nos.
        3 & 4, Summer/Fall, 1976, pp. 362-372.

        The author questions the authenticity of the labels of "Matriar-
        chy" as applied to Black family life. He believes that the con-
        cept has been erroneously applied to Blacks and as a result has
        taken on a negative stigma. Prof. Perry surmises: "The adapta-
        tions in family life that Blacks have had to make are innovative
        and are a result of complex social conditions. Whites may also
        be confronted with similar adaptations as their sex ratio becomes
        more like that of Blacks. If the word "matriarchy" is applied
        correctly, the research seems to indicate that it may be only one
        of numerous causes which might push a lower class Black male into
        deviant behavior."

369.   Robertson, Carlton.   "What a Negro Mother Faces," Forum,   Vol.
        100, No. 2, August, 1938, pp. 59-62.

        The main problem facing a Black mother is bearing a child victim-
        ized by the color of his skin. The writer notes the many prob-
        lems the child must face in education, employment, housing, and
        dealing with both a White and Black society....

370.   Young, Virginia Heyer.   "Family and Childhood in Southern Negro
        Community," American Anthropologist, Vol. 72, No. 2, April,
        1970, pp. 269-275.

        The Black family is generally interpreted as an impoverished ver-
        sion of the American White family, in which deprivation has in-
        duced pathogenic and dysfunctional features. This concept of the

family is assumed in studies of Negro personality formation which have relied entirely on clinical methods of research, states the writer. Field-work among Black town-dwellers in the Southern United States plus a reassessment of the literature yield a sharply contrasting portrait and interpretation of the Black American family on which organizational strength and functionality are found. Observations of parent-child relation in Black families show highly distinctive behavioral styles, concludes the researcher.

4. BLACK FAMILY AND EDUCATION

371. Dennis, Rutledge M. "Theories of The Black Family: The Weak-Family and Strong-Family Schools as Competing Ideologies," Journal of Afro-American Issues, Vol. 4, Nos. 3 & 4, Summer/Fall, 1976, pp. 315-328.

In this essay the author critically evaluates weak and strong theories of the Black family, analyzes the implications of the "weak" and the "strong" family theories in terms of social policy, and posits some recommendations for further research. He concludes, in part: "...If we are able to maximize the clearly polemical, we might be farther on the road to the advocacy of some prescriptive measures for the Black family."

5. BLACK FAMILY AND ECONOMICS

372. Power, Jonathan. "On The Economic Progress of Black America," Encounter (Great Britain), Vol. 39, No. 4, 1972, 79-84.

The writer analyzes the economic and social conditions of Blacks in the United States. He states there is an increase in poverty stricken fatherless (Black) families. Mr. Power suggests that the Family Assistance Program was a good thing for Black families because it helped to exacerbate Black problems in the inner-city ghetto.

6. BLACK FAMILY AND EXTENDED FAMILIES

373. Aschenbrenner, Joyce. "Extended Families Among Black Americans," Journal of Comparative Studies, Vol. 4, No. 2, Autumn, 1973, pp. 257-268.

The author points out that while the present form of the Black family may derive in many respects from early conditions in the South, it has demonstrated integrity throughout a wide variety of situations throughout history. Perhaps the ideology, and consequently, the relationships within Black families have somewhat changed through the generations, with respect for age and respectability stressed in the traditional South while egalitarianism and pragmatism are more apparent in the urban North. "Still it is only a matter of emphasis, and many personal and social needs are provided for within the extended family, which remains a

Aschenbrenner:

strong and highly adaptable institution transmitting the values of Black Americans," she concludes.

374. Barnes, Annie S. "The Black Kinship System," Phylon, Vol. 42, No. 4, December, 1981, pp. 369-370.

Prof. Barnes states that her analysis of interaction in the Black middle-class kinship system has shown that kinship groups are still-viable institutions kept alive by letter writing, telephoning, personal contact, mutual help, and ritual. Another conclusion is that socioeconomic factors influence interaction in kinship groups; hence, women are more involved than men in kin relations, which suggests that after marriage men may be more involved in in-law relations than in consanguineal behavior, states the author. If, indeed, this is the case, improvement of relations between the women and their in-laws may increase the frequency of contact between men and their relatives. "Nevertheless, ...though kin relations are female-dominated, family reunions are male-dominated in terms of positions held in family organizations and number of families holding reunions. Moreover, although reciprocal relations characterize Black middle-class family groups, another conclusion is that when dependency exists in some families, it places a strain on a number of family members, and, therefore may cause some family stress," she concludes.

375. Beck, James D. "Limitations of One Social Class Index When Comparing Races With Respect to Indices of Health," Social Forces, Vol. 45, No. 4, June, 1967, pp. 586-588.

The author surveys the health status and socio-cultural variables of families in North Carolina. Some findings include that Blacks were less likely to be married, more separations, more likely to live in an extended family, have more children and twice as likely to be living in extremes of household size (from very large to living alone). When Whites and Blacks were compared on family variables within the same group, it seems evident that their way of life differs, according to the researcher.

376. Fischer, Ann, et al. "The Occurrence of the Extended Family at the Origin of the Family Proceration: A Developmental Approach to Negro Family Structure," Journal of Marriage and the Family, Vol. 30, No. 2, May, 1968, pp. 290-300.

This is a study of New Orleans families from a structural and developmental point of view. Significant difference between Black and White in the distribution of family types is accounted for by the number of Black families which begin with the birth of an illegitimate child, state the researchers. Studied associations between race, class, age, and living with relatives at origin of family and sequence of family type in which women lived after an illegitimate birth, conclude the authors.

377. Gans, Herbert J.   "The Negro Family: Reflections on the Moynihan
      Report," Commonweal,   Vol. 83, No. 2, October 15, 1965, pp. 47-51.

      The writer states that the problems of Black families are the re-
      sult of previous inequalities which began with slavery and are
      maintained by racial discrimination. Report does not offer any re-
      commendations on policy proposals arguing that first the problems
      must be defined properly to prevent programs that do not meet the
      needs of the people. The author stresses the need for some pro-
      grams such as more employment, equality of income, adequate hous-
      ing and a research program on the structure of the Black family....

378. Geerken, Michael, and Walter R. Gove.   "Race, Sex, and Marital
      Status: Their Effect on Morality," Social Problems,   Vol. 21,
      No. 4, April, 1974, pp. 567-579.

      The authors investigate the hypothesis of the Black family to have
      a matrifocal structure relative to the white family. They found
      no sharp differences in marital roles of Blacks and Whites. How-
      ever, differences that occur are that marriage is better for white
      men than for Black men and better for Black women than white wo-
      men, conclude the writers.

379. Irvine, Russell W.   "The Black Family and Community: Some Prob-
      lems in the Development of Achievement Values," Negro Educational
      Review,   Vol 29, Nos. 3 & 4, July-October, 1978, pp. 249-254.

      Almost without exception students of the Black family have identi-
      fied the source of Black family achievement as emanating equally
      from within the family complex and through the mutually supportive
      community network available to the family. Reference, for example,
      is made to the support and encouragement given by such individuals
      as high school teachers and principals, trusted elders, neighbors,
      and so forth as decisive individuals in turning Black youth toward
      high achievement, according to Prof. Irvine. The bifurcated fea-
      tures of systems analysis allows for the adaptation of this ori-
      entation to explicating sources of white achievement development
      as well as Black achievement development. According to the author,
      what is rarely made clear in discussions of achievement, particu-
      larly achievement within a Black context, is whether the term or
      the phenomenon has the same meaning for two or more groups in
      American society. Put somewhat differently, will the fostering of
      achievement or motivating achievement be likely to have the same
      consequences for two or more groups? Will achievement, under-
      stood for the moment in conventional terms, have deleterious ef-
      fects on the structure and content of the community from which
      achievers derive? The writer addresses these questions.

380. Johnson, Robert C.   "The Black Family and Black Community Develop-
      ment," Journal of Black Psychology, Vol. 8, No. 1, August, 1981,
      pp. 35-52.

      Black family life is discussed in the context of Black community

Johnson:

development. The author contends that mutual, interactive actions
by Black families and Black community institutions could benefit
both. The familial functions of socialization (including racial
consciousness) and economical functioning are reviewed, and the
ways that Black families can assist in the development of the Black
community through efficient use of family resources are explored.
The author argues that more judicious resource utilization and allocation by Black organizations could contribute to increased family well-being.

381. Malson, Michelene. "The Social-Support Systems of Black Families,"
      Marriage and Family Review, Vol. 5, No. 4, Winter, 1982, pp. 37-57.

The contemporary literature on Black families' social-support systems has developed as an extension of the cultural variant perspective on Black families, states the author. This theoretical perspective views the mutual aid and emotional support exchanged by
members of the support system as a strength of the social system.
Within this conceptual framework, the support systems of Black
families are seen as a constructive adaptation, concludes the researcher.

382. Matthews, Basil. "The Black Family in America," New Directions,
      Vol. 3, No. 1, January, 1976, pp. 4-7.

The author discusses family values, the extended family, the fune-
ral, mental health and tries to distinguish how the Black family
is uniquely different from all other ethnic groups....

383. McAdoo, Harriette Pipes. "Factors Related to Stability in Up-
      wardly Mobile Black Families," Journal of Marriage and the Family,
      Vol. 40, No. 4, November, 1978, pp. 761-778.

The impact of upward mobility over three generations, on the extended kin network of Black parents in the mid-Atlantic area was
examined. Extensive involvement had been maintained by those born
in both the middle and working classes and those living in urban
and suburban sites. The reciprocal obligations of the help exchange patterns were not perceived as excessive, but were stronger
for those born in the working class. Educational achievement and
maternal employment peaked in the generation in which mobility occurred. Kin interaction was high with low geographic mobility.
Results indicate that extended help patterns are culturally rather
than solely economically based, states Dr. McAdoo. She asserts
that the areas of support developed by Black families are probably
the very types of internal support that will need to be developed
within non-Black families: i.e., shared childrearing and shared decision-making. The necessity for such changes has been brought
about by increasing divorce, inflation and employment of both parents of young children. The sociologist concludes: "Black families have managed to sustain their families under pressures that

McAdoo:

are now being shared by a growing number of non-Black families.
Many other American families are adopting and developing lifestyles and parenting approaches that are similar to those that
have been present for a long time within the extended kin-help
patterns of the Black community."

384. _____. "Impact of Extended Family Structure on Upward Mobility of Blacks," Journal of Afro-American Issues,, Vol. 3, Nos.
3 & 4, Summer/Fall, 1975, pp. 291-296.

The author strongly argues that we need to examine the life patterns of Blacks who have "made it", using whatever criteria you
wish, to begin to better understand the actual impact that the
extended family structure has on the viability of Black family
in the American system.

385. Nobles, Wade W. "Africanity: Its Role in Black Families,"
Black Scholar, Vol. 5, No. 9, June, 1974, pp. 10-17.

The sense of "Africanity," we contend, is the hidden strength in
Black families and has served as the underlying force in the
"struggle", states Prof. Nobles. It is, however, only when the
interpretative framework for one's analysis is based on the nature
of Black people as suggested by Professor X, that the varied expressions of that hidden strength are revealed. For instance,
overarching the notion of family is the concept of kinship which
as a system was based on the philosophical principle of the "One-
ness of Being" or one with nature. According to the author, "Be-
haviorally and structurally this principle translated into the idea
of interdependence." He concludes: "That is, all elements are
interdependent and interconnected. Structurally, the individual
is embedded in a web of "interdependent" relations with all the
other elements of the family. The idea of family or kinship consequently assigned to each individual their position in the system
of descent and marriage, while at the same time it defined attitudes, functions and behaviors."

386. _____. "African Root and American Fruit: The Black Family,"
Journal of Social and Behavioral Sciences, Vol. 20, No. 2, Spring,
1974, pp. 52-64.

The author gives a critical review of approaches in the study of
Black families, and a model which describes Black families as "tri-
balarchies" is presented. The functional character of the Black
family unit can be divided into two areas: the pragmatic functions
and the psychological functions. These functions are carried out
with the total kinship group as a frame of reference. Prof. Nobles
made suggestions for future research, training, and service.

387. Riessman, Frank. "In Defense of the Negro Family," Dissent, Vol. 13, No. 2, March-April, 1966, pp. 141-144.

The writer argues that the Daniel Moynihan Report represents a highly inappropriate approach to the development of programs and policy to fulfill the rights of the Negro. The author also points out that in response to the deficiencies of the system, the Negro has developed his own informal system and traditions in order to cope and survive, including the...extended family....

388. Smith, Raymond T. "The Nuclear Family in Afro-American Kinship," Journal of Comparative Family Studies, Vol. 1, No. 1, Autumn, 1970, pp. 55-70.

The author argues that while the "nuclear family" is an integral part of the Kinship system of all West Indians and all Americans, it does not constitute a normative role system for the lower class in either region. He concludes: "...Appearances to the contrary, there is nothing inherently 'disorganized' about Afro-American Kinship and family life...."

389. Staples, Robert. "The Black Family in Evolutionary Perspective," Black Scholar, Vol. 5, No. 9, June, 1975, pp. 2-9.

In pursuing the struggle for liberation, we must not lose sight that the Black family has many residual strengths which we can tap. They include a group of strong, supportive women, an extended kinship system and children with a great deal of resilience. At the moment is it hard to predict the future of the Black family because it is not easy to see the direction Black people are presently taking, states the educator. It appears that a certain type of cultural assimilation is gaining ascendency while a minority are consciously attempting to retain a Black folk culture. He concludes, in part: "Many Blacks have simply not adjusted their behavior in either way. This may be in error because changing times do require individual and group adaptations. Whatever happens in the future, we can continue to see the Black family as an institution whose status mirrors our struggle for dignity and liberation."

390. Wilson, Melvin N. "Mothers' and Grandmothers' Perceptions of Parental Behavior in Three-Generational Black Families," Child Development, Vol. 55, No. 6, November, 1984, pp. 1333-1339.

This study was designed to investigate perceptions of normal interactions between grandmother and grandchild and between mother and child in Black families. Grandmothers, mothers, and children between the ages of 8 and 14 were interviewed. For the 60 participating families, there were 2 levels of family structure, single-parent or dual-parent, and 2 levels of grandmother's domicile, living with the family or living in the local community. The results indicate that grandmothers perceived themselves and were perceived as having more active involvement with children when

Wilson:

they live with their single adult daughter than in the other conditions. Also, grandmothers living in the community perceived
their single adult daughters as having less active involvement
with their children than in the other conditions, declares the
author. He concludes: "Generally, these findings indicate that
Black family patterns are more complex than previously assumed,
and that extended family involvement in child rearing supports the
strength/resilience approach to Black family research."

7. BLACK FAMILY AND GENOCIDE

391. Turner, Castellano B. and William A. Darity. "Fears of Genocide
Among Black Americans As Related to Age, Sex, and Region," American Journal of Public Health, Vol. 63, No. 12, December, 1973, pp.
1029-1034.

The authors' study indicates that Black Americans, especially young
Black males, are suspicious that genocide is the aim of family
planning programs controlled by whites. However, it is not apparent that Black Americans are against family planning in particular. They conclude: "On the contrary, there is considerable evidence that Black women (if not Black men) are even more positively
inclined towards family planning than white women...."

8. BLACK FAMILY AND HOMOSEXUALITY

392. Butts, June Dobbs. "Is Homosexuality a Threat to the Black Family?" Ebony, Vol. 36, No. 6, April, 1981, pp. 138-140, 142-144.

The author argues that in her "opinion that homosexuality is not a
threat to either the stability or the future of the Black family."
She concludes: "Our internal problem and the real threat to the
Black family - is the violence of a few of us and the seeming indifference of the multitude. We need to "come home" to touch base
with ourselves by being men and women who respect one another for
the ways in which we are alike as well as for the ways in which we
are different.... "Gay" and "straight" we are the Black family.
And we will survive!"

9. BLACK FAMILY AND HOUSING

393. Ashby, William M. "No Jim Crow in Springfield Federal Housing,"
Opportunity, Vol. 20, June, 1942, No. 6, pp. 170-171, 188.

The author discusses the acts of violence occurring in the more
"liberal" cities over the issue of housing. One area where little
violence occurred was in Springfield, Illinois where the John Hay
Homes (low-cost housing project) was built. White and Black families live side by side in harmony. The writer looks at the step
taken in planning the integrated neighborhood and some of the problems they had before most problems were ironed out, and the equal

Ashby:

participation of Blacks and Whites in planning, building, maintaining and housing....

394. Brooks, Gwendolyn. "Why Negro Women Leave Home," Negro Digest,
Vol. 9, No. 3, March, 1951, pp. 26-28.

The author attempts to explain why wives leave home to either work
or start another life on their own. Some of the problems are that
they do not like to beg their husbands for money, problems of in-
laws, and marital problems, states the author.

395. Cagle, Laurence, and Irwin Deutscher. "Housing Aspirations and
Housing Achievement: The Relocation of Poor Families," Social
Problems, Vol. 18, No. 2, Fall, 1970, pp. 243-256.

For lower income Blacks, urban renewal has failed to provide alternative housing which meets their needs. Relocation is more
problematic for fatherless families and they were less successful
in obtaining public housing on a permanent basis, states the writer.

396. Comstock, Alzada P. "Chicago Housing Conditions, VI: The Problems of the Negro," American Journal of Sociology, Vol. 18, No.
2, September, 1912, pp. 241-257.

This study indicates that Black tenants pay disproportionately
high rents for their apartment and find it in poorer repair than
their immigrant neighbors. One problem is that the Black families
try to maintain a standard of living similar to that of the native-
born white citizen, even though their income is much smaller than
the whites and immigrants. Blacks also want housing near their
place of employment and will not live in cramped conditions as
does the immigrant so as to pay lower rent, concludes the researcher.

397. Edwards, Ozzie L. "Patterns of Residential Segregation Within a
Metropolitan Ghetto," Demography, Vol. 7, No. 2, May, 1970, pp.
185-193.

Residential segregation of families by income and by stage of
family life cycle in Milwaukee's Black community resembles both
pattern and degree of that in the white community. The greater
the difference in income, the more dissimilar are the distribution
by census tract. Segregation by income is greater than by family
type. Those family types which differ most in life types are more
segregated from each other, according to Prof. Edwards.

398. Evans, William. "Federal Housing Brings Segregation to Buffalo,"
      Opportunity, Vol. 20, No. 4, April, 1942, pp. 106-110, 124.

      Housing in Buffalo during the 1940's was not regulated by restric-
      tive covenants but housing segregation existed. Since migration
      of Blacks began, they have been confined to two areas with high
      rents. Slum clearance programs did not materialize. The author
      discusses the many sites chosen and then abandoned because of ra-
      cial and political friction. He also discusses the effects it has
      on the Black family....

399. Kain, John F. "Housing Segregation, Negro Employment, and Metro-
      politan Decentralization," Quarterly Journal of Economics, Vol.
      82, No. 2, May, 1968, pp. 175-197.

      The author examines the relationship between housing market segre-
      gation and the distribution and level of Black employment. Racial
      segregation in metropolitan housing may further reduce employment
      opportunities for Blacks. Prof. Kain finds that the rapid posi-
      tion suburbanization of metropolitan employment has further under-
      mined the position of Blacks and their family life style....

400. LaBarre, Maurine. "The Strengths of the Self-Supporting Poor,"
      Social Casework, Vol. 49, No. 8, October, 1968, pp. 459-466.

      This article is based on a study of thirty-six Black families from
      a housing project in Durham, North Carolina. Prof. LaBarre con-
      cludes that the Black families described in this essay are not
      "disorganized in poverty": they are maintaining, valiantly and com-
      petently, the stability of their family strengths....

401. McKee, James B. "Changing Patterns of Race and Housing: A Toledo
      Study," Social Forces, Vol. 41, No. 3, 1963, pp. 253-260.

      A study of Black housing in Toledo, Ohio tested some common assump-
      tions about race and housing and discovered a post-war transition
      from renter to owner status for Blacks. This study explored the
      means by which Black families had financed purchases of homes, the
      quality of the homes, comparative prices, and the economic status
      of the Black families concerned. The writer points out that Blacks
      are becoming owners of the very slums they inhabit. He concludes:
      "The spread of home-buying among Blacks in the oldest and decaying
      section of the city, including a relatively high proportion of sub-
      standard units, is likely to produce a new and difficult set of
      political relations between Black citizens and the community's
      political and civic leadership, especially in eliciting support
      for projects intended for the rebuilding of the community."

402. Smith, Robert H. "Family Life and Housing Environment in the Lin-
      coln (Tallahassee, Fla.) Neighborhood Community," Journal of So-
      cial and Behavioral Sciences, Vol. 18, Nos. 1 & 2, 1971-1972,
      pp. 80-89.

Smith:

The writer argues that Black family life in this Southern city is
stable and there seems to be little evidence of extended family
situations. The author points out that the families of the Lincoln Neighborhood often seek help when they are confronted with
problems they believe they are incapable of resolving alone.

10.   BLACK FAMILY AND ILLEGITIMACY

403.   Dixon, Richard D. "'The Illegitimacy Runs in Families' Hypothesis
       Reconsidered," Journal of Black Studies, Vol. 11, No. 3, March,
       1981, pp. 277-287.

       This article was based on a study of a sample of young, poor, ur-
       ban, first-conception, Black American females in Atlanta, Georgia
       between 1973-1975.

404.   Frazier, E. Franklin. "An Analysis of Statistics on Negro Illegi-
       timacy in the United States," Social Forces, Vol. 11, No. 2,
       December, 1932, pp. 249-257.

       Statistics showed a slight upward trend in illegitimate births
       from 1917-1928. Despite this general trend, the rates have gone
       down in recent years. There is a marked difference in rates for
       Northern and Southern states with Northern states having a lower
       rate, states the scholar.

11.   BLACK FAMILY AND OCCUPATIONS

405.   Aldous, Joan. "Wives' Employment Status and Lower-Class Men as
       Husband-Fathers: Support for the Moynihan Thesis," Journal of
       Marriage and the Family, Vol. 31, No. 3, August, 1969, pp. 469-
       476.

       Data forming this survey found that wives' employment status does
       not have a negative effect on the white man's participation in the
       family. On the other hand, data for Black men showed that if they
       had working wives, the husband was less active in household task
       performances and decision-making. If a Black wife has to work be-
       cause her husband is unemployed, he is even less apt to fulfill his
       responsibility as husband-father, concludes the researcher.

406.   Allen, Walter R. "Family Role Occupational Status, and Achieve-
       ment Orientations Among Black Women in the United States," Signs:
       Journal of Women in Culture and Society, Vol. 4, No. 2, Summer,
       1979, pp. 670-686.

       The author discusses a variety of topics concerning Black women
       and their occupational statuses. He suggests that Black women's
       marital and family roles affect their occupational status....

407.   Axelson, Leland J. "The Working Wife: Difference in Perception
        Among Negro and White Males," Journal of Marriage and the Family,
        Vol. 32, No. 3, August, 1970, pp. 457-464.

        This study was done in Florida of the difference in perception of
        the working wife between Black and White adult men. Results showed
        a marked difference of perception of wife working, her relationship
        to her husband, and her relationship to husband's career.

408.   Batchelder, Alan B. "Decline in the Relative Income of Negro Men,"
        Quarterly Journal of Economics, Vol. 78, November, 1964, pp. 525-
        548.

        During the 1940's Black occupational position moved closer to
        White, but 1949-1959 saw no increase in the Black to White median
        income. This trend seems to be holding in the 1960's. Because
        Black men do not make as much money as White men, they cannot pro-
        vide for their families as well as White men, states the researcher.

409.   Bock, W. Wilbur. "Farmer's Daughter Effect: The Case of the Ne-
        gro Female Professional," Phylon, Vol. 30, No. 1, Spring, 1969,
        pp. 17-26.

        The professions have been mainly dominated by White males. Lack
        of necessary business skills and training have hampered the en-
        trance of Blacks into the professions. Black females have had
        more opportunities to advance in the professional world. Contrary
        to the white population, Black families are more willing to edu-
        cate the girls than boys because they find better employment.
        This has become known as the "farmer's daughter effect." More re-
        search is needed before the noted visibility of Black professional
        women can be utilized and more attention should be given to women
        contributing to the advancement of Blacks of both sexes, concludes
        the writer.

410.   Duncan, Beverly, and Otis Dudley Duncan. "Family Stability and
        Occupational Success," Social Problems, Vol. 16, No. 3, Winter,
        1969, pp. 273-285.

        There is a tangled web of relations among economic conditions and
        family structure. The powerlessness of the Black male is traced
        back to the matriarchal family. This powerlessness with respect
        to occupational achievement is the heart of the problem of the
        Black family stability, assert the authors.

411.   Frazier, E. Franklin. "Family Impact of Urban Civilization Upon
        Negro Family Life," American Sociological Review, Vol. 2, No. 5,
        October, 1937, pp. 609-618.

        The author surmises that as long as there is a semi-feudal agri-
        cultural system in the South, there would be roving bands of Blacks
        living a lawless sex and quasi-family life. Fate of migrants to

Frazier:

cities will depend on economic and cultural resources, asserts Dr.
Frazier.

412. _____. "Occupational Classes Among Negroes in Cities," American Journal of Sociology, Vol. 35, No. 5, March, 1930, pp. 718-
738.

Dr. Frazier analyzes statistics for the distribution of occupa-
tions for selected Northern and Southern cities and shows that
there are considerable differences in occupational classes apparently related to the extent of Black participation in the whole
community. Black's lack of economic control over his community
was responsible for the inability of the higher occupational classes to escape completely from the lower occupational groups, concludes the sociologist.

413. Fuentes, Sonia. "Job Discrimination and The Black Woman," Crisis,
Vol. 77, No. 3, March, 1970, pp. 103-108.

Black women are at the very bottom of the economic totem pole.
Most Black women are service workers with unemployment being severe, especially for teenage girls. More Black women and mothers
are in the labor force with earnings accounting for a larger percentage of family income. The writer discusses some of the proposed legislation to aid women find employment and some organizations helping in the fight.

414. Harwood, Edwin, and Claire Hodge. "Jobs and the Negro Family,"
Public Interest, Vol. 23, No. 3, Spring, 1971, pp. 125-313.

The authors reappraise the theory that Black women are able to
find more and better work than Black men. As far back as 1890
men held more diversified jobs than women. The only reason there
are more Black women in white-collar jobs is because more cashiers,
clerks, etc. are employed than lawyers, doctors, etc., and more
women are in these clerical jobs, state the writers.

415. Haynes, Elizabeth Ross. "Negroes in Domestic Service in the
United States," Journal of Negro History, Vol. 8, No. 4, October,
1923, pp. 384-442.

From 1870-1900 there was a steady increase in domestic workers.
Since then there has been a decline. More Blacks are entering
trade, transportation, manufacturing and mechanical pursuits.
Little advance has been made. Wages are still below those in in-
dustry and hours are longer. Very little unionization and many
employment agencies exploit them. Little attention is given to
health and social family life of domestics, states the author.

416. Johnson, Charles S. "Present Trends in the Employment of Negro
      Labor," Opportunity, Vol. 7, May, 1929, pp. 146-148.

      This article was concerned with the industries which have been a
      refuge for Black workers and how employment had reached a slump.
      Main reasons were influx of White workers from other fields and
      the number of women entering the labor force. It was also con-
      cerned with how many displaced Blacks were being absorbed into
      other lines of work and the effects these less than meaningful
      jobs have on Black family life.

12. BLACK FAMILY AND POLYGAMOUS FAMILY

417. Kunstader, Peter. "A Survey of the Consanguine or Matrifocal
      Family," American Anthropoligist, Vol. 65, February, 1963,
      pp. 56-66.

      In earlier studies E. Franklin Frazier considered the matrifocal
      family as primitive, but this survey states that this is not so
      since this family type depends on the existence of a complex di-
      vision of labor. Data in this survey also found that in communi-
      ties the nuclear family is deemphasized or may even be absent as
      a strongly functional group. More research is needed on why the
      patrifocal family is not emphasized, concludes Prof. Kunstader.

13. BLACK FAMILY AND POST-RECONSTRUCTION

418. Agresti, Barbara Finlay. "The First Decades of Freedom: Black
      Families in a Southern County, 1870-1885," Journal of Marriage
      and the Family, Vol. 40, No. 4, November, 1978, pp. 697-706.

      Data on family residential patterns for Blacks in a Southern farm-
      ing county in 1870 and 1885 are discussed. The 1870 data show
      high percentages of Black families in nonfamily or non-nuclear
      family households, which lends support to traditional sociological
      beliefs. In 1885, however, the two-parent family was the norm and
      there were no important family structural differences between
      Blacks and whites in the county, states the author. "The findings
      are related to other recent writings on Black family history, to
      changes in the social and economic environment, and to the pre-
      vailing system of agriculture which, it is argued, affected the
      relationship of Blacks to whites and the structure of Black fami-
      lies," concludes the researcher.

419. Gutman, Herbert G. "Persistent Myths About the Afro-American
      Family," Journal of Interdisciplinary History, Vol. 6, No. 2,
      Autumn, 1975, pp. 181-210.

      The author reexamines certain major themes in E. Franklin Fra-
      zier's classic study, The Negro Family in the United States and
      presents new evidence concerning Afro-American family and house-
      hold composition at a given moment in several parts of the United
      States, but especially in the South between 1860 and 1880 and in
      one northern city, Buffalo, New York, between 1855 and 1925....

420. Harris, William. "Work and the Family in Black Atlanta, 1880,"
      Journal of Social History, Vol. 9, No. 3, Spring, 1976, pp. 319-
      330.

      The writer insists that most Black families, in Atlanta in 1880,
      were not in an obvious or structural way "matriarchal or matrifo-
      cal"; they were rather like other families of the same place,
      social class, and time. He states that there can be no doubt,
      however, that the two-parent household predominated among Blacks
      throughout the country in the years following the Civil War....

421. Shifflett, Crandall A. "The Household Composition of Rural Black
      Families: Louisa County, Virginia, 1880," Journal of Interdisci-
      plinary History, Vol. 6, No. 2, Autumn, 1975, pp. 235-260.

      According to the researcher, Black families provided homes for
      the aged, the homeless, and the unemployed at points in the fami-
      ly's development when economic burdens were less intense, though
      certainly still very real. "These people sought such homes because
      their life chances were inexorably bound up with those of family
      and friends, and because no alternative sources of employment, in-
      come, accommodation, protection, or social welfare were available.
      The burden of poverty induced Black families to rely on kinship
      networks and to become their brothers' keepers," concludes Dr.
      Shifflett.

422. Simms-Brown, R. Jean. "The Female in the Black Family: Dominant
      Mate or Helpmate?" Journal of Black Psychology, Vol. 9, No. 1,
      August, 1982, pp. 45-55.

      Two views of the Black woman as having a special position, power,
      and dominance during and after slavery are presented. An exami-
      nation of each school of thought reveals that the Black woman has
      been strong, but not dominant. Instead, she has been more of a
      "helpmate" in the family's quest for survival. In addition, the
      matriarchal myth regarding the Black woman has been created and
      maintained by certain psychological/historical mechanisms. The
      author stated that the Black woman is unique, but also has posi-
      tive and negative traits as do her fellow human beings.

423. Smallwood, James M. "Emancipation and The Black Family: A Case
      Study in Texas," Social Science Quarterly, Vol. 57, No. 4, March,
      1977, pp. 849-857.

      The writer argues that the United States Census would suggest that
      by 1870 the Black Family in Texas had acquired a remarkable degree
      of stability. He also points out that except for the high per-
      centage of Black women and children working and varied occupation-
      al patterns based largely on racial lines, the Black family close-
      ly resembled the white. Legalization of marriages along with the
      actions of well-intentioned bureau agents and preachers and tea-
      chers, both Black and White, helped stabilize the Black family.
      In addition, more freedmen apparently had strong familial instincts-

Smallwood:

at least as strong as their white counterparts, concludes Dr.
Smallwood.

14.   BLACK FAMILY AND POVERTY

424.   Brodber, Erna and Nathaniel N. Wagner. "The Black Family, Poverty,
and Family Planning: Anthropological Impressions," Family Coordinator, Vol. 19, No. 2, April, 1970, pp. 168-172.

The essay is an attempt to understand, through anthropological
techniques, the social structure of Black American families living
on welfare. The senior author, a Black female anthropologist from
Kingston, Jamaica, lived in the households studied as anthropolo-
gists traditionally have lived with "native peoples" in anthropological field work. As someone raised in a different sociocultural
milieu and trained in anthropological methods, she viewed the families with an absolute minimum of cultural value judgments. The
households were all in the "central area" of a large West Coast
city. Implications of these patterns for family planning are discussed.

425.   Radin, Norman and Constance K. Kamil. "The Child Rearing Attitudes of Disadvantaged Negro Mothers and Some Educational Implications," Journal of Negro Education, Vol. 34, No. 2, Spring,
1965, pp. 138-146.

The lower-class Black mother has a difficult life and sees herself
as responsible for the rearing of her children, with the assistance of neither a stable husband nor a friendly society. In con-
trast, the middle-class mother believes that children need defi-
nite limits that youngsters express their thoughts and make their
own decisions, argue the researchers.

426.   Reissman, Frank. "Low-Income Culture: The Strength of the Poor,"
Journal of Marriage and the Family, Vol. 26, No. 4, November,
1964, pp. 417-421.

According to the author, neither supporters nor detractors of the
"noble savage" image recognize the real strengths of the Black
poor. Their strength developed through efforts to cope with disadvantages, states the author. Implications for the educational
system and for work with low-income families are cited and illus-
trated.

15.   BLACK FAMILY AND PRISON

427.   Spain, Johnny. "The Black Family and The Prisons," Black Scholar,
Vol. 4, No. 2, October, 1972, pp. 18-34.

The writer contends that there is no Black family in American

Spain:

society. He believes, however, that a Black family can be built.
He states that no Black family exists today (1972) because of the
wage slavery, and because of the process of wage slavery in prison....

16.   BLACK FAMILY AND PUBLIC POLICY

428.   Darity, William A., Jr. and Samuel L. Myers, Jr.   "Public Policy
and the Condition of Black Family Life," Review of Black Political
Economy, Vol. 13, Nos. 1 & 2, Summer-Fall, 1984, pp. 165-187.

The authors point out that if authentic change is to come about,
it must be generated by the initiative of those who directly face
the pressures of a world in flux. The Black women who must raise
families alone and the Black men who are being left out of the new
age must define their own agenda. They may find it advantageous
to seek out new alliances, perhaps to the disquietude of their
often paternalistic public and private protectors, state the writers. For this very reason the ambitious efforts of the Black
leadership to resolve the Black family problem by "stressing the
traditional strengths as well as values and resources that have
been used to improve the lives of Black people" should be approached with caution. They conclude: "The crisis of the Black family
cannot be resolved for the better by those forces that have contributed to the development of the crisis. The victims, joined by
those who are also beginning to experience the same stress and are
beginning to diagnose the source in the same fashion, must not be
denied the potential to influence the very politics that will affect their lives."

17.   BLACK FAMILY AND RACISM

429.   Robinson, Charlotte. "Black Marriages-Victims of The Affluent
Rat Race," San Francisco Examiner, April 25, 1976, p. 24.

The writer points out the problem of the Black family has changed
from living in a racist, segregated society to coping with a racist, integrated society.

430.   Ryan, William. "Savage Discovery: The Moynihan Report," Nation,
Vol. 210, No. 17, November 22, 1965, pp. 380-384.

This psychologist argues that discrimination and segregation are
the major causes of the conditions which the Moynihan Report la-
bels "family instability" and "tangle of pathology." We must not
forget to end discrimination or all our good works will amount to
very little, concludes Prof. Ryan.

18. BLACK FAMILY AND SEX

431.   Lewis, Diane K. "The Black Family: Socialization and Sex Roles,"
        Phylon, Vol. 36, No. 3, September, 1975, pp. 221-237.

        The author contends that later socialization, depending on the
        conditions under which the families live, is more adaptive to
        particular situations of opportunity or exclusion as they operate
        for males and females. For example, in a matrifocal family in the
        inner city, where wider societal pressures are crucial, a mother's
        expectations for and consequent behavior toward her sons may be
        quite different than in a nuclear family in a small New England
        town, states Professor Lewis. These variations in role expecta-
        tions would operate not only spatially, but temporarily. She con-
        cludes: "Thus, in the past, when Black women had better employ-
        ment opportunities than men, the Black family adapted by providing
        preferential education opportunities for daughters. Now as wider
        educational and employment opportunities are opening for Blacks
        of both sexes, this should begin to be reflected in family pat-
        terns of later childhood training and role expectations."

19. BLACK FAMILY AND SINGLE FAMILIES

432.   Comer, James P. "Single-Parent Black Families," Crisis, Vol. 50,
        No. 10, December, 1983, pp. 42-45.

        According to Dr. Comer there are no quick, precise and easily
        achieved solutions to the problem of single-parent-mostly young,
        poor and uneducated-families. Other social problems such as
        crime, welfare dependency, school underachievement are largely a
        product of the same dynamics suggests a Black community structure,
        focus and process that can begin to make a difference, states the
        writer.

433.   Staples, Robert. "Beyond the Black Family: The Trend Toward Sin-
        glehood," Western Journal of Black Studies, Vol. 3, No. 3,
        Fall, 1979, pp. 150-156.

        The sociologist argues that the crisis of the Black family stems
        from more than poverty alone. It is also due to the problem of
        acculturation, the acceptance of values - alien values - which do
        not conform to the structural context of Black society. Despite
        all that was said about the lack of acculturation being the major
        cause of Black family weakness, it is becoming all too clear that
        Blacks' unique cultural moorings were functional for their situa-
        tion. He concludes: "Now Blacks stand at the crossroads of a
        major decision about which way they will proceed to order their
        lives. Will it be the organic family unit built on a Black ethos,
        or the materialism and individualism of Euro-American culture?"
        Whatever that decision may be, Black people should not be deluded
        into believing that the consequences are individual ones. The
        future of the race may be at stake."

20. BLACK FAMILY AND STERILIZATION

434. Slater, Jack. "Sterilization: Newest Threst To The Poor," Ebony,
Vol. 28, No. 12, October, 1969, pp. 150-151.

It was implied that states and governments in the United States
can control Black people, and the Black family by sterilizing
young, poor and uneducated Black females. Many Blacks sued several states and the federal government for sterilizing their daughters....

21. BLACK FAMILY AND STRESS

435. Peters, Marie F. and Grace Massey. "Mundane Extreme Environmental
Stress in Family Stress Theories: The Case of Black Families in
White America," Marriage and Family Review, Vol. 6, Nos. 1 & 2,
Spring-Summer, 1983, pp. 193-218.

It was suggested that Black Americans' lives are encumbered by the
constand threat and actual periodic occurrences of intimidation,
discrimination, or denial because of race. The stresses which
Black families face -- sometimes subtle, sometimes overt -- are
pervasive, continuous, and debilitating, states the author. Black
families in America are perennial "refugee" families. Yet they
vary from family to family and across life spans, both in their
vulnerability to racist conditions and in their regenerative abi-
lities and strategies. They have developed internal patterns for
coping with racial oppression, strategies proven to be effective
in the past, that are incorporated into their own socialization
processes, assert the writers. The researchers conclude: "...
They have access to community-based programs and shared experiences which not only buffer the potential of psychological damage
that is the impact of never-changing status, but also provide
perspectives, support, and leadership in addressing the illegali-
ty, inhumanity, and unfairness of discriminatory issues...."

22. BLACK FAMILY AND THE BLACK AGED

436. Anderson, Peggye Dilworth. "Family Closeness Between Aged Blacks
and Their Adult Children," Journal of Minority Aging, Vol. 6,
Nos. 3 & 4, 1981, pp. 56-66.

The author found, as other researchers have, that the majority of
aged Blacks, like their White counterparts, interact frequently
with their children as well as express feeling close to them.
The respondents' perceptions and descriptions of closeness to
their children stem primarily from having a reliable exchange of
support system and feeling needed and wanted by them. Therefore,
a close relationship means that the subjects have dependable, concerned and devoted children who show affection for and sensitivity toward their parents. She concludes that not only do we know
how often elderly Blacks interact with their children, we also
better understand the affective aspects of their interaction. In
addition, the findings made in this study provide us with insight

Anderson:

into the role children play in providing their aged parents with economic, social and psychological support. These findings can be instrumental to policy makers and social planners when attempting to provide support to elderly Blacks. We suggest that consideration be given to integrating the psychosocial support children provide their parents with other support mechanisms. Further, because elderly Blacks greatly depend on their children for support, we need to find ways to assist in maintaining and strengthening family relationships, concludes the writer.

437.   Cazenave, Noel A. "Family Violence and Aging Blacks: Theoretical Perspectives and Research Possibilities," Journal of Minority Aging, Vol. 4, No. 4, September-December, 1979, pp. 99-108.

This article served as a prolegomenon for the development of research strategies for the study of aging and family violence. A conflict approach to minority aging should offer many insights into day-to-day interactions, family development and societal transactions affecting their lives. Research on family violence and aging Blacks can serve as the prototype for all subsequent research on violence and aging, states Prof. Cazenave. The aged can be studied as family violence controllers or agitators, victims or aggressors. The extended nature of many Black families should make research on aging in multi-generational households and the effectiveness of potent support systems particularly fruitful, according to the author. He concludes:"Finally, because of the many social and economic restraints impinging on the full expression of masculinity for Black males, Black men can provide key insights into the relationship between middle age and aging developmental crises and marital violence. In brief, Black aging families provide an important arena from which a wide range of ecological and developmental variables related to violence and aging can be studied. In crossing the currently unexplored frontier of aging and family violence, the study of Black aging or of minority aging should provide heuristic insights that will prove useful in blazing new trails into this heretofore neglected area."

438.   Engerman, Stanley L. "Black Fertility and Family Structure in the United States, 1880-1940," Journal of Family History, Vol. 2, No. 2, Summer, 1977, pp. 117-138.

According to the authors while the situation of American Blacks in the years between 1880 and 1940 was in many ways clearly different from that of other groups, it seems that in the cross-sectional differences, as well as in the movements over time, much of the Black fertility pattern resembles that of whites in the United States and elsewhere, as well as that of free Black populations in other parts of the Americas. While it may be possible to separate analytically the problem of explaining changes in Black fertility from that of explaining changes in Black family structure, there are obvious important relationships between the two. Not only may both respond to similar social and economic forces, but different

Engerman:

family patterns have traditionally been associated with differing
fertility levels. While changes in family structure have not been
sufficient to explain most of the past movements in Black fertility, it requires close investigation, asserts Prof. Engerman.

439. Gillespie, Bonnie J. "The Black Family in the American Economy,"
     Journal of Afro-American Issues, Vol. 3, Nos. 3 & 4, Summer/Fall,
     1975, pp. 324-335.

     The author discusses the role of the Black elderly in the Black
     family and the impact that the American economy has on its life.
     He concludes, in part, about the Black elderly: "Poor Health and
     Low Income and Substandard Housing = POVERTY."

440. _____. "Black Grandparents: Childhood Socialization," Jour-
     nal of Afro-American Issues, Vol. 4, Nos. 3 & 4, Summer/Fall,
     1976, pp. 432-441.

     The writer argues that the Black extended family or multigenera-
     tional family exist today-although not in large numbers, and
     grandparents play significant and important roles in such fami-
     lies. The Black maternal grandmother was indicated in the arti-
     cle as being the main factor in Black childhood and adolescent
     socialization outside of the immediate nuclear family....

441. Jackson, Jacqueline J. "Aged Blacks: A Potpourri Toward the Re-
     duction of Social Inequities," Phylon, Vol. 32, No. 3, September,
     1971, pp. 260-280.

     Dr. Jackson describes the Southern urban Black grandparents' roles
     to emphasize certain implications for current policies surrounding
     the Black aged. She notes the role of the National Caucus on
     Black Aged in dramatizing the plight of the Black aged and gives
     proposals to reduce minimum age requirements for OASDHI recipients
     and improve their benefits since Blacks put a large sum of their
     life-savings into social security and often die earlier before re-
     ceiving full benefits. She also discusses the roles of the Black
     grandmother in the Black family.

442. _____. "Aging Black Families and Federal Policies: Some
     Critical Issues," Journal of Minority Aging, Vol. 5, No. 1, Sep-
     tember-December, 1979, pp. 162-169.

     Concerned about the unwarranted consequences of federal policies
     which are not colorblind upon aging Blacks, this article deals
     with the issues of the need for differential age-eligibility re-
     quirements by race for primary beneficiaries of Social Security
     retirement pensions and issues arising from the 1978 report of the
     Human Resources Corporation to the Federal Council on Aging. It
     also stresses the insufficiency of current data for making

Jackson:

definitive and comprehensive recommendations about federal policies and programs for aging Blacks as they relate to familial support, as well as the likely probability that the U. S. Civil Rights
Commission would not be able to produce a valid and reliable study
of racial and ethnic discrimination in aging programs, as mandated
by 1978 federal legislation. Finally, some recommendations related to the federal government and aged Blacks are offered, with
the most important ones being that no ethnic-specific legislation
nor set-asides in the areas of research, training and services be
set up, that at least in the South area agencies on aging should
not ignore feasible cooperation with existing anti-poverty agencies, and that the Federal Council on Aging should take appropriate caution, so that strategies they propose for minority aged
will not, in fact, slow up the movement of them into the mainstream, concludes Dr. Jackson.

443.   _____. "The Economic Well-Being and Financial Security of
Black Elderly Families," Journal of Minority Aging, Vol. 5, No.
4, March-October, 1980, pp. 306-317.

It was stated that the economic well-being and financial security
of Black elderly families have improved somewhat over time. However, the Black elderly families remain a group whose socioeconomic status, in comparison to that of Black males and white females
throughout their adult lives remains unenviable....Dr. Jackson
presents six Tables to support her position....

444. Reiff, Janice L., Michel R. Dahln, and Daniel Scott Smith. "Rural
Push and Urban Pull: Work and Family Experiences of Older Black
Women in Southern Cities, 1880-1900," Journal of Social History,
Vol. 16, No. 4, Summer, 1983, pp. 39-45.

The researchers conclude that the immediate impact of the city was
not negative for these older Black women, at least in the first
years after emancipation. The city was not a destroyer, instead
it provided options that were not available to Black women living
in the country. This essay contended that urban effects should be
understood by contrasting the conditions in the rural areas of origin to the special features of the urban environment itself. Old
women, particularly old widows and most especially those without
living children, were partially pushed from their rural homes.
Although they found only modest economic opportunity in the city,
their chances there were superior to what was available in the
country. Moving to the city made sense to them, and it should
make sense to historians, conclude the authors.

23. BLACK FAMILY AND THE BLACK CHURCH

445. Bims, Hamilton. "The Black Family: A Proud Reappraisal,"
Ebony, Vol. 24, No. 5, March, 1974, pp. 118-121, 123, 125, 127.

Bims:

This article states that the Black family is a unique cultural form enjoying its own inherent resources. Authority channels in large Black families often transcend households, with strong individuals assuming leadership roles, suggests Bims. He also believes that church activities are among the factors of cohesion in which Black extended families preserve their continuity....

446. Lincoln, C. Eric. "The Black Family, The Black Church and the Transformation of Values," Religion in Life, Vol. 47, No. 4, Winter, 1978, pp. 486-496.

The author suggests that the Black family has managed to maintain integrity despite the massive stress of unremittant social exigence unique to the Black experience. The most potent resource of the Black family is the Black church, according to Dr. Lincoln. He concludes, in part: "The roots of the Black family lie deep in the genesis of the Black experience, and from the very beginning the church was the principal anvil upon which the integrity of the Black family was forged."

24. BLACK FAMILY AND THERAPY

447. Hallowitz, David. "Counseling and treatment of the Poor Black Family," Social Casework, Vol. 56, No. 8, October, 1975, pp. 451-459.

The thesis of this article is that professional counseling and therapeutic services are needed and wanted by poor Black families. Among the technical problems involved in the white therapist-Black client therapeutic relationship and process are the need for the therapist's being aware of and dealing with his own subtly prejudicial attitudes and the distrust and hostility which the Black client may have toward him. Although working with poor Black families is different from working with poor white families, there is also a great similarity: basic counseling and treatment principles, concepts and methods apply to both groups, states the author. The same holds true for all families, regardless of racial origin and socioeconomic status, in which conditions precipitate maladaptive behavior, emotional disturbance, and mental breakdown, concludes Hallowitz.

448. McAdoo, Harriette Pipes. "Family Therapy in the Black Community," American Journal of Contemporary Psychotherapy, Vol. 9, No. 1, Summer, 1977, pp. 15-19.

The author recounts that the many cultural dimensions of Black families are not fully taking into account the literature used by family therapists. Prof. McAdoo reviews the literature on the Black family. She suggests that there needs to be a systematic approach of acquiring the statistical data, that will explore the Black personality, so that practitioners have an accurate picture with which to form theories and treatment modalities....

449. _____. "Family Therapy in The Black Community," American Journal of Orthopsychiatry, Vol. 47, No. 1, January, 1977, pp. 75-79.

The author argues that Black, upwardly mobile families face all the stresses experienced by other families dealing with developmental crises and economic changes, but are subject to the additional strain of discrimination. Support, often unavailable from the community, is received instead from the family and others involved in the kinship network. Dr. McAdoo points out that a link is needed between the mental health worker and the Black family. She concludes: "One possibility is greater use of Black paraprofessionals who have both practical knowledge of the people and of current techniques of therapy...."

450. _____. "Stress Absorbing Systems in Black Families," Family Relations, Vol. 31, No. 4, October, 1982, pp. 479-488.

The research found that in spite of the stress and the frequency of changes in their lives, Black families exhibited a high level of satisfaction with their family life situation. These families studied preferred not to seek help outside of their wider family because they felt community agencies were unsympathetic to their unique stresses, and because of the tradition of reliance upon family members....

25. BLACK FAMILY PLANNING

451. Beasley, Joseph D., et al. "Attitudes and Knowledge Relevant to To Family Planning Among New Orleans Negro Women," American Journal of Public Health, Vol. 56, No. 11, November, 1965, pp. 1847-1857.

Information obtained from these Black New Orleans women indicates that they were unknowledgeable about reproductive physiology, the ovulatory cycle, and effective means of contraception. Excluding the 9 women who had sterilization operations, 57 percent used no method of family planning during their most recent years of cohabitation. It was shown that about three-fourths of these women did not want to become pregnant again, two-thirds of them wanted more information about how to keep from getting pregnant, and nine-tenths thought they should have the right to plan the size of their families....

452. Bogue, Donald J. "Family Planning in the Negro Ghettos of Chicago," The Milbank Memorial Fund Quarterly, Vol. 48, April, 1970, pp. 283-307.

Bogue's study of family planning in Chicago deals with ideas of reproduction, Black sexual behavior, attitudes toward family planning, and knowledge and use of contraceptives.

453.   Campbell, Arthur A.   "Fertility and Family Planning Among Non-White Married Couples in the United States," Eugenics Quarterly, Vol. 12, No. 3, September, 1965, pp. 124-131.

It was pointed out that in every educational category, including the college group, non-white couples have shown less success in family planning than white couples.   Their level of completely planned fertility is lower, and their level of excess fertility is higher.   Prof. Campbell states that planning status is one fertility variable in which non-whites differ consistently from whites, regardless of socioeconomic status.   The white-non-white differentials vary in magnitude, but they are in the same direction in all education groups and all regions of the country.   He concludes: "It is clear that non-white wives do not want as many children as they expect to have.   They want about the same number as white wives or fewer...."

454.   Cochrane, Carl M. et al., "Motivational Determinants of Family Planning Clinic Attendance," Journal of Psychology, Vol. 84, No. 1, May, 1973, pp. 33-43.

The writers suggest that family planning may offer one avenue by which Black women, who were classified as Actives, Dropouts or Never-Beens, can successfully act to control and order events in their lives.   In some cases, conclude the researchers, the wish to avoid having more children in a partnership of questionable stability may be a more specific motive.

455.   Crokey, Elizabeth.   "Family Planning Program for the Low-Income Family," Journal of Marriage and the Family, Vol. 26, No. 45, November, 1964, pp. 478-480.

This is a study of the North Carolina birth control clinic, its history, methods of birth control prescribed, and the clients' responses.   The author found a desire of low-income families to limit the number of children.

456.   Darity, William A., et al.   "An Exploratory Study of Barriers to Family Planning: Race Consciousness and Fear of Black Genocide As a Basis," Advances In Planned Parenthood, Vol. 7, 1972, pp. 20-32.

The author found that the highest degree of concern and negative attitudes were observed in the 30-and-under group with regard to purpose and objectives of birth control services.   The same negative attitudes were observed in the case of abortions and sterilization among this age group, as compared with the females of all ages, conclude the researchers.

457.   _____, and Castellano B. Turner.   "Attitudes Toward Family Planning: A Comparison Between Northern and Southern Black Americans: A Preliminary Report," Advances in Planned Parenthood, Vol. 8, 1973, pp. 13-20.

Darity and Turner:

The researchers discuss some preliminary comparisons of respondents from Philadelphia and Charlotte, North Carolina on several important attitudes relating to family planning. They found little or no differences in family planning in the two geographic regions. Their data demonstrated strong support in the Black community for sex education programs in public schools....

458. Harrison, A.O. "Family Planning Attitudes Among Black Females," Journal of Social and Behavioral Sciences, Vol. 22, No. 3, Winter, 1977, pp. 136-145.

It was stated that the Black population is growing at a slower rate in the 70s when compared to the 60s. Nation-wide, Black females of all socio-economic levels desire smaller families. Major reasons cited are economics and an increased desire by women to control their bodies. However, those who are most effective in realizing this goal are urban middle class Blacks. These women have access to private physicians who dispense the most successful birth control methods. In addition, fertility rates for Blacks are declining because of trends in urbanization among the Black population, improved socio-economic conditions, and an increase in availability of birth control information. The writer concludes: "These findings suggest that Black females are not accepting the idea that to use birth control is to participate in the genocide of the Black population. It seems that the major issue is how to assist Black females in their expressed goals of limiting the size of their families."

459. Walters, Ronald. "Population Control and the Black Community," Black Scholar, Vol. 5, No. 9, 1974, pp. 25-31.

Dr. Walters asserts that it is inadvisable, particularly for members of the Black community, to accept unchallenged the existing assumptions and practices of the population limiting movement as it affects their own interests. This is an implicit reference to the view that the leadership and the individual in the Black community should blindly trust neither government nor health professionals to plan for the positive development of family life because the status of families and individuals is directly related to the status and well-being of the whole group and its survival in America, according to the author. He states that this conclusion takes into consideration such factors germane to this entire presentation as the role of government and its priorities, the direction and composition of the World Population movement, the nature of the assumption upon which the family planning movement is based, and the still-to-be-answered charge of genocide....

26. BLACK FEMALE ROLE IN THE FAMILY

460. Blauvelt, Mary Taylor. "The Race Problem: As Discussed by Negro Women," American Journal of Sociology, Vol. 6, No. 4, March, 1901, pp. 662-672.

Blauvelt:

The article was not as interested in the discussion of the race problem by the Michigan State Federation of Colored Women's Clubs as it was with the fact that Black women could be as beautiful, clean, knowledgeable, articulate and businesslike as white women and that Black women would make better mothers and wives than Whites.

461.   Myers, Lena Wright. "Mothers from Families of Orientation as Role Models for Black Women," Northwest Journal of African and Black American Studies, Vol. 2, No. 1, Winter, 1974, pp. 7-9.

The writer argues that for Black women, the mothers from the families of orientation are effective role models. Dr. Myers surmises that the biased concept of instability among families as defined by White middle class standards does not inhibit the existence of effective role models for Black women. The author concludes that the traditional White model of evaluation should not be the only evaluative yardstick employed in pursuit of research on Black women and the Black family....

462.   Staples, Robert. "The Myth of the Black Matriarchy," The Black Scholar, Vol. 2, No. 9, June, 1971, pp. 2-9.

White America will continue to perpetuate the myth of the impotent Black male as long as it serves their purpose, concludes the scholar.

463.   TenHouten, Warren. "The Black Family: Myth and Reality," Psychiatry, Vol. 33, May, 1970, pp. 145-173.

The author argues that the data from the empirical study do not show lower-class Black husbands to be powerless in either their conjugal or their parental roles. Black wives do appear to be powerful in their parental roles, but there is no indication that this emasculates the Black husband-father. The writer concludes that, on the contrary, this can be seen as a positive resource for Black youth, and as a strength in Black families.

464.   Valien, Preston and Albetta Fitzgerald. "Attitudes of the Negro Mother Toward Birth Control," American Journal of Sociology, Vol. 55, No. 3, November, 1949, pp. 279-283.

Of 136 Black mothers in Nashville, Tennessee, approximately one-half had unfavorable attitudes toward birth-control practices. Religious or moral reasons and a belief that birth-control practices are inefficient or injurious to health were the chief reasons given. Age, number of children, urban or rural birthplace, and amount of education appear to be associated with differential attitudes toward birth control.

27.   BLACK LOWER-CLASS FAMILY

465.   Babchuk, Nicholas and John A. Balweg. "Black Family Structure and
Primary Relations," Phylon, Vol. 33, No. 4, Winter, 1972, pp. 334-
347.

When this study was undertaken, the authors were predisposed toward the popular and widely held view that lower- and working-
class Black American couples would maintain most friendships
apart, to find the male somewhat isolated from primary contacts,
and to find women to be especially integrated in the extended family system. The current emphasis on the Black American "problem
family," the family in which the female is the dominant figure and
the male an "appendage" undoubtedly encourages this view. The
data provide no support for it, according to the researchers. "To
the contrary, the evidence suggests that the primary-group resources of lower- and working-class couples are not only greater than
is generally believed, but ordinarily mutual for the pair. The
male is not outside of the structure but an important force within it. Moreover, the evidence encourages belief that there are
not great differences in the primary resources nor patterns of
establishing or maintaining such resources among Black Americans
nor between Black and white Americans," conclude the writers.

466.   Bell, Robert R. "The Lower-Class Negro Mother's Aspirations for
Their Children," Social Forces, Vol. 43, No. 4, May, 1965, pp.
493-500.

This data supports the hypothesis that it is possible to distinguish different subgroups among Black lower class. The lower
class mother's values and aspirations for her children are very
influential for her children's future. Significant differences
were found in answers of "low status" and "high status" lower-
class mothers when questioned about their aspirations for their
children, concludes Prof. Bell.

467.   _____. "Lower Class Negro Mothers and Their Children,"
Integrated Education, Vol. 2, No. 12, December, 1964-January,
1965, pp. 23-27.

The researcher suggests that the closer the mother's aspirations
for her children are to the bottom level of the lower-class value
range, the less likely are her children to be greatly influenced
by other agencies and persons reflecting more middle-class values.

468.   Billingsley, Andrew. "Family Functioning in the Low-Income Black
Community," Social Casework, Vol. 50, No. 9, December, 1969, pp.
563-572.

The author notes three patterns of family functioning: (1) family
holds themselves together and meets child's needs, (2) family functions marginally and children on verge of difficulty, and (3) state
of confusion with child suffering most scars of racism, poverty and

Billingsley:

family disruption. Factors affecting family functioning are: (1) economic viability, (2) education of family head, and (3) man in household. Some families held together by network of intimate interrelationships of mutual aid and social integration with neighbors and kin. Social workers must build programs based on resourcefulness and strengths of Black communities and families, concludes the researcher.

469.   Dietrick, Katheryn T. "A Reexamination of the Myth of Black Ma-
        triarchy," Journal of Marriage and the Family, Vol. 37, No. 2,
        May, 1975, pp. 367-374.

Previous arguments that matriarchy is a myth in the Black lower classes are reviewed and an additional argument is presented: the irrelevance of heretofore employed decision-making measures for lower-class Blacks. This study employs seemingly more relevant measures to examine conjugal decision-making and decision-imple-mentation in predominantly lower-class Black families in five me-tropolitan populations and two non-metropolitan populations in the U.S. Role-patterning by specific decision-areas and composite power configurations are analyzed. The results call into question presumptions that matriarchy is normative in the Black lower class. In both decision-making and decision-implementation, the husband's role was primarily perceived to be that of a sharer rather than an autonomous agent. Sharing of decision-making was the majority re-sponse with respect to all decisions except decisions about the wife working, and syncratic authority type was consistently the modal decision-making structure, states the author. When interac-tion of decision-making and decision-implementation was considered, the predominant structures were syncratic cooperation (BaBd) and syncratic division of functions where decision-making was shared but decision-implementation was performed by the wife (WaBd), con-cludes Prof. Dietrick.

470.   Drake, St. Clair, "The Social and Economic Status of the Negro in
        the United States," Daedalus, Vol. 94, No. 4, 1965, pp. 771-814.

Various references are made to the Black family throughout this article. The writer compares the lower-class Black family with the middle-Class Black family. He concludes that the life styles of the Black upper-class family are similar to those of the White upper middle-class, but it is only in rare instances that Blacks have been incorporated into the clique and associational life of this group.

471.   Edwards, Harry. "Black Muslims and Negro Christian Family Rela-
        tions," Journal of Marriage and the Family, Vol. 30, No. 4, No-
        vember, 1968, pp. 604-611.

This article compared families affiliated with the Nation of Islam to those matched families affiliated with various lower-class

Edwards:

Negro Christian churches. The specific areas of family life co-
vered included husband-wife relationships; family-extended kin relationships; parent-child relationships; and relationships between
the families and various types of social groups and community agencies. The results indicated different patterns of family life
existing between the two groups. Of particular interest was the
tendency for the Muslim families to exhibit middle-class values
and behavior patterns to a greater degree than did the Christian
families.

472.   Ford, Beverly O. "Case Studies of Black Female Heads of Households in the Welfare System: Socialization and Survival," Western
Journal of Black Studies, Vol. 1, No. 2, June, 1977, pp. 114-120.

The purpose of this essay is to provide insights into how eight
Black women who head families perceive their own womanhood, how
they define it, what models of womanhood operate for them, and how
their views of themselves are shaped by the values, norms, and
traditions of the Black community.

473.   Gwyn, Felisha S. and Alice C. Kilpatrick. "Family Therapy with
Low-Income Blacks: A Tool or Turn-Off," Social Casework, Vol.
62, No. 5, May, 1981, pp. 259-266.

The low-income Black family has needs that are not being met by
traditional family therapy approaches. This article examines the
literature on the effectiveness of typical treatment methods, presents an illustrative case study, and then describes more speciali-
zed family therapy methods of engagement that are deeply rooted in
the family's world, which reflect the family's priorities rather
than the therapist's need to be developed in order for family therapy to be a tool rather than a turn-off for low-income Black families. Additional research is also necessary to determine which
innovations are proving most effective and where improvements can
be made, assert the researchers.

474.   McGhee, James D. "A Dream Denied: The Black Family in the Eigh-
ties," Urban League Review, Vol. 7, No. 1, Winter, 1982/1983, pp.
25-37.

The author asserts that there are subtle but very real reasons why
the impending destruction of the present Black middle class and
the denial of the means and opportunity for low and very low income Blacks to improve their lot represents more than just financial disaster for a relatively small group of people. He concludes: "While many low-income Blacks often derogate membership in
the middle-class, what they object to are attitudes that are perceived as foreign to them, not the lifestyle that a middle-class
income brings. That lifestyle is almost universally desired and
its availability to some Blacks gives hope to others who have not
yet achieved it...."

475.   Osmond, Marie W.   "Marital Organization in Low Income Families: A
        Cross-Race Comparison," International Journal of Sociology of the
        Family, Vol. 7, No. 2, July-December, 1977, pp. 143-156.

        Patterns of marital interaction, that are associated with differ-
        ential probabilities of marital dissolution, are analyzed in a
        Black and in a white subsample of 227 low-income families. Struc-
        tured interviews with one or the other of the spouses were conduc-
        ted in a sample of welfare applicants/recipients in the states of
        Florida, Georgia, West Virginia and New Jersey. In a multivariate
        analysis of the data, two "family polity" variables emerge as of
        overriding importance in predicting marital intactness: mode of
        decision making and strategy of conflict resolution. Marital de-
        cision making, or who actually makes the decisions, has the high-
        est association with marital intactness for whites. For Blacks,
        however, the most important indicator of family "power" is conflict
        resolution, or whose decision prevails when the spouses' interests
        conflict. A greater number of Black respondents report husband
        dominance in marriage and about equal numbers of Blacks and whites
        report "democratic" decision making. The author concludes: "There
        is no evidence of "Black matriarchy," neither normative nor beha-
        vioral. There is a greater polarization of significant others for
        Black spouses than for white. Background variables (degree of
        homogamy in terms of fathers' occupations and spouses' educational
        attainment) are differentially related to marital intactness for
        Blacks and whites. Conclusions underscore the variety of condi-
        tions which can be associated with both intact and dissolved mar-
        riages for each racial group."

476.   Robinson, Ira E., et al.   "Self Perception of the Husband/Father
        in the Intact Lower Class Black Family," Phylon, Vol. 66, No. 2,
        June, 1985, pp. 136-147.

        Contrary to what might be expected, the authors argue, their re-
        search indicated clearly that the husband/fathers are the main
        providers for their families - a position that contradicts the idea
        lower-class Black husbands are unable to fulfill this role in their
        family. "The husbands/fathers depicted themselves as being active
        in the process of decision making relative to purchasing applian-
        ces and selecting residences. They also indicated that they - ba-
        sically in conjunction with their wives - should be active in the
        decision-making process regarding residences," conclude the re-
        searchers.

477.   Rodman, Hyman, et al.   "Lower Class Attitudes Toward 'Deviant'
        Family Patterns: A Cross-Cultural Study," Journal of Marriage
        and The Family, Vol. 31, No. 2, May, 1969, pp. 315-321.

        The article was based on research done on Black women systemati-
        cally selected from a Detroit low income housing project. The
        data indicate that very few lower-class Black women were norma-
        tively favorable to nonlegal marriage...and that somewhat fewer
        than half respond that illegitimacy is "not wrong". According to
        the researchers, in the lower-class there are environmental pres-
        sures to modify conventional middle-class values and attitudes....

478. Schienfeld, Daniel R. "Family Relationships and School Achieve-
     ment Among Boys of Lower Class Black Families," American Journal
     of Orthopsychiatry, Vol. 53, No. 1, January, 1983, pp. 127-143.

     The researcher suggests that mothers of high achievers express
     ideals for their sons that emphasize self-motivated, active, learn-
     ing engagement with the world; mothers of low achievers express
     ideals that emphasize constraint, conditions encountered by a
     large proportion of lower-income Blacks thus tend to become trans-
     lated into low academic achievement of children, concludes the
     author.

479. Schwartz, Michael. "The Northern United States Negro Matriarchy
     Status Versus Authority," Phylon, Vol. 26, No. 1, Spring, 1965,
     pp. 18-24.

     The essay was based on a study of a sample of 510 lower-class
     Black boys, 100 Southern with migrant families, and 30 middle-
     class Black families. Prof. Schwartz concludes: "To be sure, the
     mother holds the family together, but the cognitive strains that
     are found reflected in the perceptions of the boys seem to be
     enough to drive these families apart and in many instances they
     even cease to exist. In many respects the effects of urbanism
     seems to be much more severe, dislocating and dysfunctional for
     lower-class Negro families than for lower-class Southern white
     families."

480. Schulz, David A. "Variation in the Father Role in Complete Fami-
     lies of the Negro Lower Class," Social Science Quarterly, Vol. 49,
     No. 3, December, 1969, pp. 651-659.

     The author observes that the father in the lower-class Negro fami-
     lies does not appear to be simply subordinate to his wife, as the
     term "matrifocal" might imply. His status, these data suggest,
     depends not only upon his capacity to earn a living and his fur-
     ther willingness to share that living with his family, but also
     upon the degree of his adherence to the norms of monogamous mar-
     riage, his ability to cope with the harsh realities of the ghetto,
     and his capacity to be a pal to his children. Dr. Schulz concludes:
     "The family that seems best able to survive as a family unit in a
     situation where there is little hope of upward mobility or of suf-
     ficient income from legitimate sources is the family that is best
     able to cope with its environment as it presents itself. In such
     a family the father is typically the discreet free-man."

28. BLACK MALE ROLE IN THE FAMILY

481. Hampton, Robert L. "Husband's Characteristics and Marital Dis-
     ruption in Black Families," Sociological Quarterly, Vol. 20, No.
     2, Spring, 1979, pp. 255-266.

     Throughout the 1960s and the 1970s a great deal of scholarly and
     popular literature has addressed the status of Blacks in American

Hampton:

society, some of it concerned with the stability of Black family
life. This article is concerned with the relationship between
husband's characteristics and marital disruption, and focuses on
575 intact Black families and identifies several factors associated with disruption. Although husband's age is the strongest bi-
variate predictor of marital disruption, husband's income is the
most important predictor; and husband's employment problems and
religiosity are also strong predictors. A causal model of marital
disruption shows that education, employment and age at marriage
influence marriage disruption through their influence on income.
Only age, income and religiosity had a significant direct effect,
states the researcher. The majority of Black families remained
stable during the author's study period. This is important given
the often distorted view of marital stability among Blacks. Families, irrespective of racial and ethnic background, go through a
period of "disruption proneness" or a period in which they are trying to establish the viability of the marital union. "Given the
age at which most marry, this period tends disproportionately to
be during their twenties. The young may worry that they will never
find a niche in the society, or at least not one that commands
their own respect and that of others, both as they try to establish their own families' identities and find meaningful employment. This makes the stress and strains on young Black families
all the greater, for in addition to the normal problems associated
with establishing an intimate dyadic relationship, Blacks must
also deal with the racial and economic inequities in our society,"
concludes the author.

482. Hare, Nathan. "The Frustrated Masculinity of the Negro Male,"
      Negro Digest, Vol. 13, No. 8, August, 1964, pp. 5-9.

      The author relates the frustration of Black males in playing the
      masculine role of providing for the family and protecting them.
      Also the Black male may feel inferior to his wife because she had
      more education and a better job. White supremacists have used
      the myth of Black male superior sexuality as an excuse to cas-
      trate and lynch him, concludes Dr. Hare.

483. Moynihan, Daniel P. "Employment Income and the Ordeal of the
      Negro Family," Daedalus, Vol. 94, Fall, 1965, pp. 745-770.

      The writer argues that the cumulative result of unemployment and
      low income, and probably also of excessive dependence upon the in-
      come of women, has produced an unmistakable crisis in the Negro
      family, and raises the serious question of whether or not this
      crisis is beginning to create conditions which tend to reinforce
      the cycle that produced it in the first instance. The crisis
      would probably exist in any event, but it becomes acute in the
      context of the extraordinary rise in Negro population in recent
      years, concludes Dr. Moynihan.

484. Parker, Seymour and Robert J. Kleiner. "Social and Psychological
      Dimensions of the Family Role Performance of the Negro Male,"
      Journal of Marriage and the Family, Vol. 31, No. 3, August, 1969,
      pp. 500-506.

      The researchers assumed that if deviance in Negro male family role
      performance is actually normative, then conscious dissatisfaction
      with family role performance, i.e., discrepancies, would not be
      related particularly to generalized feelings of failure and hope-
      lessness. The fact that such a relationship did exist leads to
      the possible conclusion that those Negro males who perceive them-
      selves as relative failures, i.e., low achievers, with little hope
      of success, are also more prone to feel that they are failing in
      their family role performance. These findings cast further doubt
      on the idea that "deviant" family behavior among Negro males is a
      reflection of a distinct subculture. They conclude: "A more
      adequate interpretation of these data would involve the hypothesis
      that the problems encountered by the Negro male in the areas of em-
      ployment, housing, and general social discrimination result in
      feelings of failure and inadequacy and an inability to perform his
      family role adequately."

485. Sizemore, Barbara A. "Sexism and the Black Male," Black Scholar,
      Vol. 4, Nos. 5, 6 & 7, March-April, 1973, pp. 2-11.

      The author stresses the fact that in American society the value of
      male superiority is held; women are considered inferior, and are
      relegated to the lowest rungs on economic and social ladders.
      Last to be hired, first fired, Black women are discriminated
      against in pay, hiring and by laws. And this attitude has a neg-
      lected effect on the Black family, argues the writer.

486. Staples, Robert. "Educating the Black Male at Various Class
      Levels for Marital Roles," Family Coordinator, Vol. 19, No. 2,
      April, 1970, pp. 164-167.

      This article explores the necessity and feasibility of preparing
      the Black male at various class levels to take on the marital
      roles of husband and father and offers some observations about
      what the author considers the most pragmatic approach to the prob-
      lem. Dr. Staples argues that Black males may best be prepared
      for their future marital roles by the inculcation of pride in
      their African heritage by a reminder of their forefathers' patri-
      lineal and patriarchal form of family organizations. The writer
      concludes that, hopefully, this will generate those changes in the
      Black family which will enable the Black husband and father to
      play the role required of him....

29.   BLACK MIDDLE-CLASS FAMILY

487. Landry, Bart and Margaret P. Jenchek. "The Employment of Wives in
      Middle-Class Black Families," Journal of Marriage and the Family,
      Vol. 40, No. 4, November, 1978, pp. 787-798.

Landry and Jenchek:

Many studies of the employment of Black and white wives have compared rates and patterns among all Black and all white wives. The
present study focuses primarily upon wives in Black middle-class
families, with comparisons made to wives in middle-class white and
working-class Black families. A model with 11 independent variables is presented, and multiple regression analysis used to predict the probability that a wife will be employed. Findings support the hypothesis of both race and class effects upon the employment of wives. Black middle-class wives were found to have
higher employment rates than both white middle- and Black working-
class wives. At the same time, patterns of influence among factors affecting employment differed between Black and white middle-
class wives, as well as between Black middle- and working-class
wives. Results of the regression analysis and contingency analysis of relevant data suggest that Black middle-class wives have
higher employment rates because of economic need, state the authors.

488. Little, Monroe H. "Class and Culture: A Reassessment of E. Frank-
      lin Frazier's Black Experience," Western Journal of Black Studies,
      Vol. 4, No. 2, Summer, 1980, pp. 122-131.

      Prof. Little argues that E. Franklin Frazier did not use careful
      methods in developing a historical explanation for the rise and
      condition of the Black middle class. Frazier's impatience with
      objective measures of class, his inability to deal with social
      change satisfactorily, and his blindness to the order and meaning
      of modern Black undergraduate behavior, sentiments, and values
      distorted and omitted important aspects of Afro-American student
      life, according to the author. He concludes: "Interpretation of
      the contemporary Black community requires assumptions about its
      past. The choice is between historical reality, based on a ri-
      gorous examination of sources and historical fantasy, rooted in
      ideological preconceptions and uncritical acceptance of group
      mythology."

489. McAdoo, Harriette Pipes. "Upward Mobility and Parenting in
      Middle-Income Black Families," Journal of Black Psychology, Vol.
      1, No. 1, August, 1981, pp. 1-22.

      In this essay the roles of dual-parent employment, high mobility
      aspirations, and discrimination in parenting are covered. In a
      sample of 178 families with 305 parents, the extended family help
      network was found to be still an important source of support, from
      kin and fictive kin, for newly mobile and those one or two genera-
      tions of middle-income status, yet the reciprocal obligations for
      help received were not felt to be excessive, states Prof. McAdoo.
      A review of the various cycles in research on non-poor Black fami-
      lies is related to various movements within the Black community.
      The relevance of various SES classifications and characteristics
      of economically mobile families are explored by the author.

30. BLACK POLYGAMOUS FAMILY

490.   Allen, Walter R. and Bamidele, A. Agbasegbe. "A Comment on
(Joseph) Scott's 'Black Polygamous Family Formation,'" Alternative
Lifestyles, Vol. 3, No. 4, November, 1980, pp. 375-381.

This brief article takes a critical look at Joseph W. Scott's
article "Black Polygamous Family Formation." While Scott's research is seen as helpful, several problems in his treatment of
plural mating and marriage arrangements among Black Americans are
discussed. Major conceptual problems are created by Scott's use
(or misuse) of the concept "polygyny." Significant methodological
problems are also posed by his sampling approach, operationaliza-
tion of concepts, and analytic strategies. Studies such as
Scott's are of optimal value when their exploratory nature, and
consequent limitation, are clearly acknowledged, state the authors.

491.   McAdoo, Harriette Pipes. "Commentary of Joseph Scott's 'Black
Polygamous Family Formation,'" Alternative Lifestyles, Vol. 3,
No. 4, November, 1980, pp. 383-388.

The essay critiques the polygyny model of Joseph Scott in terms
of the pressures felt by young, poor Black women with children
who often enter into extramarital unions with married men as they
attempt to find economic and emotional security.

492.   Scott, Joseph. "Black Polygamous Family Formation: Case Studies
of Legal Wives and Consensual Wives," Alternative Lifestyles, Vol.
3, No. 1, February, 1980, pp. 41-64.

This study examines how eleven legal wives and eleven consensual
wives drifted into polygamous (man-sharing) relationships. The
study also examines how the declining sex ratio may be influencing
these and other demographic developments in the Black communities
across the United States. A case in point is the rising number of
out-of-wedlock births among Black teenagers and their subsequent
drift into man-sharing arrangements due to the circumstances of
the rating-dating-mating marketplace, states the author.

31. BLACK RURAL FAMILY

493.   Beasley, Joseph D. and C. L. Hunter, A. Fischer. "Attitudes and
Knowledge Relevant to Family Planning Among New Orleans Negro
Women," American Journal of Public Health, Vol. 56, No. 11,
November, 1966, pp. 1847-1857.

This survey found that for women age 15-45 in metropolitan New
Orleans, there is substantial ignorance of reproductive physiology and birth control. Most did not want to become pregnant again
and wanted family planning clinics. The absence of a paternal family head and the instability of the family structure was a major
problem of Blacks not only in New Orleans but across America, conclude the researchers.

494. Henderson, Donald. "The Negro Migration, 1916-1918," Journal of
      of Negro History, Vol. 6, No. 4, October, 1921, pp. 383-398.

      The maladjustments of Blacks to their environment in the South
      caused them to flee to another locality. They could not overcome
      economic and social barriers of race prejudice. The author discus-
      ses the many motives for this migration, new opportunities open to
      them, and the obstacles migrants faced and the effects it had on
      the Black family.

495. Jacques, Jeffrey M. "Self-Esteem Among Southeastern Black-American
      Couples," Journal of Black Studies, Vol. 7, No. 1, September,
      1976, pp. 11-28.

      This study found that unlike earlier reports, there is no negative
      self-esteem among Black Americans and no evidence that spouse's
      self-esteem related to other spouse's color. Increased interest
      in Black Studies may reflect a change in perception. More Blacks
      in decision making positions and more opportunities open to them.

496. Lystad, M.H. "Family Patterns, Achievements, and Aspirations of
      Urban Negroes," Sociology and Social Research, Vol. 45, No. 3,
      April, 1961, pp. 281-288.

      This study involved 100 Black families in New Orleans, Louisiana.
      The author found varying family patterns in his study. He also
      points out that family types were related to some differences in
      social performance. As children, the respondents achieved a
      higher educational level in those families in which the father was
      both present in the home and active with children. The writer
      concludes that Blacks in all family types held expectations for
      their children which were much higher than their own achievements
      or participation.

497. Young, Virginia Heyer. "Family and Childhood in a Southern
      Negro Community," American Anthropologist, Vol. 72, No. 2, April,
      1970, pp. 269-288.

      Dr. Young suggests that children usually remain with their mother
      while she may have a series of unions; this makes the ties between
      mother and child strong and culturally significant. The Negro man,
      however, has a role in the system. His absence from the household
      of his own children and his periodic moves to different households,
      at least while he is young, is not a measure of psychic inadequacy,
      according to the author. It is his role in a functional system,
      the values of which are free response to emotions and true and
      continuing compatibility between man and woman. She states that
      Negro marriage and family practices provide social and psychologi-
      cal security for childbearing and child training; they embody cul-
      tural values and serve human needs. As such, they deserve to be
      recognized as functionally integral parts of an American Negro
      culture. "To interpret these practices as deteriorated forms of a
      general American culture introduces an ethnocentric bias and ob-
      scures some of the values and inner working of Negro society," con-
      cludes the researcher.

32. BLACK URBAN FAMILY

498. Berger, Curtis J. "Law, Justice and the Poor," Academy of Political Science Proceedings, Vol. 29, July, 1968, pp. 52-59.

The prevailing mood of the ghetto is one of alienation. Social justice for the poor requires a broader sharing of the nation's plenty, and a social system in which they feel they can contribute. Black families in the ghetto do not believe that society has any interest in their plight, states the writer.

499. Boggs, James. "Blacks in the Cities: Agenda for the 70's," Black Scholar, Vol. 4, No. 4, November-December, 1972, pp. 50-61.

The writer discusses the many problems Blacks face in the city: bad housing, poor transportation, drugs, inadequate health care, lack of training facilities, and the conditions of the Black family. Blacks must work within their own communities to change these conditions politically, socially, and economically, concludes the author.

500. Brody, Eugene. "Color and Identity Conflicts in Young Boys: Observations of Negro Mothers and Sons in Urban Baltimore," Psychiatry, Vol. 26, No. 12, May, 1963, pp. 188-201.

The study of Black mothers and sons revealed that many of the boys had conflicts involving anxiety or guilt-laden wishes to be white and some were uncertain as to their identities. Mothers also exhibited conflict about their skin color and role as a Black. The function of Black mothers as models for their sons was emphasized. The author found that it was unlikely that a relationship with a mother, no matter how secure, can be an adequate basis for the development of a stable social identity in a boy....

501. Farley, Reynolds. "Fertility Among Urban Blacks," The Milbank Memorial Fund Quarterly, Vol. 48, April, 1970, Part 2, pp. 183-214.

The author looks at trends in urban and rural fertility, factors explaining fertility trends and current differentials in fertility. The author sees fertility rates as continuing to drop especially with urban Blacks....

502. Feagin, Joe R. "A Note on the Friendship Ties of Black Urbanites," Social Forces, Vol. 49, No. 21, December, 1970, pp. 303-308.

Contrary to popular beliefs about Black urbanites, they did form friendship ties with people in their neighborhoods, states the author. Most wives, because of large families and low incomes, seem to have an intensive contact with friends. They were also involved in kinship and neighboring networks, concludes Prof. Feagin.

503. Frazier, E. Franklin. "Ethnic Family Patterns: The Negro Family in the United States," <u>American Journal of Sociology</u>, Vol. 53, No. 61, May, 1948, pp. 435-439.

The Black family developed into a matriarchal family because of loss of the African cultural heritage and the requirements of slavery, states Prof. Frazier. Urbanization has caused much family disorganization because they could not function effectively in the city. The deviations in the character of the Black family are strongly associated with his social isolation and economic position. As he becomes more accepted and participates in his society, his family lifes becomes more stable, concludes the scholar.

504. _____. "Negro Harlem: An Ecological Study," <u>American Journal of Sociology</u>, Vol. 43, No. 1, July, 1937, pp. 72-88.

This detailed study tells how Blacks came to live in Harlem, the population distribution, marital status, birth and death rates, crime, and distribution of institutions in the area and how each has affected the lives of its residents. The study showed that the organization and disorganization of Black family life in the Northern city were closely tied to the economic and social structure of the Black community, states Dr. Frazier.

505. _____. "Some Effects of the Depression on the Negro in Northern Cities," <u>Science and Society</u>, Vol. 2, No. 1, Fall, 1938, pp. 489-499.

The effects of the Depression on Blacks in Northern cities has laid bare the general economic insecurity of the Black masses. It destroyed their foothold in industries they gained during the war. One of the chief effects of the Depression upon the thinking of Blacks has been the spread of radical ideas among working class Blacks through cooperation with white workers as they became allies in the struggle for work and relief, concludes the sociologist.

506. Furstenberg, Frank F., Jr., et al. "The Origins of the Female-Headed Black Family: The Impact of the Urban Experience," <u>Journal of Interdisciplinary History</u>, Vol. 6, No. 2, Autumn, 1975, pp. 211-233.

The researchers argue that they do not wish to imply that the institution of slavery was <u>not</u> brutalizing and dehumanizing. Yet, one must not convert a sense of moral outrage into a monolithic interpretation of the Black experience, assert the authors. They conclude: "Once we recognize that the matrifocal Black family is a product of economic discrimination, poverty, and disease we cease to blame the distant past for problems which have their origins in more recent times. It was, and still is, much easier to lament the sins of one's forefathers than to confront the injustices of more contemporary socioeconomic systems."

507.   Hiday, Virginia A. "Parity and Well-Being Among Low-Income Urban
        Families," Journal of Marriage and the Family, Vol. 37, No. 4,
        November, 1975, pp. 789-797.

        The author found that among Black families in inner city neighbor-
        hoods characterized by poverty, parity was found to have strong,
        consistently negative relationship with family well-being. The
        writer argues that the weight of empirical evidence shows structu-
        ral factors to be the primary cause of poverty within urban areas
        of industrial nations. The purpose of this study was to indicate
        within broad structural constraints the extent to which an indivi-
        dual can control her fertility has significant effects on her
        family's well-being.

508.   Jackson, Jacquelyne J. "Ordinary Black Husbands: The Truly
        Hidden Men," Journal of Social and Behavioral Sciences, Vol. 20,
        No. 2, Spring, 1974, pp. 19-27.

        Studies of the Black family have paid very little attention to the
        employed or retired Black husband. This article attempts to as-
        sist in correcting this imbalance. The data in this study were
        collected in 1968 and 1969 from approximately 73 percent of all
        male household heads or all males 21 or more years of age in an
        urban renewal area and 79 percent of adult male subjects randomly
        selected from designated blocks in areas peripheral to the urban
        renewal area. The data contradict the usual stereotype of the
        relative insignificance of the father in Black families, and, per-
        haps more important, the extent of his power within his family.
        Black males tend to exercise stronger power within their families
        than do white males....

509.   Johnson, Everett. "A Study of Negro Families in the Pinewood
        Avenue District of Toledo, Ohio," Opportunity, Vol. 7, No. 8,
        August, 1929, pp. 243-245.

        The author studied families in Toledo's major Black district. The
        Black population is small compared to other cities. Its size and
        Black residential areas are scattered all over the city. Johnson
        studies the population, migration, housing, conditions of property,
        sanitary conditions, religious life, and industrial status of the
        Black in Toledo.

510.   Jones, Eugene Kinckle. "Negro Migration in New York State,"
        Opportunity, Vol. 4, No. 1, January, 1926, pp. 7-11.

        This is a study of Blacks in the North, what led them to migrate
        to New York and the social complexion of the Black population in
        New York. Because Blacks migrated to New York, political power is
        strengthened, church and social service organizations providing
        better programs and New York became the center of intellectual and
        cultural life among Blacks in America, concludes the writer.

511. Kain, John F. "The Big Cities Big Problem: The Growth of Huge
      Racial Ghettos Exacerbates Already Existing Problems Ranging from
      Finance to Transportation," Challenge, Vol. 15, September-October,
      1966, pp. 408.

      With the rise of white suburbanization, there has been a rapid
      growth and expansion of Black city ghettos, especially in the bus-
      iness districts. Since ghetto redevelopment programs are costly,
      programs should emphasize expansion of suburban housing opportuni-
      ties and provide Blacks with education and jobs to break out of
      the ghetto. The Black family has been hurt by the lack of proper
      housing and meaningful jobs, argues the researcher.

512. Kephart, William, and Thomas P. Monahan. "Disertion and Divorce
      in Philadelphia," American Sociological Review, Vol. 17, No. 4,
      December, 1952, pp. 719-727.

      The writers found that Blacks were underrepresented in divorce ac-
      tions in Philadelphia and overrepresented in desertion and non-
      support cases. Percentage of divorce among white families is
      higher than non-whites. There is a backlog of non-white families
      characterized by separation or desertion for which no formal di-
      vorce proceedings have been initiated, conclude the authors.

513. Ladner, Joyce and Walter W. Stafford. "Black Repression in the
      Cities," The Black Scholar, Vol. 1, No. 2, April, 1970, pp. 38-52.

      One major problem of cities with large Black populations in the
      1970s is the racist structure in the organizations crucial to
      Black survival. These organizational goals can only be changed if
      Blacks control the pattern of influence and establish new rules.
      Who shall control is the big issue facing urban Blacks. They must
      constantly re-evaluate theories of urbanization and racism and the
      effects it has on the Black family, assert the writers.

514. Lammermeier, Paul J. "The Urban Black Family of the Nineteenth
      Century: A Study of Black Family Structure in the Ohio Valley,
      1850-1880," Journal of Marriage and the Family, Vol. 35, No. 3,
      August, 1973, pp. 440-456.

      The author's basic conclusions are two-fold: (1) the urban Black
      family structure during the nineteenth century was basically a
      two-parent, male-headed family that showed little evidence of re-
      taining structural characteristics of the slave family, and (2)
      despite the increasing trend towards residential segregation, the
      only sign of a lessening of the two-parent family is a rise in the
      proportion of female-headed extended families.

515. Savage, James E., et al. "Community-Social Variables Related to
      Black Parent-Absent Families," Journal of Marriage and the Family,
      Vol. 40, No. 4, November, 1978, pp. 779-786.

Savage, et al.:

The researchers provided some objective data from a large sample
of Black parent-absent families in an urban setting. It was found
that in order to cope with parent-absence significant role adjustments were made by different members of the family. This was particularly evident when observing factors influencing parent-child
relationships and family cohesiveness, state the authors. In addition, a variety of community-social variables were demonstrated
to affect the attitudes and behaviors of these families. "Finally,
perception of the impact of these variables differently influenced
the parent-absent family groups. These results will have important implications for psychologists, sociologists and other professionals who must deal with the growing phenomenon of the Black
parent-absent family," conclude the writers.

516. Stack, Carol B. "Black Kindreds: Parenthood and Personal Kin-
      dreds Among Urban Blacks," Journal of Comparative Family Studies,
      Vol. 3, No. 3, Autumn, 1972, pp. 194-206.

      This article was based on field work the author did, between 1968-
      1970, among second generation welfare families in a midwestern
      city in the United States. She concludes: "...the adaptive base
      of operations of the poorest Black people can be attributed to
      personal Kinship network as well as networks of friends."

517. Wolf, Ann Marie. "A Personal View of Black Innercity Foster Fami-
      lies," American Journal of Orthopsychiatry,   Vol. 51, No. 1,
      January, 1983, pp. 144-151.

      This article uses the personal experience of a 21 year-old, white,
      middle-class medical student living in a Black inner-city neigh-
      borhood as a basis for observations on the special form of exten-
      ded family that flourishes in this neighborhood. The author be-
      lieves that there is no longer a white cultural counterpart of the
      Black extended family. Dr. Wolf concludes: "That if the child is
      of the Black inner-city culture, it is possible that being 'foster'
      has no particular meaning. The child may be the great-niece of
      the foster parent, or the granddaughter of a former next-door
      neighbor. It is likely that the child feels as much a part of the
      family as any other child born into the household. In this study
      were shown relatively few differences between Black and white
      women...."

33. COMPARATIVE FAMILIES

518. Aug, Robert G., and Thomas Bright. "Study of Wed and Unwed Mother-
      hood in Adolescents and Young Adults," Journal of the American
      Academy of Child Psychiatry, Vol. 9, No. 6, October, 1970, pp.
      577-594.

      This study involved the rural white population and the urban Black
      population of Lexington-Bluegrass area. The authors note case

Aug and Bright:

studies of how girls viewed themselves and their babies, past experience and their relationships with family and husbands/boyfriends.

519.   Balkwell, Carolyn, Jack Balswick and James W. Balkwell. "On Black and White Family Patterns in America: Their Impact on the Expressive Aspect of Sex-Role Socialization," Journal of Marriage and the Family, Vol. 40, No. 4, November, 1978, pp. 743-748.

This research investigates the hypothesis that expressive aspects of sex-roles are learned in the early socialization of the child. Literature on the Black family emphasizes the dominance and strength of the mother as a model of behavior, hence, one might expect less dimorphism in sex-roles among Blacks than among whites if, indeed, these behaviors are learned as the child internalizes the roles of the parents, state the authors. Expressiveness of fondness, sadness, pleasure, and antipathy were operationalized by composite scales based upon responses to 16 Likert-type items which were administered to 1190 high school students. They conclude: "Black students tended to have lower levels of expressiveness of each of the four emotions than white students. Males were more expressive of antipathy, while females tended to be more expressive of fondness, pleasure, and sadness. There was less sexual dimorphism among Blacks than among whites in the expressiveness of pleasure - but not in the expressiveness of the other three emotions."

520.   Baritz, Karen W. and Elaine S. Levine, "Childrearing By Black Parents: A Description and Comparison to Anglo and Chicano Parents," Journal of Marriage and the Family, Vol. 40, No. 4, November, 1978, pp. 709-719.

This essay describes the childrearing attitudes and behaviors of Black parents living in a lower working-class neighborhood. Interview data from 160 Black mothers and fathers are compared to similar data from 152 Chicano and 143 Anglo parents living in the same neighborhood. Black parents are typified as expecting early autonomy, not allowing wasted time, being both highly supportive and controlling, valuing strictness and encouraging equalitarian family roles. The Black parents differed from either the Anglo and/or the Chicano parents on several dimensions of childrearing, state the authors. Basically, the Black parents in this study can be typified as believing in the value of strictness, expecting early assumption of responsibility by a child for his or her own body functions and personal feelings, expecting that a child's time will be used wisely and not wasted, encouraging a child's involvement in decision-making and exhibiting loving concern and care while also desiring to closely monitor a child's behavior to assure certain goals, i.e., obedience, achievement, conclude the researchers.

521. Bauman, Karl E. and J. Richard Udry. "The Difference in Unwanted
      Births Between Blacks and Whites," Demography, Vol. 10, No. 3,
      August, 1973, pp. 315-328.

      Blacks are more likely than whites to have unwanted births. A com-
      mon explanation for that difference is that Blacks use less effec-
      tive contraceptive methods, use contraception less effectively,
      and use contraception less often than whites. Analysis of data
      from 17 cities in the researcher's family planning evaluation pro-
      ject suggested that, among women living in low-income neighbor-
      hoods, the Black-white difference in unwanted births was not due
      to (1) Blacks reaching desired completed parity at younger ages
      than whites, (2) differences in age or parity in our Black and
      white samples, (3) Black-white differences in current use of
      physician-administered contraception, or (4) Blacks being more
      likely than whites to adopt physician-administered contraception
      after having an unwanted birth. Black-white differences which
      might have contributed to relatively more unwanted births among
      Blacks were (1) Blacks desired fewer children, (2) Blacks were
      less likely than whites to use nonphysician-administered methods
      and more likely than whites to use no contraception, and (3)
      Blacks had higher failure rates than whites subsequent to the
      adoption of physician-administered methods and when not using
      those methods. Comparisons are made with the 1965 and 1970 Na-
      tional Fertility Studies, and program implications of the findings
      discussed. The authors state that their finding that the Black-
      white difference in unwanted fertility is due to a Black-white dif-
      ference in desired completed parity, rather than actual parity,
      suggests that lowering Black unwanted fertility relative to white
      might be accomplished by raising the desired completed parity of
      Blacks rather than lowering their parity.

522. Baumrind, Diana. "An Exploratory Study of Socialization Effects
      on Black Children: Some Black-White Comparisons," Child Develop-
      ment, Vol. 43, No. 1, March, 1972, pp. 261-267.

      In a study of current patterns of parental authority and their
      effects on the behavior of preschool children, the data for the
      16 Black children and their families were analyzed separately
      since it was thought that the effect of a given pattern of paren-
      tal variables might be affected by the larger social context in
      which the family operates. The major conclusion from this explo-
      ratory analysis was that if the Black families were viewed by
      white norms they appeared authoritarian, but that, unlike their
      white counterparts, the most authoritarian of these families pro-
      duced the most self-assertive and independent girls.

523. Beckett, Joyce O. and Audrey D. Smith. "Work and Family Roles:
      Egalitarian Marriage in Black and White Families," Social Service
      Review, Vol. 55, No. 2, June, 1981, pp. 314-326.

      The researchers state that although Black families have made more
      progress in role sharing than white families, most employed wives
      in all families still have two jobs - one in the marketplace and

Beckett and Smith:

one in the home - while their husbands essentially have only the
outside job. Moreover, Black husbands, compared with white husbands, are also more likely to share the domestic and child-care
roles traditionally assigned to the wife.

524. Bell, Robert R. "The Lower-Class Negro Family in the United
      States and Britain: Some Comparisons," Race, Vol. 11, October,
      1969, pp. 173-181.

      This is a study of the Black family in the U.S. and the West
      Indian migrant to Britain. It shows that both seem to have simi-
      lar attitudes and values. Noteworthy factors found that West In-
      dian women had a more positive definition of marriage. Both had
      high number of illegitimate births without social stigma. West
      Indian women had a more equal view of marriage and sexual rights.
      U. S. women had larger families at an earlier age. Child rearing
      is chiefly mother role in the U.S., whereas the West Indian family
      did this jointly because more fathers were present in their homes.
      West Indian mother had higher aspirations for their children.
      The author feels that ghetto life in the U.S. is a major cause of
      family disorganization, concludes the writer.

525. Berger, Alan S., and William Simon. "Black Families and the Moy-
      nihan Report: A Research Evaluation," Social Problems, Vol. 22,
      No. 2, December, 1974, pp. 145-161.

      The authors argue that in their research on Black and white 14-18
      year olds in Illinois, few differences were found in the ways that
      families treated their children, and these differences were not
      concentrated in the lower-class. They conclude: "Even in the
      lower-class broken family, there was no indication that Black
      families are dramatically different from white families. Thus, in
      terms of delinquency, perceptions of the education desired by the
      parents, self conceptions, and notions, of appropriate gender role
      behavior of adults, the empirical evidence does not provide ade-
      quate support for the conclusion of the (Daniel) Moynihan Report."

526. Bernard, Jessie. "Marital Stability and Patterns of Status Varia-
      bles," Journal of Marriage and the Family, Vol. 28, No. 4, Novem-
      ber, 1966, pp. 421-439.

      The author makes comparisons from 1960 census of White and non-
      white marriages. Variables used were income, schooling and occu-
      pation. For men 45-54, both showed increase in stable marriages
      with increased income, schooling and occupation. Proportions of
      stable marriages were higher for whites in all status levels.
      Defects in data, incompatibility of variables, and cultural and
      social-psychological variables may explain some of the disparity
      of the information, observes Dr. Bernard.

527. _____. "Notes on Educational Homogamy in Negro-White and White-Negro Marriages," Journal of Marriage and the Family, Vol. 28, No. 3, August, 1966, pp. 274-276.

Interracial marriages in 1960 were about as homogamous as intra-marriages; where differences did occur. Blacks usually married up rather than down, a tendency much more pronounced in Black women than men. White men tended to marry down while White women showed about the same percentage marrying up as down. Average number of wives' schooling, Black and White rated higher than husbands both Black and White, concludes the researcher.

528. Biller, Henry. "A Note on Father Absence and Masculine Develop-ment in Lower-Class Negro and White Boys," Child Development, Vol. 39, No. 3, September, 1968, pp. 1003-1006.

The relation of father absence and sociocultural background to mas-culine development was explored. Subjects were 6-year old, lower-class Negro and white boys. In terms of projective sex-role ori-entation (Brown's IT scale), white father-present boys were the most masculine; there was no significant difference between white father-absent and Negro father-present boys; and the Negro father-absent boys were the least masculine, states the author. No sig-nificant differences relating to either direct sex-role preference or teacher's ratings of masculinity on a multidimensional scale were found. The results suggested that underlying sex-role orien-tation is more influenced by father availability and family back-ground than are more manifest aspects of masculinity, concludes the writer.

529. Blau, Zena Smith. "Exposure of Child Rearing Experts: A Structu-ral Interpretation of Class-Color Differences," American Journal of Sociology, Vol. 69, No. 6, May, 1964, pp. 586-608.

According to the author, Black mothers expose themselves to child rearing literature less than white mothers. Black mothers express favorable attitudes toward child rearing experts. Economic dis-crimination and social segregation of Blacks are major impediments to acquiring urban middle class culture, states the researcher.

530. Blood, Robert. "Negro-White Difference in Blue-Collar Marriages in a Northern Metropolis," Social Forces , Vol. 48, No. 1, September, 1969, pp. 59-64.

Comparison of Black and White blue-collar marriages show signifi-cant differences in many variables toward greater deprivations for Black wives, according to the author. They have to make most family decisions alone, get less help from husbands at home, less interaction between husband and wife, and have a greater dissatis-faction with their husbands, states the researcher.

531. Bonner, Florence. "Black Women and White Women: A Comparative Analysis of Perceptions of Sex Roles for Self, Ideal-Self and the Ideal Mate," The Journal of Afro-American Issues, Vol. 2, No 3, Summer, 1974, pp. 237-246.

Women were tested on three scales (self perception, ideal woman and ideal man) plus ten biographical questions on a Black group and a White group. Black females are usually thought to differ from white females. This is perceived to be linked to their race and their inter-relationship to the Black male which is believed to be different than the white male/female relationships. Findings suggest that how the self is viewed in relation to other significant variables within and between the groups. More study should be done in this area, states the researcher.

532. Bould, Sally. "Female-Headed Families: Personal Fate Control and the Provider Role," Journal of Marriage and the Family, Vol. 39, No. 3, May, 1977, pp. 339-349.

The researcher states that overall, Black female-headed families are similar to white families in the proportion of income which they receive from various sources with the exception of the relative importance of Aid to Families with Dependent Children to expand the concept of income to include source as well as amount. She concludes: "Income which has a clear legal, moral and practical right is probably important in providing mothers the freedom and autonomy to plan for their children, with some sense of assurance and certainty."

533. Cavan, Ruth Shonle. "Negro Family Disorganization and Juvenile Delinquency," Journal of Negro Education, Vol. 28, No. 3, Summer, 1959, pp. 230-239.

Black delinquents originate in the same type of families as White delinquents, but unfavorable conditions are more frequently found in Black families, states the writer. Delinquency prone children tend to develop a concept of themselves as deviants and of their families as below average. Parents of these children often feel that they are bad and have the same low feeling of their family, concludes Prof. Cavan.

534. Cosby, Arthur. "Black-White Differences in Aspirations Among Deep South High School Students," Journal of Negro Education, Vol. 40, No. 1, Winter, 1971, pp. 17-21.

According to the writer, aspiration levels of students, even disadvantaged students, are quite high. Black students had higher level aspirations in comparison between groups with similar socioeconomic backgrounds. This may be true because of changed attitudes toward Black pride and optimism about future attainment of goals, concludes the author.

535.   Cummings, Michele and Scott Cummings. "Family Planning Among the
       Urban Poor: Sexual Politics and Social Policy," Family Relations:
       Journal of Applied Family and Child Studies, Vol. 32, No. 1, Janu-
       ary, 1983, pp. 47-58.

       The researchers point out that Blacks used abortion less than
       either Whites or Mexican-Americans. The authors state that their
       data is clear in that conservative arguments which focus solely
       on the alleged sexual improprieties of Black women are grossly
       distorted and deserve to be flatly dismissed. They conclude that
       "most of the evidence presented in this study showed relatively
       few differences between Black and white women, and when differen-
       ces did emerge, they were not large....

536.   Edwards, G. Franklin. "Marriage and Family Life Among Negroes,"
       Daedalus, Vol. 95, Winter, 1966, pp. 1-23.

       It was pointed out that during the 1950's the status of the Black
       family was unchanged and compared with White families, lost ground.
       Non-whites became more urban, there were more separations, divorces
       and deaths, and birth rates remained high, greater unemployment
       and underemployment. The status of the Black family has an im-
       portant bearing on the child. He will have less economic and emo-
       tional support and will likely have lower aspirations in life,
       states the author.

536a. _____ . "Marital Status and General Family Charac-
       teristics of the Nonwhite Population of the United States,"
       Journal of Negro Education, Vol. 22, Summer, 1953, pp. 280-296.

       This study found that the nonwhite family at mid-century had many
       of the same characteristics noted by E. Franklin Frazier in ear-
       lier studies. Interrelated factors of low economic status and
       high proportion of broken homes created a bad atmosphere for the
       child. One of the greatest changes is the urbanization of the
       Black. As other institutional patterns affecting the family
       change, so will the status of the Black family, concludes the
       researcher.

537.   Farley, Reynolds, and Albert I. Hermalin. "Family Stability: A
       Comparison of Trends Between Blacks and Whites," American Sociolo-
       gical Review, Vol. 36, No. 1, February, 1971, pp. 1-17.

       This study concludes that contrary to beliefs, most Black families
       are husband-wife families, majority of Black children live with
       both parents, more whites are in the category indicative of fami-
       ly stability, and changes over the years suggest both trend to-
       ward greater stability in some families and a trend in the oppo-
       site direction for some families....

538.   Geismar, Ludwig, et al. "Social Class, Ethnicity, and Family
       Functioning: Exploring Some Issues Raised by the Moynihan Report,"
       Journal of Marriage and the Family, Vol. 30, No. 2, August, 1968,
       pp. 480-487.

       This research reports on the relationship between social function-
       ing of urban families and their ethnic status. The authors asses-
       sed the influence of social class on the way ethnic group member-
       ship affects family behavior. The researchers' results show that
       social status overshadows ethnicity in determining the nature of
       family functioning.

539.   Golden, Joseph. "Characteristics of the Negro-White Intermarried
       in Philadelphia," American Sociological Review, Vol. 18, No. 2,
       April, 1953, pp. 177-183.

       This study done for the years 1922, 1927, 1932, 1937, 1942 and
       1947 found most marriages were between Black men and White women.
       The author also studied occupational status of couples, age of
       marriage, previous marital status, education, and religious pre-
       ference.

540.   Gustavus, Susan O. and Kent G. Mommsen, "Black-White Differen-
       tials in Family Size Preference Among Youth," Pacific Sociological
       Review, Vol. 16, No. 1, January, 1973, pp. 107-119.

       The researchers found that the Black youth do desire to limit their
       family size and, more often than whites, think that their parents
       had too many children. Further, they were concerned with econo-
       mic reasons for limiting family size, as are whites. They con-
       clude: "Since 1957, both white and Black fertility rates have de-
       clined, but there has been a slightly larger drop for Blacks. If
       the present data on the family size preferences of Black youth are
       at all representative, white and Black fertility rates may con-
       tinue to converge."

541.   Hartnagel, Timothy F. "Father Absence and Self Conception Among
       Lower Class White and Negro Boys," Social Problems, Vol. 18, No.
       2, Fall, 1970, pp. 152-163.

       Within racial categories, no differences were found between father-
       absent and father-present boys. Effects of father absence vary by
       children's age. Sometimes father absence is not as critical as
       the family's response to the absence. Then too, frequent father
       movement in and out of the home may pose more of a problem than
       father absence, concludes the researcher.

542.   Hays, William C. and Charles H. Mindel. "Extended Kinship Pat-
       terns in Black and White Families," Journal of Marriage and the
       Family, Vol. 35, No. 1, February, 1973, pp. 51-57.

       This essay compares and explains the differences in extended fami-
       ly cohesion of Black and white families. The Black family is not

Hays and Mindel:

approached as deviant or pathological, but from the view of a separate subculture within a pluralistic society. Comparisons were
made in terms of both intensity and extensity of interaction of
Black and white families with their extended kin. Specific comparisons were made of contact and help patterns, number of kin
living in the household, and salience of kin. It is shown that
the extended kin network is a more salient structure for Black
families than it is for white families. Black families also received more help from more of their extended kin in child care and
to get this type of help more often than whites. They conclude:
"This would seem to indicate that the extended kin would be much
more likely to play an important role in the socialization of the
child in Black families than is the case with white families, and
this would tend to bind the kin network more tightly together for
Black families than for white families."

543.   Heer, David M.   "Negro-White Marriage in the United States,"
       Journal of Marriage and the Family, Vol. 28, No. 3, August, 1966,
       pp. 262-273.

       The writer analyzes the trend of Negro-white marriage in Califor-
       nia, Hawaii, Michigan and Nebraska. An upward trend was noted in
       all states. Higher Black-white marriage in areas where residen-
       tial segregation is low and there are minimal status differences
       between Black and White population, concludes the researcher.

544.   Herzog, Elizabeth.   "Is There a 'Breakdown' of the Negro Family?"
       Social Work, Vol. 11, No. 1, January, 1966, pp. 3-10.

       Controversy of the Black family centers on (1) whether the Black
       family is crumbling; (2) whether breakdown is due to poverty, cul-
       tural inheritance or to a cycle of self-perpetuating pathology;
       and (3) whether remedy is sought through improving the status of
       the Negro or helping the Black family directly. The author notes
       that slavery is not the only reason for Black family disorganiza-
       tion. Low-income white families also have the same problems. Not
       all Black families are female dominated, low-income and highly
       unstable, states the author.

545.   Hill, Robert.   "The Illusion of Black Progress," Black Scholar,
       Vol. 10, No. 2, October, 1978, pp. 18-24, 49-52.

       The essayist declares that the gap between Black and white family
       income has significantly widened in recent years. Between 1975
       and 1976 for example, the median income for all Black families re-
       lative to the income of all white families fell from 62 percent to
       59 percent. He concludes, in part: "The decline is primarily due
       to the sharp increase in the number of Black families with heads-
       male as well as female- who are unemployed or not in the labor
       market. Consequently, many Black families are more likely to be
       poor today than they would have been in the past."

546. Kanno, Nellie B. "Comparative Life Styles of the Black Female in the United States and the Black Female in Lesotho," The Journal of Afro-American Issues, Vol. 2, No. 3, Summer, 1974, pp. 212-217.

Kanno's thesis that the twin "adversities" of being both female and Black have produced a group of women determined to succeed in societies which have oppressed them and in which it is assumed that the Black female is head of a deteriorating family structure. The Lesotho woman has suffered from the same forms of oppression and discrimination. If their status is to change, it will have to proceed on three fronts: Political, economic, and educational. All of which seem very remote, states the author.

546a. King, Karl. "A Comparison of The Negro and White Family Power Structure in Low-Income Families," Child and Family, Vol. 6, No. 2, Spring, 1967, pp. 65-74.

According to Prof. King, all-in-all there appears to be more involvement of the Negro father in the decision-making areas under study, with less mother dominance than has been historically presented. This must be considered in light of the fact that this is only one measure of family power structure. While limited in scope, it does serve as one indication of the status of the urban low-income intact Negro family, suggests the writer.

547. King, Mae C. "The Politics of Sexual Stereotypes," Black Scholar, Vol. 4, Nos. 6 & 7, March-April, 1973, pp. 12-23.

The writer discusses the stereotyped images of Black women: non-feminists, depreciated sex objects, lower image. These female racial stereotypes are indispensable to the maintenance of racially stratified order in America. Although these stereotypes are generally untrue, they still are effective in achieving the political power purposes that they serve. These negative stereotypes have an effect on the role of the Black woman in the family, concludes the author.

548. Mack, Delores E. "The Power Relationship in Black Families and White Families," Journal of Personality and Social Psychology, Vol. 30, No. 3, September, 1974, pp. 409-413.

The author states that her research indicates that Black and white working- and middle-class couples have very similar ideas about decision-making power and dominance in the family. These data indicate that the notion of equality or near equality between the husband and wife is a pervasive one in American society. The most important finding of this study is that class differences far outweigh any racial differences, states Prof. Mack. She concludes: "Class differences were found in two out of the three situations examined; no comparable racial differences were found. The absence of racial differences and the importance of class suggest that a more careful analysis of these factors as determinants of various aspects of the marital relationship is needed...."

549. _____. "Where the Black-Matriarchy Theorists Went Wrong,"
Psychology Today, Vol. 4, No. 8, January, 1971, pp. 24, 86-87.

Dr. Mack contends that in her own studies there is no such power-
distribution difference between Black and White families. She declares that her work has shown that Blacks and Whites do not differ on their perceptions and uses of power in a marriage relationship. Prof. Mack concludes: "...social class is more important
than race in determining the power structure within a marriage."

550. Middleton, Russell and Snell Putney. "Dominance in Decisions in
the Family Race and Class Differences," American Journal of Sociology, Vol. 65, No. 6, May, 1960, pp. 605-609.

The authors found that in the making of minor family decisions
among forty married couples in four groups -- White professors,
Black professors, White skilled workers and Black skilled workers--
no significant differences were found in the relative dominance of
husband and wife. Neither were there significant differences in
dominance between groups on specific problems. Contrary to expectation, the equalitarian pattern appeared to predominate in all
four groups. The writers conclude that a comparison of families
with working wives and families with non-working wives were more
dominant in decision-making than the working wives in all areas
studied except purchases and living standards, where there was no
significant difference.

551. Parker, Seymour. "Characteristics of Negro Mothers in Single
Headed Households," Journal of Marriage and the Family, Vol. 28,
No. 4, November, 1966, pp. 507-513.

This article contrasts the adjustment and attitudes of mothers in
broken and intact families and evaluates the possible effects of
those characteristics on their children. Data analyzed in this
study was based on interviews conducted in Philadelphia, Pennsylvania. Mothers in the two types of family situations were compared on educational status, prevalence of psychoneurotic symptoms,
scores on self-esteem index, reference group behavior, and measures
of goal-striving stress associated with goals for self and hypothetical son. The writer argues that in general, these analyses
indicated that compared to mothers in intact families, mothers in
the broken family situation had poorer psychological adjustment
and less involvement in goals for self and a hypothetical son.
These characteristics may have important implications for the
achievement related attitudes of children raised in female-headed
households, concludes the researcher.

552. Pope, Hallowell. "Negro-White Differences in Decisions Regarding
Illegitimate Children," Journal of Marriage and the Family, Vol. 31,
No. 4, November, 1969, pp. 756-764.

Data from a sample of unwed mothers in North Carolina indicate racial differences regarding the disposition of their illegitimate

Pope:

children and their postbirth marital behavior: Negroes less often
married after the birth, less often wanted to marry their sex partners (if not planning marriage beforehand), less often had their
illegitimate children adopted, more often were advised to keep
them; but, if not yet married, had more contact with the alleged
father. Possible reasons were discussed for these findings: (1)
Negro women perceive fewer advantages than white women in holding
the marital rather then the single status; (2) Negroes receive
fewer rewards for moving toward marriage; (3) Negroes may not have
as normative an orientation toward legitimacy and marital sex relations as whites.

553. _____. "Unwed Mothers and their Sex Partners," _Journal of
Marriage and the Family_, Vol. 29, No. 3, August, 1967, pp. 555-
567.

Data from 387 White and 552 Black women who were not married when
they had their first child were used to characterize the prepreg-
nancy relationship between unwed mothers and the fathers of their
children. The data supported the conclusion that, in general,
their "courtships" cannot be characterized as deviant, exploita-
tive, or lacking in exposure to the normal social controls. Reasons were discussed for Blacks less often planning to get married
at the time of their pregnancies even though in comparison to
Whites, they were more frequently in a long term courting relationship....

554. Reeder, Amy L. and Rand D. Conger. "Differential Mother and Father Influences on the Educational Attainment of Black and White
Women," _Sociological Quarterly_, Vol. 25, No. 2, Spring, 1984,
pp. 239-250.

This article examines the impacts of maternal and paternal influences on the educational attainment of women and whether these
parental effects operate similarly for white and Black women. Specifically, the study measures the differential effects of mother's
and father's education, occupation, and encouragement. Using data
from the National Longitudinal Survey of Labor Market Experience
(NLS), 428 white and 145 Black women were examined. Findings indicate different patterns in the way mothers and fathers affect
their daughters' educational attainments. For both groups of
women, father's education was found to be a generally better predictor than mother's education, while mother's occupation was more
important than father's occupation. Mother's occupation and parental expectation variables were relatively more important for
Black women, and parental education variables were more important
for white women, conclude the researchers.

555. Scanzoni, John. "Sex Roles, Economic Factors, and Marital Soli-
darity in Black and White Marriages," _Journal of Marriage and the
Family_, Vol. 37, No. 1, February, 1975, pp. 130-144.

Scanzoni:

Based on data from a regional sample of husband-wife marriages,
Black and white husbands and wives are compared on measures of
sex role norms, self-concept, and task-performance evaluation of
wives. Blacks emerge as more egalitarian on the more innovative
and behavioral measures of sex roles, but less egalitarian on the
neo-traditional and more ideological sex role dimensions. According to Dr. Scanzoni, Blacks also tend to score as more instrumental and more expressive than whites. In addition, Black wives
are evaluated more positively than white wives in terms of task-
performance; and they are also perceived to possess greater marital authority than Black husbands," concludes the author.

556. Smith, Howard P. and Marcia Abramson. "Racial and Family Experi-
      ence Correlated with Mobility Aspiration," Journal of Negro Educa-
      tion, Vol. 31, No. 4, Spring, 1962, pp. 117-124.

      Thirty-three Blacks and 33 White high school students, matched
      for age, sex, intelligence, and social status, served as subjects
      to test the relationship between mobility and aspiration. The re-
      sult as a whole showed no consistent relationship or association
      between the independent variables and mobility aspiration as they
      relate to the family life styles.

557. Spaights, Ernest. "Some Dynamics of the Black Family," Negro
      Educational Review, Vol. 24, Nos. 3 & 4, July-October, 1973, pp.
      127-137.

      The author argues, and rightfully so, that it is time that the
      differences between white and Black family groupings be recognized.
      It is a mistake to continue to apply the indices of social disor-
      ganization and pathology to a total group of people. All of the
      behavior which permeates low-income Black existence should not be
      interpreted as pathological, states the writer. He concludes:
      "Because the white social scientist has culturally encapsulated
      himself, the time has arrived when the Black behavioral scientist
      possesses a more thorough fund of knowledge about white social
      interaction than whites have about Blacks. But most important of
      all, it is time that the great strengths of the Black family be
      recognized throughout American society."

558. Tausky, Curt and William J. Wilson. "Work Attachment Among Black
      Men," Phylon, Vol. 32, No. 1, Spring, 1971, pp. 23-30.

      This study suggests that: (1) Society work norms are as widely
      endorsed among Black workers as among white workers; (2) all seg-
      ments of the Black population desire jobs that enhance occupation-
      al status; and (3) less than satisfactory work habits among new
      recruits and trainees may be more a function of adjustment prob-
      lems and fear of dead-end jobs than disaffection from work norms.
      These norms have a neglected effect on Black family life style,
      according to the authors.

559.   Terrell, Henry S. "Wealth Accumulation of Black and White Fami-
        lies: The Empirical Evidence," Journal of Finance, Vol. 26, No. 2,
        May, 1971, pp. 363-377.

        It was stated that the evidence appears overwhelming that the net
        wealth position of Black families is substantially poorer than
        that of white families in similar characteristics. The reason
        does not appear to be related to a lack of thrift among Black fa-
        milies, since the bulk of consumption studies show that Blacks
        save more at any given level of income, but rather to the fact
        that Black families at any observed income level appear to have
        had a past history of lower average income than white families of
        that same income level, according to the author. He also suggests
        that the general findings on wealth accumulation demonstrate the
        pervasive effect of the past on the current economic status of
        the Black minority population. Current income data alone which
        generally show Black families having roughly three-fifths as much
        income as white families are very misleading because they fail to
        account for the substantially poorer net wealth position of Black
        families. "These rather stark findings on wealth accumulation sug-
        gest that economic equality for Black families will not be achieved
        when the current annual income gap will remain as a legacy of past
        economic deprivation," concludes the writer.

560.   Whitaker, Barbara. "Breakdown in the Negro Family: Myth or
        Reality?" New South, Vol. 22, No. 4, Fall, 1967, pp. 37-47.

        The author believes that if there has been no significant change
        in family structure during the past two decades, then there are no
        grounds for claiming that a new "tangle of pathology" has set up a
        degenerative process from within, over and above response to the
        long continued impact of social and economic forces from without;
        and that this process is specific to a Negro "culture inherited
        from days of slavery." The author concludes: "Only as we find a
        way to reach, welcome, and include all children, all young people,
        all women, all men--regardless of race, income level, source of
        income, or family status--in a way of life which our Judeo-Chris-
        tian ethic dictates, will we really succeed in solving the essen-
        tial problems of the isolated disadvantaged family. New forms of
        participation, in new kinds of jobs, as new kinds of volunteers,
        in new kinds of civic responsibility are needed to open the path
        to genuine integration."

561.   Willie, Charles V. and Susan L. Greenblatt. "Four 'Classic' Stu-
        dies of Power Relationships in Black Families: A Review and Look
        to the Future," Journal of Marriage and the Family, Vol. 40, No.
        4, November, 1978, pp. 691-697.

        Studies of Black families in varying social classes are reviewed
        to determine the prevailing power relationship between spouses.
        In general, Black families appear to be more equalitarian than
        white families; the middle-class Black family is more equalitarian
        than any other family type. Rigid role-differentiation for hus-
        bands and wives most frequently occurs in middle-class white

Willie and Greenblatt:

families according to studies reviewed here. Social scientists are cautioned against projecting upon Black families behavior more frequently observed in their own race or social class group. The sociologists conclude: "The traditional two-parent nuclear family was never the only viable family unit in Western culture, and in our rapidly changing society, it can no longer be viewed as the ideal arrangement which all families should be encouraged to emulate...."

562. _____. "The Black Family and Social Class," American Journal of Orthopsychiatry, Vol. 44, No. 1, January, 1974, pp. 50-60.

The sociologist comes to the following conclusions: (1) that Black and white families in America share a common value system, (2) that they adapt to the society and its values in different ways, largely because of racial discrimination, and (3) that the unique adaptation by Blacks is further differentiated by variations in style of life by social class. It was also pointed out that the author's initial assumption that the way of life of Blacks in America can be understood independent of their involvement with whites appears to be unwarranted, states the writer. Moreover, the life-styles of different social classes cannot be understood apart from the rest of society. "Our revised version emphasizes both personal action and social reaction. We assert that the difference between the families of racial groups in the United States, and the difference between the families of various social classes within the racial groups are a result of how each family acts as well as how each family is treated," concludes Dr. Willie.

563. Yancey, William L. "Going Down Home: Family Structure and the Urban Ghetto Trap," Social Science Quarterly, Vol. 52, No. 4, March, 1972, pp. 896-906.

The author concludes: (1) that the relationship between low income and family instability is stronger in urban than in rural areas, and (2) that white migrants are more likely to return to rural areas than Black migrants, it follows that Black families are more vulnerable to urban poverty than white families. The writer states, if the research reviewed above can be generalized, then the proportion of broken families among the Black urban poor should be much higher than among the white urban poor. In rural areas the author found fewer broken families and smaller differences in the rate of family disruption between Blacks and whites....

34.   RESEARCH AND THE BLACK FAMILY

564. Allen, Walter R. "The Search for Applicable Theories of Black Family Life," Journal of Marriage and the Family, Vol. 40, No. 4, February 1978, pp. 117-129.

This essay attempts to identify appropriate theoretical frameworks

Allen:

for the study of Black family life. It is argued that theory in
the area generally consists of both "objective" (conceptual approach) and "subjective" (ideological perspective) components.
Competing conceptual approaches (structural-functional, interac-
tional and developmental) and ideological perspectives (cultural
equivalent, cultural deviant and cultural variant) in the literature are critically evaluated. Unification of the developmental
approach with the cultural variant perspective in future studies
is then proposed as one strategy for enhancing our understanding
of Black family structures and processes in this society. The
author concludes by calling upon Black family researchers to become more sensitive to inherent "objective/subjective" biases in
contemporary theorizing about Black families.

565. Billingsley, Andrew. "Black Families and White Social Science,"
      Journal of Social Issues, Vol. 26, No. 3, Summer, 1970, pp. 127-
      142.

      Dr. Billingsley argues that Black families who have fared so ill
      historically in white American society have fared no better in
      white American social science, and largely for the same reasons.
      For American social scientists are much more American than social
      and much more social than scientific. They reflect all the pre-
      judice, ignorance and arrogance which seems to be endemic to
      Americans of European descent. Furthermore, because of their
      skills at communication and their acceptance as authorities on
      race relations, social scientists do even greater damage to the
      understanding of Black family life than do ordinary citizens,
      states the scholar. He concludes, in part: "Still, Black fami-
      lies, who have survived some of the most severe oppression at the
      hands of white society, also show signs of surviving the treatment
      they have received in social science."

566. _____, and Amy Tate Billingsley. "Negro Family Life in
      America," Social Service Review, Vol. 39, No. 3, September, 1965,
      pp. 310-319.

      The authors discuss six crises for the Black family: (1) from
      Africa to America, (2) from slavery to emancipation, (3) from
      rural to urban areas, (4) from the South to the North and West,
      (5) from negative to positive social status, (6) from negative to
      positive self-image. They conclude: "We must create that se-
      quence of generations" able to help the Negro family teach its
      members how to be Negro and American and human at the same time....

567. Cross, William E., Jr. "Black Family and Black Identity: A
      Literature Review," Western Journal of Black Studies, Vol. 2,
      No. 2, Summer, 1978, pp. 111-124.

      The author argues that for the period in which most studies on
      Black identity have been conducted, the composition of the typical

Cross:

Black family was a two-parent household embedded in a well-organi-
zed, cohesive, and supportive kinship system. This finding suggests that up until the 1970's, sustained poverty did not have the
dramatic adverse effect on Black family composition that had once
been assumed, but there does remain the question of how well these
families functioned, states the writer.

568. Dill, Bonnie T. "The Dialectics of Black Womanhood," Signs:
      Journal of Women in Culture and Society, Vol. 4, No. 3, Spring,
      1979, pp. 543-555.

      The author discusses the Black woman and her role in the Black
      family structure. Prof. Dill argues that serious historical re-
      search promises to provide new information regarding the structure
      and organization of Black families at different historical periods
      and in different regions of the United States. He concludes, in
      part: "Information about values, attitudes, and the vicissitudes,
      of daily life will remain, however and other descriptive reports...."

569. Gullattee, Alyce C. "Psychiatric Factors to Consider in Research
      on the Black Woman," The Journal of Afro-American Issues. Vol. 2,
      No. 3, Summer, 1974, pp. 199-203.

      To what do we attribute the strengths of the Black woman and how
      does a Black female child develop a meaningful image of herself?
      In answering these questions, Gullattee stresses the need for a
      methodology for studying the effects of social class on mental ill-
      ness in the Black community. We need to know about depression
      among Blacks, and more about the ego so as to develop methods for
      treatment. Dr. Gullattee notes that those in the academic and so-
      cial struggle must share their knowledge with the young. The
      Black woman is vital to this process for she helps to provide the
      strength for the Black family and community, states the author.

570. Hampton, Robert L. "Institutional Decimation, Marital Exchange,
      and Disruption of Black Families," Western Journal of Black
      Studies, Vol. 4, No. 2, Summer, 1980, pp. 132-139.

      This writer documented several factors which are associated with
      marital disruption in Black families and placed these factors with-
      in the context of institutional decimation. The data show that
      the majority of Black families remained stable during the study
      period. This is important given the often distorted view of
      marital stability among Blacks. Future work in this area should
      be devoted to a description and analysis of various coping stra-
      tegies employed by Black families to combat the stress of living
      in a racist society and maintain their functional integrity, con-
      cludes Prof. Hampton.

571.   Hare, Nathan.   "What Black Intellectuals Misunderstand About the
Black Family,"   Black World, Vol. 25, No. 5, March, 1976, pp. 4-

Dr. Hare argues that the strength-of-Black-families school has
misled the Black movement away from an attack on the suffering of
Blacks in their family situation and related conditions. In the
name of a false racial pride, they pretend that all is well with
the Black family in America, despite our recognized economic, educational and political deprivation, states the author. In the
process, the strength-of-Black-families dogma minimized and neglected the psychological effects and the social destruction of
the Black male's unemployment and underemployment, of the instability provoked by the siphoning of the Black male labor-market
surplus into prisons and military camps. He concludes: "In so
doing, these intellectuals turned their backs on Black reconstruction and the belated restructuring of the Black family as a
springboard, or at least a link in the chain of struggle for
Black socio-economic elevation...."

572.   Hayes, Floyd W., III. "In Support of The Afro-American Family,"
Los Angeles Sentinel,   August 2, 1984, p. A-7.

The writer states that the historic and contemporary assault on
the Black family represents the policy and practice of "divide
and rule." He also suggests that where there is no familial integrity and group bonding, nor any hope for institutions and personal worth, material provisions solely can hardly raise a people
above chattel conditions.....

573.   Hill, Mozell E. "Research on the Negro Family," Marriage and
Family Living, Vol. 19, No. 2, February, 1957, pp. 25-31.

The author takes a look at the historical approaches to the Black
family, socialization of Black youth, moral approach to family
background of the caste-class hypothesis, cultural determinism,
family background of Black soldiers, social change and Black family behavior, organization of Black family, the limitations of
Black family research and the need for a multi-disciplinary approach to the study of family behavior.

574.   Johnson, Leanor B. "The Search for Values in Black Family Research," Western Journal of Black Studies, Vol. 1, No. 2, June,
1977, pp. 98-104.

Legend, folklore, and mythology handed down through oral tradition have given definition to Black family forms. In this regard,
rich resources are available from qualitative data drawn from
printed matter -- letters, diaries, and manuscripts, as well as
from the aged Blacks who have been neglected as both source and
subject of sociological research, observes Prof. Johnson. The
author concludes: "In short, the search for values and the internal dynamics of the Black family promises to be complex and difficult, requiring precise methodological procedures, time and
money....Searches which produce fruitful returns are never easy."

575. Mathis, Arthur. "Contrasting Approaches to the Study of Black
      Families," Journal of Marriage and the Family,   Vol. 40, No. 4,
      November, 1978, pp. 667-678.

      This article examines two competing perspectives which have in-
      fluenced the study of Black families. The first perspective is
      related to the early research by E. Franklin Frazier and has sub-
      sequently impacted the formulation of social policy. This view
      assumes that Black families are patterned after the dominant cul-
      ture, states Prof. Mathis. Whereas, the other perspective holds
      that at least part of Black family life is linked to African forms
      of culture. Theoretical and empirical studies are presented in an
      attempt to show where future research would be most useful in de-
      veloping a cohesive view of the nature of Black families.

576. McNair, Charles L. "The Black Family Is Not a Matriarchal Family
      Form," Negro Educational Review, Vol. 26, Nos. 2 & 3, April-July,
      1975, pp. 93-100.

      The author believes that if the Black family is a matriarchal fa-
      mily form, it varies markedly from the definition. In fact, this
      investigation has uncovered strong evidence to the contrary. This
      evidence is succinctly summarized in the following findings states
      the researcher:

      1. Contrary to widespread belief in a "matriarchy" among Blacks,
          the research data reveal that most Black families, whether
          low-income or not, are characterized by an equalitarian pat-
          tern in which neither spouse dominates, but shares decision-
          making and the performance of expected tasks.
      2. National data from the U. S. Census reveal that over seventy
          percent of the heads of Black families are males, as opposed
          to less than thirty percent female heads of Black families.
      3. National earnings data do not support the popular conception
          that wives' earnings in most low-income Black families are
          greater than the husband's. Recent Bureau of Labor Statis-
          tics data indicate that the husband's earnings surpassed the
          wife's. The Black husband provides the majority of the Black
          family's income, whether poor or non-poor.
      Considering the forestated findings, one can generalize that the
      Black family, despite institutionized opposition, has striven with
      much success toward attaining the family standards set by the do-
      minant culture. Contrary to the Frazierian thesis of 1939, the
      Black family in America today is not matriarchal, concludes the
      researcher.

577. Nobles, Wade W. "Toward An Empirical and Theoretical Framework for
      Defining Black Families," Journal of Marriage and the Family, Vol.
      40, No. 4, November, 1978, pp. 679-690.

      The author declares that the analytical framework developed to
      "understand" the phenomena within a culture must be "sensitive"
      to the dictates of that culture. Consistent with the axiomatic
      contention of a continued African world-view operating within the

Nobles:

> cultural milieu of white American culture, we suggest that the
> Black family system should be thought of as African in "nature"
> and American in "nurture". He concludes, in part: "The intrin-
> sic nature of integrity of Black family systems is, therefore,
> African. This "integrity" of Black families, we have termed the
> sense of 'Africanity'...."

578. Peters, Marie F.   "The Black Family - Perpetuating the Myths: An
      Analysis of Family Sociology Textbook Treatment of Black Families,"
      Family Coordinator, Vol. 23, No. 4, October, 1974, pp. 349-357.

      A serious issue in the family sociology field is the inadequacies
      of both research and testbooks in the treatment of Black American
      families. The contemporary view of the Black family usually em-
      phasizes concepts of (1) deviancy, (2) pathology, and/or (3) un-
      controlled sexuality. College family sociology textbooks in the
      family sociology field are analyzed in order to demonstrate how
      all family sociology textbooks should be examined as to their
      treatment of Black family literature. Most are found to be inac-
      curate and unacceptable; only a few meet acceptable criteria, con-
      cludes the author. A guide is presented for evaluating college
      family sociology textbooks.

579. Reynolds, Bertha C.   "A Way of Understanding: An Approach to
      Case Work with Negro Families," The Family, Vol. 12, No. 7,
      November, 1931, pp. 203-208.

      The author argues that there are three methods of approach to
      deal with Negro cases: (1) Constant individualization; (2) Con-
      stant relating of behavior to the social setting, and (3) Con-
      stant search for the WHY some differences occurred....

580. Rubin, Roger H.   "Matriarchal Themes in Black Family Literature:
      Implications for Family Life Education," Family Coordinator , Vol.
      27, No. 1, January, 1978, pp. 33-41.

      A review of the research literature on Black family life revealed
      that matriarchal themes are recurrent in describing male-female
      relationships, states the author. This was found in studies on
      family structure, identification, out-of-wedlock births, parent-
      hood, marriage, sexuality, and peer groups. Research limitations
      were an evident source of the distortions eventually reflected in
      family life textbooks. He concludes: "Recognition of these li-
      mitations should serve as a guide to search for more representa-
      tive resources in order that greater accuracy in portraying Black
      family life can be achieved."

581. Scott, Patricia Bell.   "Sex Roles Research and Black Families:
      Some Comments on the Literature," Journal of Afro-American Issues,
      Vol. 4, Nos. 3 & 4, Summer/Fall, 1976, pp. 349-351.

Scott:

Dr. Scott states that there are several statements that can be made about sex role development in Black families. They are:

1. The attitudes of Blacks toward the roles of husband, father, wife, and mother are unclear; however, the role of parent is a significant indicator of one's adulthood, masculinity, and femininity.
2. The concept of power and those indicators of this concept are defined differently in the Black community. The variables used in white society cannot be used to measure power in Black families.
3. There are available Black male role models in the community. Many of these men are integral, supportive members of families, yet not visible members of households.
4. Socialization of Black children into sexual and sex role behavior begins at an early age. There is some evidence which supports the notion that there is less differential treatment of male and female children among Blacks.

582. _____. "Teaching about Black Families Through Black Literature," Journal of Home Economics, Vol. 68, No. 2, March, 1976, pp. 22-23.

The writer discusses a number of myths and misconceptions about Black families in the United States. She concludes: "...Black literature is an exciting medium through which both instructors and students can explore the vitality, uniqueness, and diversity of the Black family experience in American society."

583. Spaights, Ernest. "The Evolving Black Family in the United States, 1950-1974," Negro Educational Review, Vol. 27, No. 2, April 1976, pp. 111-128.

The process of Black family evolution during 1950-1974 has created a more complex family structure, but also one with awakening potential. People in Black families have more and greater opportunities for advancement and self-development than at any previous time. He concludes: "Although outside destructive forces seem more menacing, the growing strength of people in Black families will enable them to find the required tools for family survival and enrichment. It is my feeling that these crises will pass and the Black family will emerge stronger and better than before."

584. Staples, Robert. "Research on Black Sexuality: Its Implications for Family Life, Education, and Public Policy," Family Coordinator. Vol. 21, No. 2, April, 1972, pp. 183-188.

Dr. Staples believes for those Black women who happen to have a child out-of-wedlock, the family life practitioner should seek a public policy which assures that child an equal life chance in this society. The family professional should not be part of any

Staples:

endeavor that punishes children for the conditions of their birth.
In a practical sense, this means seeking an end to legal discrimi-
nations against the out-of-wedlock child including the designation
of legitimacy on birth certificates, states the sociologist. He
concludes: "The research on Black sexual behavior reveals some
salient deviations from white, middle-class norms. By his recognition of these differences, the family life and sex educator will
be better prepared to deal with an educational program that will
effectively meet the needs of his students and American society."

585.   _____. "Research on the Negro Family: A Source for Family
Practitioners," Family Coordinator, Vol. 18, No. 3, July, 1969,
pp. 202-210.

The writer points out that research on the Black family demonstrates
that it has undergone certain changes in adapting to the circumstances in which it found itself. Yet it has survived as an important social unit to fortify its members against the vicissi-
tudes of American racialism. Dr. Staples concludes that the hope
of the future partly lies with the family life educator's understanding of Black family organization which will benefit both
Blacks and society in general....

586.   _____. "The Black Family Revisited: A Review and a Preview,"
Journal of Social and Behavioral Sciences, Vol. 20, No. 2, Spring,
1974, pp. 65-78.

The purpose of this article is to review the past stages of Black
family research and the social conditions extant at the time. Alternative conceptual models for studying Black families are proposed. An analysis is made of future trends in selected aspects
of Black family life. He concludes: "The control of Black family studies is now in the hands of those whose destiny is affected
by the nature of what we choose to investigate and the problems
that seek resolution. If the Marxist dictum that the knowledge
of a society reflects the needs of its ruling class, we must stand
fast to his other maxim: That some men seek to understand society,
our task is to change it."

587.   _____. "The Matricentric Family: A Cross-Cultural Examination," Journal of Marriage and the Family, Vol. 34, No. 1,
February, 1972, pp. 156-165.

Among Afro-American families, role synthesis on the part of Black
women was necessary because of the society's denial to Black men
of sufficient job and economic opportunities to carry out their
role requirement, suggests the scholar. Unlike other societies
where role synthesis is seen as a necessary adaptation to economic exigencies, the female-headed household among Blacks has been
labeled a form of pathology. The evidence for this assertion is
quite weak since without the role integration that took place in

Staples:

some Black families, their mere survival was doubtful, argues Dr. Staples. He concludes: "The ethnocentric assumption of many Americans is that there is something inherently wrong with a female-dominated family structure. As we have seen from our other examples of the matricentric family system, they can be, and are, very functional units which can maintain the stability of the social system. The problems female-headed Black families face are often attributable to the limited opportunities available to the female which place her at a distinct disadvantage with male-headed households."

588. _____. "Towards a Sociology of the Black Family: A Theoretical and Methodological Assessment," Journal of Marriage and the Family, Vol. 33, No. 1, February, 1971, pp. 119-138.

This essay is a summary and analysis of research and theory on Black families in the past decade. In the macro-sociological section the theories on Black family life are critically analyzed for their theoretical and methodological validity. The second section presents micro-sociological research findings on Black family life and is more of a summary of the research literature on this subject. These research findings are presented according to the typical family stage sequences of Black family life, from dating behavior to parental roles and socialization processes. In his overall assessment of works on the Black family the author concludes that the imposition of ethnocentric values on the analysis of Black family life preclude the application of much of the current research and theory to the development of a viable sociology of the Black family.

589. Swan, L. Alex. "A Methodological Critique of the Moynihan Report," Black Scholar, Vol. 5, No. 9, June, 1974, pp. 18-24.

Dr. Swan points out that the rate of family instability is higher in the white population than in the Black population. Moynihan does not present any data to substantiate his argument that Black social problems are a function of family instability, states the author. Even when he presents data to show that Black children who live in homes where the father is absent do poorly in school, he does not show that white children in such homes do just as poorly. He concludes: "Methodologically speaking, it is impossible for Moynihan to draw valid and useful conclusions relative to the issues he raised from the data he presents in his report. Therefore, it would behoove any reader to approach the use of this report with deliberate caution."

590. "The Black Family Summit - Facing the Challenge," Crisis, Vol. 91, No. 6, June/July, 1984, pp. 5-50.

This entitled issue is devoted to the Black family: "Developing and Mobilizing Resources For Supporting the Black Family";

The Black Family, etc.:

"Single-Parent Black Families"; "Patterns of Child Rearing and
Socialization in Black Families"; "The Black Aged"; "Crime, Violence and Black Families"; "Housing and Black Families"; "Education and the Black Family"; "Jobs and Economic Security"; and
"Healthy Black Families."

591.   Turner, Clarence Rollo. "Some Theoretical and Conceptual Consi-
       deration for Black Family Studies," Black Lines: A Journal of
       Black Studies, Vol. 11, No. 4, Summer, 1972, pp. 13-27.

       This article contends that any serious study of the dynamics of
       the Black family requires: (1) that research and writing in the
       area move beyond the institutional frame of reference and (2) that
       precise and exacting scholarship characterize any future investi-
       gations of the Black family with specific attempts to: (a) sur-
       pass comparative socioeconomic and demographic analysis as methods
       of adequately defining the Black family; (b) ameliorate the per-
       sistent and acrimonious debate surrounding discussions of the myth
       of reality of the Black family matriarchy; and (c) extend the in-
       quiry concerning Black sexual behavior outside of the prevalent
       notions of its problematic nature.

592.   Williams, J. Allen, Jr. and Robert Stockton. "Black Family
       Structures and Functions: An Empirical Examination of Some Sug-
       gestions Made by Billingsley," Journal of Marriage and the Family,
       Vol. 35, No. 1, February, 1973, pp. 39-49.

       Andrew Billingsley in Black Families in White America has criti-
       cized much of the previous research on the Black family, saying
       that social scientists have ignored the structural variation among
       families and have focused on a very limited number of family func-
       tions. To correct what he believes to be a distorted picture of
       the Black family, he has suggested a typology of family structures
       and a large number of family functions which should be taken into
       consideration. This essay, based upon data collected from 321
       Black households, used Billingsley's typology to examine the asso-
       ciation between family structures and functions. It is concluded
       that a few modifications of the typology would expand its utility,
       that more detailed information about family structure does reduce
       the chances of distortion and contribute to greater understanding,
       and that Billingsley may have overemphasized the capacity of many
       Black families to deal with their functional problems..., state
       the authors.

593.   Zeul, Carolyn R. "The Integration of Blacks in Suburban Neigh-
       borhoods: A Reexamination of the Contact Hypothesis," Social
       Problems, Vol. 18, No. 4, Spring, 1971, pp. 462-474.

       The basic concern of this article was the process by which isola-
       ted Black families were integrated into predominantly White sub-
       urban neighborhoods. It dealt with those cases where panic-

Zeul:

selling and rapid out-migration of White residents did not occur, i.e., where Blacks were accepted -- at least physically -- into the neighborhoods. It sought an explanation of how such physical integration was transformed into social integration. The writer argues that improving the attitudes of residents before Blacks enter lower-status neighborhoods is the key to furthering social integration in these areas. The author concludes that an effort could be made to acquaint the public with the positive effect of Black in-migration on property value as well as the social and economic characteristics of the typical in-coming Black family....

Dissertations

1. BLACK FAMILY AND SLAVERY

594. Jones, Bobby Frank. "A Cultural Middle Passage: Slave Marriage and Family in the Antebellum South." Unpublished Doctoral Dissertation, University of North Carolina, 1965. 273 pp.

According to Dr. Jones, plantations frequently used familial organization as a disciplinary tool to regulate the male sex drive, as is demonstrated by the family's initiation which usually was accomplished by the master's assigning a mate to a male slave upon request. With such tenuous foundations, the primary familial bond tended to be the mother-child relationship, but matricentrism was not as extensive as sociologists have previously presumed. A male surplus assured every household would have an adult serving in the father's role. Under the tenant-like organization of farms, slave families tended toward patricentrism with males as recognized heads of households. These families constitute the cultural bedrock of the American Negro family, concludes the author.

595. Toliver, Susan D. "The Black Family in Slavery, the Foundation of Afro-American Culture: Its Importance to Members of The Slave Community." Unpublished Doctoral Dissertation, University of California, Berkeley, 1982. 220 pp.

This paper is an attempt to address some fundamental questions pertaining to slave family life in the Antebellum South. In particular, the author is concerned with the nature of slave family relations, and that which was valued by these families. Dr. Toliver concludes that the slave family was organized as opposed to disorganized, monogamous, responsible for instrumental and expressive needs of its members, bonded by durable ties of affection, guided by a code of morals, disrupted most often by sale or death of a member as opposed to desertion or other voluntary reasons.

2. BLACK FAMILY AND ADOPTION

596. Wachtel, Dawn D. "Adoption Agencies and the Adoption of Black
      Children: Social Science and Equal Opportunity in Adoption."
      Unpublished Doctoral Dissertation, University of Michigan, 1972.
      199 pp.

      Because of the high correlation found between employment of Black
      social workers and agency involvement in Black adoptions, an at-
      tempt was made to find out why some agencies employed Black social
      workers and others did not. Using Simon's method, three models
      were tested. The model which best described the situation was a
      straight line model in which social worker involvement in hiring
      decisions led to few Black social workers being hired and conse-
      quently high agency involvement in Black adoptions. This finding
      led to a consideration of the role of the social work profession.
      The data revealed an unexpected finding: agencies employing social
      workers more oriented toward the profession were less likely to be
      involved in Black adoptions, while agencies employing social work-
      ers who were less oriented toward the profession were more likely
      to be involved in Black adoptions, declares Dr. Wachtel. It was
      concluded that in terms of policy, the data strongly suggest that
      adoption agencies interested in finding Black adoptive homes
      should proceed with the following: hiring Black social workers;
      utilizing television and other outreach techniques; and streamlin-
      ing processing procedures. The data used in the analysis were
      gathered from 24 adoption agencies located in the Washington, DC.
      and Baltimore metropolitan areas.

597. Warner, Victoria E. "The Adoption of Black Children: Retrospect
      and Prospect." Unpublished Doctoral Dissertation, Florida State
      University, 1974. 223 pp.

      This research attempts to examine two aspects of adoption prac-
      tice for Black children: (1) research, special programs and pro-
      jects designed to increase the adoption opportunities prior to
      1972 and (2) the status of adoption opportunities for Black
      children in Florida for the period 1968-72. Among the early pro-
      jects reviewed are parochial programs (1930-1945), the National
      Urban League Project (1953-1955), Adopt-A-Child Project (1955-
      1959) and MARCH (1956-1958). Consideration is given to the in-
      fluence on the total practice of adoption by family planning pro-
      grams and the War on Poverty, both commencing in the 1960's.
      These nationwide programs produced a decrease in the number of
      white babies available for adoption and subsequent focus on older
      children, medically deficient children, single-parent and foster-
      parent adoptions. Possibly the most unexpected consequence of
      these programs was the movement toward transracial adoptions, a
      pattern given rather exhaustive attention in the review of eleven
      (11) studies, four (4) major projects, three (3) international con-
      ferences, eight (8) magazine articles and two (2) novels, states
      the researcher. For the agencies participating in the study, an
      overall decrease in total adoptions was noted and only a slight
      increase in adoptions for Black children was evident. The mean
      number of Black children adopted annually during the period 1968-
      1972 was 49.8, which was 9.37 percent of the total adoptions com-
      pleted, but an infinitesimal number of state population of more

Warner:

than a million Black persons. Agencies varied in the applicabili-
ty of the eight variables tested; four agencies experiencing only
one each and one agency accounting for six of the eight variables.
Using the Mann Whitney 4 Runs Test, the only variable which could
be positively correlated with increased opportunities for the
adopting of Black children, was the use of Black staff, concludes
Dr. Warner.

3.   BLACK FAMILY AND CHILDREN

598.   Anderson, Mable B. "Child-Rearing Practices of Negro Migrant
Mothers in Three Pennsylvania Counties." Unpublished Doctoral
Dissertation, Pennsylvania State University, 1965. 225 pp.

This work describes domestic agriculture migratory families to
find out sources from which mothers obtain parental care and child
rearing information.

599.   Benjamin, Rommel. "Conceptions Of The Familial Role By Black Male
Youth." Unpublished Doctoral Dissertation, Mississippi State
University, 1971. 139 pp.

The purpose of this research was to test the general hypothesis
that young Black males vary in regard to their conception of the
Black male familial role. Also, tests were made to see if these
conceptions were significantly associated with several other selected variables. The respondents' conceptions constitute the dependent variable while the independent variables are: age, father's familial role, perception of barriers to typically family
religiosity, family income, father's education, and family structure. The research hypothesis was tested on a sample of 344 college and high school males all of whom were Black and attended
Black schools. Analysis of the data showed that respondents did
vary relative to their conceptions of the male familial role.
Their conceptions were categorized as being typical if they assigned a majority of those family responsibilities which are theore-
tically male familial role responsibilities to the male. They
were low typical if the female and male roles were assigned approximately equal degrees of responsibility for these male role functions and atypical if the female role was indicated as being most
responsible for male role responsibilities. A majority of the respondents were found to have low typical conceptions of the male
familial role, asserts Prof. Benjamin. Only two independent variables were found to be significantly related to the dependent variable (respondent's conceptions). These two related independent
variables were family structure and the father's familial role,
according to the author. "Of these two the father's familial role
was most strongly related to the respondent's conception of the
male familial role. The research findings seem to substantiate
the research position that the male familial role should be given
significantly more consideration in efforts made to strengthen the
Black family relative to stability," concludes Dr. Benjamin.

600. Blue, John T., Jr. "An Empirical Study of Parent-Child Relations:
      Matricentrism in the Southern Family." Unpublished Doctoral Dis-
      sertation, American University, 1958. 429 pp.

      Study to find which parent is more closely related to the child.
      Hypothesis was that bonds between parent and child were matricen-
      tric. The effect of social and situational factors on parent-
      child relations was explored, plus sex, race and social status.

601. Carter, Charles A. "An Investigation of Self-Acceptance and the
      Perception of the Mother-Offspring Relationships of Black Educable
      Mentally Retarded and Non-Retarded Offspring." Unpublished Docto-
      ral Dissertation, Catholic University of America, 1974. 137 pp.

      Found that educators and counselors should foster higher self-
      accepting attitudes among Black educable mentally retarded off-
      spring and encourage better child-mother relations between Black
      non-retarded offspring and their mothers. Improved child-mother
      relations and self-acceptance would lead to their improved social
      and learning effectiveness in school.

602. Dean, Katherine. "Father Absence, Feminine Identification, And
      Assertive-Aggressiveness -- A Test of Compulsive Masculity Among
      Institutionalized Negro Juvenile Delinquents." Unpublished Doc-
      toral Dissertation, Florida State University, 1970. 131 pp.

      Dr. Dean asserts that father absence, for these boys, was not
      found to be associated with the evidences of compulsive masculini-
      ty that were selected for this study. It was concluded that fur-
      ther attempts to test Walter B. Miller's compulsive masculinity
      hypothesis are not now called for, and it was suggested that fu-
      ture efforts be reserved for testing hypotheses which operational-
      ly specify the process through which family structure variables
      are postulated as productive of a child's later attitudes and be-
      haviors. Noted, too, was the special importance of being able to
      identify femininity by some indicators other than a conspicuous
      absence of its usual manifestations....

603. Gordon, Margaret Taber. "Mobility and Child Rearing: A Study of
      the Achievement of Black and White Metropolitan Children." Unpub-
      lished Doctoral Dissertation, Northwestern University, 1972.
      389 pp.

      Each mother characterized into four mobility situations: stable
      middle class, upwardly mobile, downwardly mobile and stable work-
      ing class. Economic, child-rearing and psychological advantages
      related to educational and occupational attainments vary according
      to mobility situation and scholastic achievement of the children
      follow the same pattern.

604. Hendricks, Leo Edward, Jr. "The Effect of Family Size, Child
      Spacing and Family Density on Stress in Low Income Black Mothers

Hendricks:

and Their Preadolescent Children." Unpublished Doctoral Dissertation, University of North Carolina at Chapel Hill, 1977. 167 pp.

Family size, child spacing and family density were found to be poor predictors of stress in this group of low income Black mothers. Regression analysis of the mothers' personal stress level on the variables, family size, child spacing and family density, and the observable confounding variables revealed that (1) full-time employment status of the mother was found to be the most important among all the study variables in producing a change in the mothers' personal stress level, (2) family size, child spacing or family density produce the least change in the mothers' personal stress level, and (3) these variables explained no more than 20% of the variance in the personal stress level of the mothers, concludes Dr. Hendricks.

605. Horton, Ralph George. "Black Parent-Child Participation in Preventive-Intervention Programs; Implication for Self-Concept Values and Racial Identification." Unpublished Doctoral Dissertation, University of Michigan, 1973. 194 pp.

Dr. Horton examines link between Black parents and staff evaluation of two preschool preventive-intervention programs and the formation of a self concept value system and racial identity within the children. He also examines the Black child in relation to the Black family. Prof. Horton's findings indicate that special intervention programs for Black children and their parents have been specifically established to maintain and if necessary, alter the socialization, and control the communication system of Black people.

606. King, Jerry G. "A Study of Strengths In Black Families." Unpublished Doctoral Dissertation, The University of Nebraska-Lincoln, 1980. 153 pp.

The family members in the study indicated that commitment and understanding were the most important factors which contributed to making the marriage satisfying. God-centeredness was another salient factor that was perceived by the respondents as contributing to marital satisfaction. One major finding of this study was that members of strong Black families tend to enhance each other's self-esteem through sharing compliments and appreciation. Indeed, the parents of these strong families exhibited a pattern of expressing appreciation to their children, spending much time with them, participating in their children's activities and generally expressing a strong interest in them. So significant relationship was found to exist between perceptions concerning the degree and depth of religious faith, concludes Dr. King.

607. Lipscomb, LaFayette W. "Parental Influence In The Development Of Black Children's Racial Self-Esteem." Unpublished Doctoral

Lipscomb:

Dissertation, University of North Carolina at Chapel Hill, 1975.
173 pp.

Recent studies on racial self esteem show a reversal in the tendency for Black children to have negative self concepts. This research explored the causal explanations for such a reversal by
investigating the process by which social status, parental attitudes, and socialization practices influence the development of
Black children's racial preferences and stereotypes. Data were
obtained from interviews with 60 Black mothers of five or six
year old children in Durham, North Carolina; and from a race
awareness test of the children in the home. Factor analysis and
path analytic procedures were employed in the data analysis. The
results indicate that socioeconomic status (mother's education,
income, and mother's occupation) affects mother's child rearing
practices directly and indirectly through mother's attitudes, and
that both attitudes and socialization practices influence the self
esteem of their children. Both professional mothers and educated
mothers scored low on Americanism attitudes, were thus likely to
have more Black objects in the home, and consequently had children
who tended to prefer their own race and hold more positive Black
stereotypes, states Dr. Lipscomb. Two additional findings are especially noteworthy for their implications concerning social
change: (1) Anti-establishment attitudes and the teaching about
notable Blacks were positive predictors of preference and stereotypes; (2) Children who were taught about the extreme differences
of status among Black people tended to have less positive Black
stereotypes than other children in the sample..., concludes the
author.

608. McAdoo, John Lewis. "An Exploratory Study of Racial Attitude
Change in Black Preschool Children Using Differential Treatment."
Unpublished Doctoral Dissertation, University of Michigan, 1970.
96 pp.

This study examined the effects of positive and negative reinforcement and a Black consciousness curriculum on the racial attitudes
of Black preschool children. Sixty-five lower socio-economic
Black preschool children ages 3.5 to 5.5 were selected to participate in this study. The subjects came from three different integrated nursery schools located in Ann Arbor, Dearborn Heights, and
Ypsilanti, Michigan. Dr. McAdoo found that racial attitudes can
be changed in both a positive and negative direction. The results
supported Williams and Edwards (1967) in finding negative reinforcement to cause greater changes than positive reinforcement
and Black consciousness curriculum. No sex differences were found.
There was no difference in change scores for subjects coming from
intact and those from nonintact homes, according to Dr. McAdoo.
The racial attitudes of the subjects in this study were found to
be more positive towards their own ethnic identity than McAdoo's
(1970) and Williams and Edwards (1969) studies. The subjects from
this study chose to play with the brown doll more frequently on
the racial preference test than either in the Clark and Clark (1939),

McAdoo:

or the Asher and Allen (1969) study. Thus, results may indicate a possible shift in the Black child's feelings for his own ethnic group, concludes the researcher.

609. Moore, William Lee. "Relationships Between Partners of Family Living and School Achievement of Black Children Living in an Economically Depressed Urban Community." Unpublished Doctoral Dissertation, Purdue University, 1972. 105 pp.

The author investigates whether the family structure of the Black child living in an economically depressed community had any effect on his achievement. Results show that community setting had limited bearing on school achievement.

610. Mootry, Russell, Jr. "The Effects of Family Structure On Unemployment Among Black Youth (16-22) Living In Rural Poverty Areas." Unpublished Doctoral Dissertation, Howard University School of Social Work, 1982. 107 pp.

The purpose of this study was to examine the effect of family structure on Black youth unemployment. The writer's concern about this problem stemmed from an awareness of the serious and pervasive nature of unemployment among Black youth. Major variables in the study were derived from a review of relevant literature and studies and instruments used in the National Longitudinal Study (NLS) of the High School Class of 1972. Major variables were family structure, employment status, number of dependent children, educational status, health problems, and work experience. The major findings of the study were as follows: (1) the relationship between single-parent family units and the employment status of Black youth was not statistically significant (2) The relationship between two-parent family units and Black youth employment status was not statistically significant.

611. Peters, Marie F. "Nine Black Families: A Study of Household Management and Childbearing In Black Families With Working Mothers." Unpublished Doctoral Dissertation, Harvard University, 1976. 339 pp.

The study families were selected from the school population of a preschool program in a medium-sized city in the Northwest. Naturalistic observations of mother-child interactions were made, and through semi-structured interview-discussions with parents, this study explored many facets of the lives of nine Black families. Household management and childrearing patterns were explored and the Black employed mothers were examined from the perspective of what they did as they combined the roles of employee/homemaker/mother, as well as in terms of what they wanted; that is, their goals and aspirations as Black parents who socialize children for participation in a world which attributes special significance to racial identity, suggests Prof. Peters. Eight coping strategies

Peters:

emerged: (1) dedication to the maintenance of multiple incomes;
(2) willingness of parents to be flexible about working hours;
(3) sharing of household/child care responsibilities between spouses; (4) utilization of child care services, from relatives to
day care; (5) use of older children as responsible helpers; (6)
family teamwork and cooperation as a practical, rather than ideological response; (7) the following of intricate schedules and
routines; and (8) job stability for the husband and job flexibility for the wife which allows the husband to build up job security
and the wife to be vocationally upwardly mobile. Dr. Peters concludes: "Although these families do not in general discuss racial
issues with their children, they live the racial reality of Black
in a Black/White world and indicate that they expect their children to gradually learn from their environment what this means.
The mothers in this study are offered as prototypes of working
mothers and it is suggested that their experiences, values, and
concerns have relevance to programs and policies involving Black
families."

612.   Phillips, Mona T. "The Black Family and Community: Their Role In
the Formation of Positive Self-Concept of Working Class Black
Youth." Unpublished Doctoral Dissertation, University of Michigan, 1982. 138 pp.

According to the writer, research done in the late 1970's through
1980 showed that Blacks and whites showed "no significant difference" on various self-esteem measures. These findings caused
those interested to question old assumptions, early research and
literature. The primary goal of this study was to discover and
clarify the "intervening processes" that serve to reinterpret the
negative messages of the general society, and protect the self-
esteem of Blacks. Results indicated that (1) Self-esteem was related to intervention; (2) The kinship structure played a crucial
role in redefining the negative messages of the general society;
and (3) The Black community by its very existence acts as an effective agent of intervention. The author concludes that strategies of affirmation protect Black self-esteem because they explain
the negative messages of the society (thereby reducing their effect), and they counteract devaluation by messages intended to
bolster individual self-worth and a racial group-pride.

613.   Richardson, Barbara B. "Racism and Child-Rearing: A Study of
Black Mothers." Unpublished Doctoral Dissertation, Claremont
Graduate School, 1981, 385 pp.

This research explored the dynamics of the socialization of Black
children, taking into account the impact of racism on the child-
rearing practices of Black mothers. Using the framework of an
ecological approach which emphasized the significance of the impact of both internal and external environmental factors on individual behaviors, an interview schedule was administered to sixty-
two Black mothers of diverse socioeconomic status living in

Richardson:

metropolitan Los Angeles. Examined were: (1) the cultural/racial
characteristics of the mothers' socialization, education and parenting environments; (2) experiences with racism; (3) social reality perceptions; (4) child-rearing values and behaviors used in
raising children to cope with racism and racial oppression; and
(5) various relationships between the mothers' external (experien-
tial) environments and their child-rearing practices. Correlati-
onal data were reported identified the internal and external maternal variables which impact upon the socialization of Black
children. Conclusions drawn from these analyses indicated: (1)
cultural/racial characteristics of the mother's environment are
strongly associated with her social reality perceptions and child-
rearing values; and (2) environmental experiences and/or high educational status are associated with strategies used to prepare
the child to deal with racism. Prof. Richardson proposed a socialization process paradigm to incorporate the external and internal environmental phenomena which exist in the social reality of
Black mothers....

614.   Rubin, Roger H. "Family Structure and Peer Group Affiliation as
        Related to Attitudes about Male-Female Relations Among Black Youth."
        Unpublished Doctoral Dissertation, Pennsylvania State University,
        1970. 149 pp.

        There were ten statistically significant findings in this study.
        The most interesting was that males who were not affiliated with
        a same sex peer group were found to be more permissive in their
        attitudes toward female premarital sexual permissiveness than those
        who were affiliated. The male peer group seemed to act as a re-
        straining force, contradicting other studies on male sexuality.
        Many of these nonaffiliates may be people who "stand alone" or
        "walk alone" because of the undependability and mutual mistrust
        afforded by peers in a poor, Black community. Nonaffiliation may
        free them from the restraints of the community and increase their
        permissiveness. In addition, the presence of many peripheral peo-
        ple raises questions as to the extensiveness of the peer group
        system, states Dr. Rubin. However, the main conclusion of the
        study was that family structure, peer group affiliation, social
        class, and sex were not good predictors of attitudinal differences
        concerning male-female relations among these Black youth....

615.   Trufant, Carol Ann. "The Effects of Familial Support System on
        Black Mothers' Childrearing Attitudes and Behaviors, and on Their
        Children's Competence." Unpublished Doctoral Dissertation, Michi-
        gan State University, 1977. 161 pp.

        Dr. Trufant's subjects consisted of 53 Black mothers, with child-
        ren aged 4 and 5 years old, between the ages of 22 and 40 years
        old. All mothers were in the lower income bracket, many of whom
        were on welfare, and their children attended either Head Start or
        one of two Day Care centers in South Central Los Angeles. Re-
        sults indicated that simple nuclear family structure affected mo-
        thers' autonomy. No other significant results were found for
        mothers' childrearing behaviors. Husbands/stable males and

Trufant:

mothers alone as caretakers fostered less than optimal behaviors
in children whereas grandmothers and Others consisting mostly of
parent siblings and friends as caretakers fostered more constructive behaviors. Others, e.g., siblings as caregivers, fostered
self-confidence in children whereas mothers alone and husbands
fostered more fearfulness in children. Grandmother and Others as
caretakers did not have any effect on mothers' childrearing attitudes but educational level did. Mothers with some college, bu-
siness/trade school, and one or more years of college encouraged
independence in their child more than mothers with the lowest educational attainment (11th grade or below). Trends indicated that
mothers who completed high school handled financial stress related
to children's special needs better than mothers with some college,
and, attenuated mothers had a tendency to view parent-child relations more positively than mothers in extended families, asserts
the author. The results also suggested that, generally, single
mothers choose their men according to how well they felt the men
would get along with the child, than according to how much her
social and emotional needs were satisfied. Financial needs were
low in priority, concludes the researcher.

616.   Wyatt, Gail Elizabeth. "The Relationship of Life Changes and
       Focus of Control Attributions to Cognitive Aspects of the Black
       Mother-Child Interaction." Unpublished Doctoral Dissertation,
       University of California at Los Angeles, 1973. 187 pp.

       Interaction between mother and child, particularly her style of
       reinforcement, which mediates a large part of the child's environ-
       ment, is explored as a source contributing to a Black child's la-
       ter difficulties or successes in school. Prof. Wyatt's findings
       suggest that the direction of mothers' reinforcement was related
       to appropriations of the child's environment.

617.   Zwiebel, Sarah. "The Relation Between Maternal Behaviors and
       Aggression in Sons: Black and Puerto Rican Families." Unpublish-
       ed Doctoral Dissertation, Adelphi University, 1979. 218 pp.

       This study sought to identify the relation between the child
       rearing behaviors of Black and Puerto Rican mothers of low socio-
       economic status and the existence of aggressive behaviors in their
       latency age sons. It is also asked whether Black and Puerto Rican
       mothers differ overall in their child rearing behaviors. This
       knowledge was thought useful for the purpose of both the education
       and treatment of parents and children, and for the profession's
       understanding of differing ethnic and racial child rearing prac-
       tices among the urban poor, states Prof. Zwiebel. Puerto Rican
       mothers scored significantly higher than Black mothers on the
       Anxiety dimension. Puerto Rican mothers also scored higher than
       Black mothers on the sociability dimension, but the difference
       between the scores of the two groups only approached significance.

4. BLACK FAMILY AND COUNSELING

618. Meggerson-Moore, Joyce Ann. "A Survey of a Sample of Black Families' Views of the Counseling Profession." Unpublished Doctoral
Dissertation, Saint Louis University, 1979. 153 pp.

This study deals with Black families and the counseling process.
The study tries to determine (a) how Black families feel about the
counseling process as a means for resolution of family conflicts,
(b) what events would lead the family to counseling, (c) expectations of families of how the counseling process works and who the
"helping" person would be, (d) the relationship of education, income, number of family members, ages of parents, and length of
marriage to the types of family problems and the sources families
utilized for assistance with problems. A questionnaire was administered to 30 Black families who were chosen from a Saint Louis
County Community Services Project Program. There were three counselors and a supervisor who offered services to families who attended. This survey sought attitudes of this sample of Black families toward counseling.

619. Wade, Ernest M. "Comparative Analysis of Counselor Response to
Married and Single Black Female Parents in Terms of Acceptance,
Effective Parenting, and the Need for Further Counseling."
Unpublished Doctoral Dissertation, Michigan State University, 1983.
140 pp.

The purpose of this study was to investigate the effects of family
structure, Black two-parent family, and Black female-headed single-parent family on the perceptions of school counselors. The
effects of family structure upon responses to audiotaped counseling simulations was examined. The issue of major concern in this
study was whether counselors would respond differently to married
Black female parents than to single Black female parents. The literature supports the proposition that negative views exist about
Black families. These views are particularly negative when refer-
ring to Black female-headed single-parent families. This family
group is viewed as being not only different but also deficient in
nature. It is perceived by others, professionals and the general
community, as being pathological and incapable of producing effective children, states Dr. Wade.

5. BLACK FAMILY AND EDUCATION

620. Binderman, Murray. "Factors in Desegregation Decisions of Black
Mothers." Unpublished Doctoral Dissertation, University of North
Carolina at Chapel Hill, 1970. 215 pp.

Dr. Binderman gives data on possible factors which would distinguish integrator parents from non-integrator parents. Studied
parents in Orange County, North Carolina. Factors such as mother's
education, her level of knowledge, feelings of powerlessness, and
alienation were measured.

621.   Freeman, Hazel Joyce McElwee. "The Operative Effect of Common Va-
        riables on the Early Development of the Success Potential for Suc-
        cessful Black Adult American Males." Unpublished Doctoral Disser-
        tation, Saint Louis University, 1973. 125 pp.

        The author attempts to find common variables in the lives of suc-
        cessful Black men. Some commonality was found in role model iden-
        tification, parental attitude toward formal education, and eviden-
        ces of sustainly nurturing family relationships.

622.   Gillespie, Joanna Bowen. "Socioeconomic Status, Race, and Tradi-
        tional and Progressive Attitudes Toward Education." Unpublished
        Doctoral Dissertation, New York University, 1973. 90 pp.

        Dr. Gillespie studies relationship between socioeconomic status
        and race on parental attitudes toward education. Prof. Gillespie
        suggests that racial background by itself is an influence in shap-
        ing the educational ideology of parents in regard to traditional-
        ism or progressivism.

623.   Goodman, James Arthur. "A Study of the Use of Opportunity for
        School Integration as Related to Deprivation and Patterns of Ali-
        enation in Three Groups of Negro Families." Unpublished Doctoral
        Dissertation, University of Minnesota, 1967. 139 pp.

        Dr. Goodman's findings show that the bussed students were of high-
        er social class and less deprived than non-bussed and future bus-
        sed students. Some families and individuals will need personal
        and individual help to begin constructive interaction with social
        institutions from which they have been alienated, concludes the
        researcher.

624.   Holowenzak, Stephen Paul. "The Analysis of Selected Family Back-
        ground Achievement, and Area of Residence-School Factors Influenc-
        ing Differences in the Educational Plans and Desires of Twelfth
        Grade Males and Females from Six Ethnic Groups." Unpublished Doc-
        toral Dissertation, Catholic University of America, 1963. 290 pp.

        The following factors played a more important role in the educa-
        tional plans and desires for 12th grade males and females: family
        background rather than achievement or area of residence; family
        process rather than home background; socio-economic status rather
        than family structure; expectations for excellence rather than at-
        titude toward life or study habit; student body rather than teach-
        ing staff.

625.   McAdoo, Harriette Ann Pipes. "Racial Attitudes and Self Concepts
        of Black Preschool Children." Unpublished Doctoral Dissertation,
        University of Michigan, 1970. 175 pp.

        Dr. McAdoo found no correlation between racial attitude and self
        concept; no difference in children from intact and those from bro-
        ken homes. Prof. McAdoo concludes that boys have higher ideas of

McAdoo:

self-concept than girls.

626.   Moore, William, Jr. "A Portrait: The Culturally Disadvantaged
        Preschool Negro Child." Unpublished Doctoral Dissertation, St.
        Louis University, 1964. 293 pp.

        This study identifies and describes distinguishing characteristics
        of culturally disadvantaged pre-school Black children in St. Louis.
        Dr. Moore provides a cultural description of conditions found in
        public housing projects which influence behavior of the child.
        Home, family, health, educational climate, economic conditions,
        leisure time activities and moral and spiritual values are explo-
        red.

6. BLACK FAMILY AND EXTENDED FAMILIES

627.   Creighton-Zollar, Ann. "A Member of the Family: Strategies for
        Black Family Continuity." Unpublished Doctoral Dissertation,
        University of Illinois at Chicago Circle, 1980. 167 pp.

        In light of past conceptual and ideological problems in defining
        the Black family, this work begins without designating any speci-
        fic collectivity or persons or roles and statuses as the proper
        referant of the term family. Instead, the research imposed both
        structural and functional criteria and identified as a family
        sets of individuals who met both sets of criteria. Four unmarried
        Black males raised on welfare served as the initial informants.
        From this group, the researcher identified four sets of indivi-
        duals, the relations among whom bear designations of kinship
        (structural criteria) and who engage in a system of mutual aid in-
        volving the exchange of goods and services (functional criteria).
        In each case, the family identified is extended, spanning three to
        four generations and spread out over several households. In three
        of the four cases, the family contains both mobile and nonmobile
        members. In these cases, the interactions and interdependence
        between mobile and nonmobile family members are integrated through
        the mechanisms of generalized reciprocity and pooling, according
        to the writer. Because children are consciously taught to gene-
        rate and to interpret these mechanisms, because they are practi-
        sed ritualistically as well as in the face of necessity, and be-
        cause even the family which does not practice them espouse them
        as the way things "ought to be", these mechanisms are interpreted
        as cultural attributes rather than ad hoc idiosyncratic responses
        to conditions of urban poverty. In the fourth case, mobiles have
        disengaged from the extended family leaving it composed entirely
        of individuals who are members of the underclass. In this family
        balanced rather than generalized reciprocity characterizes the
        relationships of family members and pooling behavior is absent.
        In none of the cases can the failure of nonmobiles be attributed
        to exploitation at the hands of their kin, states the writer.
        When the family is economically differentiated, nonmobiles are on
        the receiving end of generalized reciprocity from those family

Creighton-Zollar:

members who have been mobile. "When the indirect flows of goods
and services in this type of family are taken into consideration,
it can even be seen that the mobiles are not being exploited.
When the family is homogeneously poor, the failure of an individual to save money needed for mobility cannot be attributed to the
nature of exchanges with kin, for in this situation each individual gets back from the family all that they put into it," concludes Dr. Creighton-Zollar.

628.   Martin, Elmer P., Jr. "A Descriptive Analysis of the Black Extended Family: Toward a New Perspective of Black Family Life in America." Unpublished Doctoral Dissertation, Case Western Reserve
University, 1975. 363 pp.

It was concluded that the extended family had to be capable of un-
dergoing continuous structural changes in order to fulfill basic
survival needs and to perform basic survival functions such as providing family leadership, informally adopting children and providing aid and support to extended family members. This structural
metamorphosis was also a necessary requirement for pursuing short-
range day-to-day survival goals and the long-range goals of helping family members to become economically self-sufficient, states
Prof. Martin. It appeared that the crucial role extended families
have in respect to the survival and well-being of Black family
members is diminishing in the wake of increasing secularization
and individualization of family members, the persistent exploita-
bility of Black people, and the societal pressure toward making
extended families more compatible with an urbanized, industriali-
zed, technological society. Dr. Martin concludes, in part: "Thus,
the major implications are that communal support be set up in
Black communities, by Black people, to bolster weakening extended
family structures; that extended family members reaffirm and modi-
fy extended family values in order to assure survival and in order
to maintain the roots of their cultural heritage and in order to
maintain the roots of their cultural heritage as a race...."

629.   Tuck, Inez. "An Analysis of the Intergenerational Patterns in
Two African-American Families." Unpublished Doctoral Dissertation, University of North Carolina at Greensboro, 1980. 333 pp.

This study has three purposes: (a) to examine the culture found
in two rural average African-American families as they were reconstructed for genealogical charts to determine generational patterns,
(b) to study the interaction between economic/political institutions and the two families, and (c) finally, to analyze families
in order to ascertain the degree of retention of African cultural
remnants. One family resided in rural North Carolina, an area
with considerable contact with the dominant American culture. The
other family lived in the Sea Islands, an area relatively isolated
from the dominant culture. A biography of each family was written
within the context of an ethnographic/historical community study.
Genealogical charts were reconstructed representing six generations

Tuck:

of each family and served as the source for respondents. Twenty-
four respondents, ages 16-93, were interviewed and data collected
about generational patterns. The general findings from this study
supported the theory of cultural pluralism. These African-American
families were found to have an ethnic culture which was rooted in
Africanism. The conclusion was that African-American families
have used strategies for coping with societal change which are
characteristic of the ethnic-racial group. The writer recommends
that African-American families not be studied as a deviant family
resulting from a deteriorated state of the family. The study of
average African-American families are in keeping with the tenets
of cultural pluralism, states Dr. Tuck.

7. BLACK FAMILY AND HEALTH

630. Sellers, Frank, Jr. "Impact of Sickle Cell Anemia on Attitudes
and Relationships Among Particular Family Members." Unpublished
Doctoral Dissertation, University of Pittsburgh, 1974. 128 pp.

Dr. Sellers investigates emotional difficulties of families having
a child with Sickle Cell Anemia. Prof. Sellers showed that the
Sickle Cell child affects the immediate family, especially the
mother. There are also important emotional and mental health aspects associated with this disease, concludes the researcher.

631. Van Ginneken, Jeroen K. "Social Factors Related to Utilization
of Maternal and Child Health Services by Black Families in Buffalo, New York." Unpublished Doctoral Dissertation, State University of New York at Buffalo, 1972. 196 pp.

One of the objectives of this survey carried out in 1970 was to
describe patterns of use of maternal and child health (MCH) services, in particular use of prenatal and pediatric services. Another major objective was to identify determinants of use of these
MCH services. The data were derived from interviews with 143
Black mothers living in Buffalo, New York. Socioeconomic status
and health beliefs were determinants of frequency of visits to
MCH services: patients of high socio-economic status and with favorable health beliefs were likely to make more visits than patients of low socioeconomic status and with unfavorable health
beliefs. A third determinant of frequency of MCH visits was attitudes toward MCH services: patients with positive attitudes toward MCH services were likely to make more visits than patients
with negative attitudes toward MCH services. These relationships
of attitudes toward MCH services and frequency of visits remained
when type of MCH service and socioeconomic status were controlled,
concludes the researcher.

632. Wilkie, Charlotte H. "A Study of Familial Expectations Regarding
Work for the Negro Schizophrenic Male Patient on Convalescent
Leave." Unpublished Doctoral Dissertation, Catholic University of

Wilkie:

America, 1970.   223 pp.

Study of work outcome of Black schizophrenic patients who returned
to live with family members.   The writer investigates familial
expectations of role performance of patient, plus his own expectations.   This study shows that patient expectations for own role
performance was higher than his familial expectations of him.

8.   BLACK FAMILY AND HYPERTENSION

633.   Williams, Myrna B.   "Psychological Correlates of Essential Hypertension within the Black Family."   Unpublished Doctoral Dissertation, University of North Carolina at Chapel Hill, 1980. 212 pp.

Perception of aggression and perception of life stress were inves-
tigated in 105 Black individuals from 35 Black family sets (husband, wife and one child).   The family sets were divided into
three blood pressure groups: (1) HN - 15 families - one parent
with essential hypertension, one normotensive spouse and one normotensive child, (2) NN - 15 families - both parents normotensive
and one normotensive child and (3) HH - 5 families - both parents
with essential hypertension and one normotensive child.   Each
blood pressure group was further divided into target, spouse and
child subjects.   The repressed hostility hypothesis was investi-
gated by predicting that essential hypertensives would express
less aggressive imagery than normotensives and that a recognizable
pattern of responding would exist for essential hypertensives with
them suppressing aggressive responses as aggressive cues progressed from ambiguous to more explicit.   The life stress hypothesis
was examined by predicting that essential hypertensives would report more individual stress and see life as generally more stressful than normotensives.   The pre-hypertensive hypothesis was in-
vestigated by predicting that the children of hypertensive parents
would respond similarly as what was predicted for their parents,
argues Dr. Williams.   Her findings did not support the repressed
hostility hypothesis or the life stress hypothesis.   Essential hypertensives did not express more or less inward or outward aggression than normotensive adults.   There were no differences between
essential hypertensives and normotensives in the amount of aggression expressed as aggressive cues progressed from ambiguous to
more explicit.   Essential hypertensives did not perceive their
lives to be more stressful in general than normotensives nor did
they report that more stressful events had actually happened to
them within one year of the testing.   "Like their parents there
were no significant differences between any of the children groups
in the total amount of inward or outward aggression expressed, how
stressful they perceive life in general to be or the number of
events they reported had happened to them within one year of the
testing.   There were no consistent patterns of expression of aggression for any of the children groups as aggressive cues progressed from ambiguous to explicit.   Other findings were that
children with both parents having essential hypertension had significantly higher blood pressures than children of normotensive

Williams:

parents and that more hypertensives than normotensives were over-weight," concludes the researcher.

9. BLACK FAMILY AND ILLEGITIMACY

634. Oppel, Wallace C. "Illegitimacy: A Comparative Follow-up Study.
A Matched Group of 120 Six to Eight Year-Old Negro Illegitimate
Children and Their Mothers is Compared to a Group of 120 Legiti-
mate Six to Eight Year-Old Negro Children and Their Mothers on
Measures of Child Development and Mothering Behavior." Unpublished
Doctoral Dissertation, Catholic University of America, 1969.
188 pp.

Comparisons of the legitimately born and the illegitimately born
Negro study children disclosed that the illegitimately born children had a non-significantly higher frequency of impairment on all
the measures of development used in the study except height. If
statistical significance is not used as a criterion, the relatively small quantitative differences disclosed by the data do not
easily lend themselves to an interpretation that illegitimately
born Negro study children who are reared by their mothers are at
greater risk of poor developmental outcomes than legitimately born
children, asserts Dr. Oppel. He concludes: "...Nine percent of
the legitimate group and 19 percent of the illegitimate group received at least two-thirds of their support from public welfare.
These findings do not support contentions that illegitimately born
children should be singled out for long-term agency follow-up service, nor that they should be removed from their homes on the assumption that illegitimacy is probably indicative of neglect."

10. BLACK FAMILY AND MENTAL ILLNESS

635. Meers, Dale R. "Definitions, Perceptions and Accommodations to
Mental Illness of Low Income, Ghetto Resident Black Families."
Unpublished Doctoral Dissertation, Catholic University of America,
1973. 402 pp.

Psychiatric social work carries an interdisciplinary, clinical
responsibility for assessments of developmental and family histories essential to differential psychiatric diagnosis. Since both
subcultural norms and reality stress may sustain or induce various
behaviors that are descriptively identical to symptoms of mental
illness, the social worker carries diagnostic responsibility in
making relevant distinctions. In its dependence on descriptive
psychiatric nosology, however, social work appears remiss in the
assessment of normative deviance and psychopathology in the Black
subculture. This study explores the congruence of indigenous and
psychiatric conceptions of mental illness. The absence of both
relevant outpatient treatment resources and indigenous conceptions of treatability appeared to contribute to selective perceptions that avoided conclusions of mental illness, according to
Dr. Meers. The respondents' views of the police as ineffectual

Meers:

and public welfare as indifferent, appeared to sustain lay notions
that deviant behavior did not merit treatment and that psychoses
were only treatable through institutionalization under legal du-
ress. Both private physicians and hospital staff reaffirmed lay
views that the preponderance of neurotic and psychomatic distress
were matters of either medical or moral responsibility, states the
author. Prof. Meers concludes: "In the absence of relevant and
concerned professional community distinctions on the treatability
of mental illness, these subjects' pessimistic and conservative
views of mental illness may reflect institutionalized indifference,
if not covert racism. Existing community psychiatric services
appeared as either unavailable or as irrelevant to the needs of
respondents who conceptualized their emotionsl and symptomatic
needs as outside the model of professional orthodoxy."

11.   BLACK FAMILY AND MILITARY FAMILIES

636. Keller, Ella T. "Black Families in the Military System." Unpublished Doctoral Dissertation, Mississippi State University, 1980.
288 pp.

Among the almost three million dependents affected by military policies are the families of over 150,000 Black active duty personnel. The present research effort was an exploratory study into
the nature of Black military families. Data were collected through
personal interviews with ninety-one Black active duty servicemen
and their wives. The ninety-one families were chosen from Black
military personnel stationed at two Southern military installa-
tions, Columbus Air Force Base in Columbus, Mississippi and Naval
Air Station-Memphis in Millington, Tennessee. The sample included
both officers and enlisted men from the Air Force, Navy and Marine
Corps. The average length of service was 7.4 years. These Black
military families were found to resemble other Black families in
the areas of household task allocation and decision-making structure. Husbands generally attributed more household task participation to themselves than did their wives. There was also some
evidence of role specialization along traditional lines. The
findings on decision-making support those studies which caution
against the automatic characterization of Black families as matriarchal. The predominate pattern found among these families was
equalitarian decision-making, according to Prof. Keller. She
asserts that these Black military families were similar to other
military families in terms of the characteristics of military life
which they liked, disliked or viewed with some concern. These
Black military families, however, did report infrequent use of military resources and a preference for civilian rather than military marital counseling, argues the researcher. These Black military wives also reported low participation rates in wives social
and volunteer organizations. Overall, however, these families reported generally positive attitudes toward military life which was
reflected in the number of husbands and wives favoring re-enlist-
ment, concludes Dr. Keller.

12. BLACK FAMILY AND OCCUPATIONS

637. Gordon, Joan L. "Some Socio-Economic Aspects of Selected Negro
Families in Savannah, Georgia: With Special Reference to the Effects of Occupational Stratification on Child Rearing." Unpublished Doctoral Dissertation, University of Pennsylvania, 1955.
224 pp.

Dr. Gordon studies the manner in which differentials in the occupational classification of the heads of Black families in Savannah
are associated with and affect patterns of child-rearing. She
found that differences in occupational level of family head reflect differences in social and economic factors operating in the
family. Prof. Gordon also found a functional relationship between
family head's occupational stratum and how he rears his child.

638. Jones, Barbara Ann Posey. "The Contribution of Black Women to the
Income of Black Families: An Analysis of the Labor Force Partici-
pation Rates of Black Wives." Unpublished Doctoral Dissertation,
Georgia State University, 1973. 158 pp.

Dr. Jones accesses influence of selected personal family and economic characteristics of Black wives in their decision to enter
or remain in the labor force. Factors deterring the wife are
small children and geographic mobility, declares the writer.
Schooling also exerts a negative influence, suggests Prof. Jones.

13. BLACK FAMILY AND POVERTY

639. Durbin, Elizabeth Meriel. "Family Instability, Labor Supply and
the Incidence of Aid to Families with Dependent Children." Unpublished Doctoral Dissertation, Columbia University, 1971. 280
pp.

Dr. Durbin investigates the relationship between family instability and the demand for ADC assistance and traces the subsequent effects of welfare demand on labor supply. The author feels welfare system encourages families to break up and increases in ADC
assistance reduces labor supply of unskilled males and females.

640. Henderson, Donald Mark. "A Study of the Effects of Family Structure and Poverty on Negro Adolescents from the Ghetto." Unpublished Doctoral Dissertation, University of Pittsburgh, 1967.
218 pp.

This is a study of whether family structure is more important than
poverty in determining inadequate social performance of lower
class Black children. Prof. Henderson's findings suggest that
the influence of the Black ghetto where the child lives is most
important. The ghetto is characterized by racial, physical, social and mental isolation which produces a different life style
making it difficult to perform adequately in society, concludes
Dr. Henderson.

641. Reischauer, Robert Danton. "The Impact of the Welfare System on
      Black Migration and Marital Stability." Unpublished Doctoral Dis-
      sertation, Columbia University, 1971. 167 pp.

      According to the author, the welfare system has been accused of
      being counterproductive. Results of this study found that migra-
      tion from the South was unrelated to welfare opportunities else-
      where, patterns of migration somewhat influenced by welfare oppor-
      tunities in areas of destination and availability of welfare has
      little to do with rate at which low income persons leave cities.
      Welfare-related instability arises because public assistance lo-
      wers both the benefits of marriage and the costs of disruption to
      the poor by providing subsidized alimony payments, states the re-
      searcher.

14.   BLACK FAMILY AND PRISON FAMILIES

642. Green, Alice P. "Case Studies of the Impact of Separation Due to
      Incarceration on Black Families." Unpublished Doctoral Disserta-
      tion, State University of New York at Albany, 1982. 304 pp.

      Dr. Green explores and describes the nature and extent of changes
      that take place in Black prisoners' families and the adjustments
      made by female spouses and family units after the male is separa-
      ted from his family by incarceration. The author's findings sug-
      gest that once a father/spouse is removed from his household, his
      roles and responsibilities are quickly assumed by his female
      spouse with assistance from a number of external resources that
      include kinfolk and social welfare agencies. In an effort to ad-
      just to the accompanying emotional and psychological stress, fe-
      male spouses relied upon a number of adaptive or coping mechanisms
      such as denial, increased job and educational activities, and ac-
      centuated displays of loyalty to their spouses, demonstrated most
      prominently by their compelling struggle to visit the imprisoned
      family member as often as possible. She believes that although
      most families were harmed in some fashion by the arrest and long-
      term separation, some familial and marital relationships appeared
      strengthened by the separation; this usually occurred in situa-
      tions where the male had a drug or alcohol dependency. Prof.
      Green argues that nevertheless, the wives were able to gain a new
      sense of self-reliance and independence that allowed them to main-
      tain family functions and pursue other desired goals....

15.   BLACK FAMILY AND SICKLE CELL DISEASE

643. Mazepa, James P. "Family Structure and Symptomatology in Sickle
      Cell Disease." Unpublished Doctoral Dissertation, University of
      Illinois at Chicago, 1983. 113 pp.

      This descriptive and exploratory study of a sickle cell disease
      sample looked for associations between family structure and symp-
      tomatology in the sickle cell patient. The sample was drawn from
      the pediatric sickle cell clinic at Michael Reese Hospital in
      Chicago, Illinois, and consisted of 76 families which included 83

Mazepa:

children with sickle cell disease. Single-parent families scored
significantly higher than two-parent families on the adaptability
dimension (p<.02) in the direction of chaotic types, and marginally higher on the cohesion dimension (p<.10) in the direction of
enmeshed types. Children from single-parent families lost more
days from school than children from two-parent families with the
difference approaching statistical significance (p<.058), as also
in the number of hospitalizations (p<.07). Families in the study
represented 14 of the 16 family types of the FACES instrument.
No significant differences were observed between children from
normal range and extreme range family types on the dependent variables concludes the author. However, there is a trend for children from extreme family types to have generally higher though not
statistically significant mean scores on the dependent variables,
suggests Prof. Mazepa.

16. BLACK FAMILY AND SINGLE PARENTS

644. Gorum, Jacquelyne W. "Stress-Coping Patterns and Functioning of
Black Single-Parent Families." Unpublished Doctoral Dissertation,
Howard University School of Social Work, 1983. 196 pp.

The purpose of this study was to explore the relationship between
stress-coping patterns (use of informal support, formal support)
and the functioning (problematic, nonproblematic, total) of Black
single-parent families. This study was exploratory in nature and
was designed to provide information on significant variables related to the level of functioning of Black single-parent families,
the relationship between variables, and establish the basis for
testing of hypotheses related to single-parent functioning. The
study sample comprised 62 (30 males and 32 females) Black single-
parent families from the Washington, D.C. area. Ten (10) hypotheses relating to the functioning of Black single-parent families
were tested using a variety of statistical procedures, the highest
level being multiple regression analysis. There was no reason to
reject any of the hypotheses because of lack of significance at
the .05 level of significance, declares the author. Stress, coping patterns, sex and socio-economic status as independent variables accounted for 16% of the variation in the dependent variable,
family functioning. A significant relationship between socioeconomic status and nonproblematic functioning was found. The relationship between coping patterns (use of formal support) by functioning (problematic) and sex by functioning (total) were approaching significance and with a larger sample might be significant,
according to Dr. Gorum. She concludes: "There was little variance among the participants which partially explains the lack of
significant difference on the hypotheses. They were firmly enmeshed in a support network. Thus, family network therapy or community services would help both Black single mothers and fathers."

645. Hirsch, Seth L. "Home Climate in the Black Single-Parent, Mother-
      Led Family: A Social-Ecological Interactional Approach." Unpub-
      lished Doctoral Dissertation, United States International Univer-
      sity, 1979. 178 pp.

      From the findings, generally, the author concluded that the Black,
      single-parent, mother-led family, as a family structure, is ade-
      quate for the competent rearing of children. It was also conclu-
      ded that, overall, the families evaluated in the study were
      "healthful" in both their interactional patterns and perceived
      social-ecology at home. Further, it was concluded that family in-
      teraction could be used to predict the perceived social-ecology at
      home and that the two variables can effectively assess home climate.

646. Hynes, Winifred Joyce. "Single Parent Mothers and Distress: Re-
      lationships Between Selected Social and Psychological Factors and
      Distress in Low-Income Single Parent Mothers." Unpublished Docto-
      ral Dissertation, Catholic University of America, 1979. 223 pp.

      This study utilizes a multivariate correlational design with a ran-
      domly selected sample of 95 low-income single parent mothers (63
      Black and 32 white) either living in government-subsidized public
      housing and/or receiving Aid to Dependent Children. Six major hy-
      potheses including subhypotheses for social supports and locus of
      control were tested with the following results: (1) greater so-
      cial supports (informal, natural or familial resource systems, and
      formal resource systems or membership organizations) are strongly
      related to lower distress, while greater societal resource systems
      (e.g., local community agencies, or social service programs) show
      a weak association at best with lower distress; (2) higher social
      participation is strongly related to lower distress; (3) greater
      financial independence is not related to lower distress although
      single parent mothers with lower income, no matter what the source
      of income, tend to report higher distress; (4) higher internal
      locus of control, where there is one father, is strongly related to
      lower distress, but there is no relationship between locus of con-
      trol and distress where there are two or more fathers; (5) there
      is no relationship between higher orientation to change and lower
      distress; and (6) lower lingering attachment is strongly related
      to lower distress.

647. LaPoint, Velma DeVonne. "A Descriptive Survey of Some Perceptions
      and Concerns of Black Female Single Parent Families in Lansing,
      Michigan." Unpublished Doctoral Dissertation, Michigan State
      University, 1977. 140 pp.

      The purpose of this survey was to obtain a description of the per-
      ceptions, concerns, and needs of Black female single parent fami-
      lies in the Lansing, Michigan, community. Demographic data of
      these families were identified as well as the economic and inter-
      personal concerns that selected Black female single parents en-
      counter in the Lansing, Michigan community. According to Dr. La
      Point, single parents reported a range of expressions that their
      children have said about being members of a single parent family.

LaPoint:

Some expressions included: feeling more grown up because the children were able to help the mother, feeling negative because they do
not have two parents like other children, and asking about the absent parent, observes the author. In general, self-perceptions
and reported children's expressions were positive and negative.
Single parents reported many positive aspects about their families. These included positive family interaction, good adaptability to the lifestyle of a single parent family without a spouse,
and the influence of religion that provided for a strong family
bond, concludes the researcher.

648.   Meyers, Edna O. "Self-Concept, Family Structure and School Achieve-
        ment: A Study of Disadvantaged Negro Boys." Unpublished Doctoral
        Dissertation, Columbia University, 1966. 168 pp.

        This study sought to ascertain the self concept, acceptance of ra-
        cial identity, family structure, and school achievement of disad-
        vantaged Black boys. Prof. Meyers found that Black boys would do
        well in school if at least one parent was there for guidance.

17. BLACK FAMILY PLANNING

648a.   Burke, Kenyon C. "Attitudes Toward Family Planning of Black Medi-
        cal Students at Meharry Medical College." Unpublished Doctoral
        Dissertation, Rutgers University, The State University of New
        Jersey, 1983. 368 pp.

        This study compared individual and family characteristics of Black
        medical students and their attitudes toward family planning pro-
        grams and services. As a result of this comparison, it was possi-
        ble to identify beliefs that were associated with expected resis-
        tance to the introduction and expansion of family planning servi-
        ces to Black communities in the United States. One hundred and
        forty-four female and male Black medical students who were enrol-
        led at Meharry Medical College in Nashville, Tennessee, completed
        a self-administered questionnaire. The conclusions of the study
        were that birthplace and student's year in medical school proved
        to be the most powerful predictor of attitudes toward family plan-
        ning. Student's birth control practice, church attendance, abor-
        tion experience and mother's occupation were marginal predictors
        of student's attitudes toward family planning. Results of this
        investigation indicate an overall acceptance of family planning on
        the part of Black medical students and the presence of some sus-
        picion of the intent of Government family planning policy inten-
        tions, states Dr. Burke.

649.   Fisch, Maria Alba. "Internal Versus External Ego Orientation and
        Family Planning Effectiveness Among Poor Black Women." Unpublished
        Doctoral Dissertation, Columbia University, 1973. 145 pp.

Fisch:

Thirty-four Black women on welfare were interviewed and classified
as Effective or Ineffective Planners. They were given a modified
Rotter I-E Scale to test their belief in internal/external control
of rèinforcements and the Portable Rod and Frame Test to measure
field independence. They were also asked to make human figure
drawings, which were rated according to the Peck-Goldstein Body
Sophistication Scale to measure psychological differentiation. Dr.
Fisch states that no significant differences were found between
Effective and Ineffective Planners on the measures used. There
were also no significant correlations among the measures. Since a
high degree of intrasubject variability was observed on the Portable Rod and Frame Test, asymmetrical scorers with high variability
were eliminated. The PRFT scores of the remaining Ss were revised
to reduce variability further, and were compared. After these procedures, Effective Planners were found to be less field dependent
than Ineffective Planners. It was also found that, when compared
with other populations, the Black lower income women studied, as a
group, showed a strong belief in external control of reinforcements
and a high degree of field dependents, concludes Prof. Fisch.

18.   BLACK FEMALE'S ROLE IN THE FAMILY

650.   Honig, Margerie Hanson. "The Impact of the Welfare System on Labor
Supply and Family Stability: A Study of Female Heads of Families."
Unpublished Doctoral Dissertation, Columbia University, 1971.
160 pp.

Dr. Honig analyzes relationship between proportion of the population receiving welfare under the AFDC program and the level of income available to recipients from the program relative to expected
income. Prof. Honig found that current provisions for public assistance primarily to families without male support provides a significant impetus for family disintegration which itself may lead
to intergenerational increases in the welfare program.

651.   Myers, Lena Wright. "A Study of the Self-Esteem Maintenance Process Among Black Women." Unpublished Doctoral Dissertation, Michigan State University, 1973. 135 pp.

Dr. Myers investigates literature which assumes that Black women
heads of households evaluate their situation by using the typical
white woman as their reference group. Literature also emphasizes
that the level of self-esteem of Black women in this situation
should be low, ignoring the possibility of selectivity among roles
and reference groups among Black women in the maintenance of self-
esteem. Her results show that for Black women, the reference group
used in self assessment are other Black women. The matriarchal
structured family does not lower self-esteem and self-esteem maintenance is a reference group process, concludes the sociologist.

652. Osmond, Marie Withers. "Family Stability and Economic Dependen-
      cy." Unpublished Doctoral Dissertation, Florida State University,
      1973. 414 pp.

      Regardless of race, disability, family composition or structural
      linkage, the female-headed family emerged consistently as the most
      economically disadvantaged, declares Prof. Osmond. Three major
      paths of poverty, demonstrating an increasing probability of chro-
      nic economic dependency, were discerned: white male headed with
      both spouses working; Black male headed with one working or dis-
      abled family head; female headed family with many dependents and
      some disability.

653. Phillips, Judith. "Performance of Father-Present and Father-
      Absent Southern Negro Boys on a Simple Operant Task as a Function
      of the Race and Sex of the Experimenter and the Type of Social Re-
      inforcement." Unpublished Doctoral Dissertation, University of
      Minnesota, 1966. 158 pp.

      The researcher's findings support the theory that father-absence is
      a salient determinant of the responsiveness of young Black boys to
      the race of adult reinforcement agents and the type of social en-
      forcer despensed in a test situation.

654. Rutledge, Essie Manuel. "Marital and Family Relations of Black
      Women." Unpublished Doctoral Dissertation, Michigan State Univer-
      sity, 1974. 176 pp.

      This study is concerned with describing and analyzing various as-
      pects of the marital and family (parent-child) relations of Black
      women. More precisely the effort has been to: (1) consider the
      nature of marital and parent-child relationships, (2) to note the
      extent of variations in the relationships; (3) note correlations
      between marital and parent-child relationships and other characte-
      ristics of the women and of their husbands. In pursuit of this
      effort the various aspects of the marital-family relations studied
      are: marital happiness, marital interaction goals, marital dis-
      agreement, marital instability, feelings of role inadequacies, af-
      fective relations toward spouse and children, traditional and mo-
      dern attitudes toward childrearing goals, and parental satisfac-
      tion. The major conclusions are: (1) family relations of intact
      Black families are generally indicative of "strengths"; (2) a dy-
      namic approach to studying Black families is much more realistic
      than a structural-functionist approach in that the former is more
      capable than the latter in: (a) accounting for variations in
      Black families and (b) obtaining a detailed account of Black fami-
      ly life; (3) it is much more realistic to study Black families on
      their own merits than to compare them with whites, since compara-
      tive studies of Blacks and whites result in misconceptions because
      of the racial inequalities within our society.

655. Samuels, Morris R. "A Study of Maternal Role Performance in One-
      Parent Negro Families." Unpublished Doctoral Dissertation, Colum-
      bia University, 1970. 171 pp.

Samuels:

The author's data revealed several significant findings. Children in Fatherless Families are less successful in academic school performance and school behavior than children in Father-Present Families. They also have more contact with the police. Their mothers had more difficulty with their own schooling than the Father-Present group. The writer points out that the children of the Father-Absent group however, belong to more recreational organizations, which was a highly significant finding. Fatherless families also have dinner together significantly more often than Father-Present Families. Dr. Samuels suggests that these last two activities are seen as possible coping techniques employed by the Father-Absent Family to help them deal more effectively with father-husband absence. More contact with friends and neighbors, though not significantly different, is also viewed in the realm of coping behavior. The tendency to view lower-class Negro Fatherless Families as multi-problem and disorganized may overemphasize problem areas and prevent family strengths from being evaluated, asserts Prof. Samuels. He concludes: "The fact that the research literature shows no consensus of opinion regarding the negative impact of fatherlessness, should give us sufficient reason to stop stereotyping these families, and start looking at them with a new and fresh perspective."

656. Schneller, Donald Philip. "An Exploratory Study of the Effects of Incarceration on the Families of Negro Inmates of a Medium-Security Prison." Unpublished Doctoral Dissertation, Catholic University of America, 1966. 169 pp.

The author determines the nature and extent of changes occurring in the family after family head is incarcerated. Financial and social stigma changes took place but the worst change was of an emotional nature. Dr. Schneller suggests increased use of family counseling, visiting privileges, telephone-visiting privileges, free transportation to prison for family, conjugal visits and home furloughs for select married inmates.

657. Snow, Jacquelyn E. "A Heuristic Study of Black Female Heads of Households and Black Females Who are not Heads of Households and Their Involvement with Their Children's Educational Development, Camden, New Jersey." Unpublished Doctoral Dissertation, State University of New Jersey, 1976. 139 pp.

The central theme of this study was to assess the similarities and differences between Black females who are solely heads of households and Black females who are not solely heads of households and their involvement with the educational development of their children currently enrolled in Camden, New Jersey. The following conclusions are derived based upon the findings of questions proposed: (1) There is no significant difference in the educational involvement of mothers from the one-parent group and mothers from the two-parent group with their children. The following reasons substantiate this finding. There was no significant

Snow:

difference between the two groups with regard to familiarity of
school personnel, attendance to P.T.A. parent conference meetings
and student activities. Further, there was no significant difference between reports on the educational performance of their
children and recognition of scholastic achievement. However,
there was noticeable difference on the statistics from both groups
regarding children who had failed courses. More children from the
single parent structure had failed courses than children from two-
parent structures. The cause may be attitudinal rather than lack
of support or guidance. (2) There is no difference between the
two groups in making immediate provisions for their children
which could have an impact on their educational development. Statistics were quite similar for both groups pertaining to providing
educational trips, books, a daily paper, magazines and television.
(3) An important finding of this study is that both groups re-
sponded similarly on discussing sex and drug matters with their
children. (4) Another finding is that children from one-parent
group female headed households were not involved with the police
any more than children from homes where there were two parents.
(5) Mothers from one-parent homes spend as much time with their
children as do mothers from two-parent homes, based on this study.
(6) Mothers from the one-parent families do not feel any more de-
feated than mothers from two parent families. Both groups unanimously felt their children's life situation could be changed.
There was no difference in the aspirations of the one-parent family and the two-parent family for their children....

658. Wasserman, Herbert Louis. "Father-Absent and Father-Present Lo-
      wer Class Negro Families: A Comparative Study of Family Func-
      tioning." Unpublished Doctoral Dissertation, Brandeis University,
      1968. 241 pp.

      Dr. Wasserman studied father-present and father-absent families
      to determine differences between backgrounds, attitudes and cur-
      rent behavior of mothers as well as school performance and other
      behavioral indices of one son in each family.

                    19. BLACK LOWER-CLASS FAMILY

659. Borlick, Martha M. "The Effects of a Parent Group Discussion
      Program on Parental Learnings of Unwed, Expectant Negro Adoles-
      cent Girls from Low-Income Families." Unpublished Doctoral Dis-
      sertation, University of Maryland, 1966. 235 pp.

      This study explored effects of a parent group discussion program
      on four areas of parental learning: factual knowledge concerning
      pregnancy; labor and delivery and behavior of the newborn; atti-
      tudes of self-assurance in the parent role; and performance during
      labor and delivery and performance in management of infant in the
      home. Dr. Borlick hypothesizes that at the post-stage, the mean
      level of parental learning would be greater for parent group dis-
      cussion participants then for non-participants.

660.   Butler, Carol Ann. "An In-Depth Investigation of the Vocational
        Development Patterns of Forty Black American Professional Men
        from Lower Socio-economic Level Families." Unpublished Doctoral
        Dissertation, New York University, 1970. 194 pp.

        This study of the forty men took place in the New York metropoli-
        tan area. Dr. Butler's findings show that most had been reared
        in families whose interactions, attitudes and structure were more
        similar to Black middle class family than had Blacks in general
        from lower socio-economic families. Occupation in a high level
        profession was not related to having been reared in a family with
        a middle class life style, states the researcher.

661.   Conwill, William L. "A Conceptual Analysis of Black Family In-
        stability." Unpublished Doctoral Dissertation, Stanford Univer-
        sity, 1980. 212 pp.

        This dissertation first lays out a formal analysis, outlining the
        concepts of "Black", "family", and "instability", based on a so-
        cial science perspective on the Black presence in America. It
        then proceeds to a critique of the ideology and theory behind the
        normative scholarly perception of the Black family as unstable,
        to show the process of de-legitimization of the Black family.
        Following that, it examines the economic implications of the move-
        ment of Blacks and women during the 1960s and 1970s, respectively,
        for liberation from a White male-dominated economic system. It
        relates these implications to marital instability in the White
        family as a prelude to a discussion of whether the socioeconomic
        plight of Blacks in America can be attributed to a cultural pre-
        ference for female-headed households. The author offers a moti-
        vational analysis to account for the normative scientific percep-
        tion of Blacks, and the Black family, in America. It concludes
        with some recommendations for training mental health professionals
        for working with Black lower-class urban families.

662.   George, Kochuparampil Mammen. "Family Structure and Fertility
        Among Lower Class Negroes: A Study in Social Demography." Un-
        published Doctoral Dissertation, University of Kentucky, 1970.
        145 pp.

        The general thesis of this study is that family support tends to
        weaken the desire for effective family planning and thus contri-
        bute to higher fertility. Prof. George's hypothesizes that fami-
        ly support in the extended family influences reproductive beha-
        vior of its members is correct.

663.   Kamii, Constance K. "Socio-Economic Class Differences in the
        Preschool Socialization Practices of Negro Mothers." Unpublished
        Doctoral Dissertation, University of Michigan, 1965. 159 pp.

        Dr. Kamii's investigation of specified aspects of mother-child
        interactions which appear to foster anaclitic identification
        among middle class children and hinder it among lower class

Kamii:

children. She found that inability of members of lower class to
behave in conformity with middle class standards appears to stem
from differences in socialization practices than from differences
in child rearing goals.

664.   Jones, Curtis J. "Differences and Similarities Between Two Pa-
rent and Mother-Child Black Families Residing in a Lower Socio-
Economic Status Census Tract." Unpublished Doctoral Dissertation,
Michigan State University, 1974. 203 pp.

The present study explores similarities and differences between
two parent families and mother-child Black families. The examination of specific characteristics is undertaken within a framework which facilitates a comparative and exploratory analysis of
the data focused upon. A specific effort is made to compare contrasting socio-economic-status populations. In this investigation
a population residing in a lower socio-economic-status census
tract is compared with a population of higher socio-economic-
status examined by Scanzoni in his study entitled The Black Family
in Modern Society. The analysis of data supports the conclusion
that implications of related research, which seem to support the
generalization that there are more differences than similarities
between two parent families and mother-child families, might well
be questioned and re-examined. Indeed this investigation suggests
that many more similarities, in the areas explored, than differences exist when the two family types are studied. An extension of
the findings extrapolated from this study also suggests that alleged differences between socio-economic-status levels might also
be questioned, concludes Dr. Jones.

665.   McIntyre, Jennie J. "Illegitimacy: A Case of Stretched Values."
Unpublished Doctoral Dissertation, Florida State University, 1966.
102 pp.

This study was of the valuation of marriage of a group of women
who had borne illegitimate children. Most were unhappy over illegitimate pregnancies, most preferred a boy-friend to a husband,
most had entered early sexual activity because of peer group pressures and most approve of marriage and were aware of disadvantages
of having an illegitimate child, concludes Dr. McIntyre.

666.   Moed, Lillian Weissman. "Belief Systems and Aspirations on Family Life of Lower Class Black Youths." Unpublished Doctoral Dissertation, University of California at Los Angeles, 1970. 270 pp.

Dr. Moed investigates belief systems about family life in a ghetto
community. Supplementary material included beliefs and descriptions concerning groups, school experiences, career aspirations,
race and neighborhood. An attempt was also made to identify the
strengths of lower class Black families.

667. Rydman, Edward J., Jr. "Factors Related to Family Planning Among
      Lower-Class Negroes." Unpublished Doctoral Dissertation, Ohio
      State University, 1965. 171 pp.

      Dr. Rydman's observations suggest that social and cultural factors
      may have an influence upon family planning practices. Reveals
      that there are very few factors which have a strong influence on
      family planning but many which may have a small influence. Sub-
      jects behave in many inconsistent ways and additional areas of
      cultural and social milieu need further investigation before any
      valid conclusion on contraceptive practices can be drawn, con-
      cludes the researcher.

668. Schulz, David A. "Variations in Complete and Incomplete Families
      of the Negro-Lower-Class." Unpublished Doctoral Dissertation,
      Washington University, 1968. 500 pp.

      This study described and analyzed some of the rich variety found
      in lower-class Negro families as that variety was reflected in
      ten families all of whom lived at one time in a large urban hous-
      ing project in a Midwestern city. The major criterion for selec-
      ting these families was that five of them be complete and five be
      fatherless. The families were also in about the same stage of de-
      velopment. All families had one or both parents between the ages
      of thirty and fifty-five, and all had three or more children. All
      but two families had teen-age children, states Dr. Schulz. A ty-
      pology based on the relative degree of adult male marginality to
      each family was developed and seven types were discerned. Four
      types of boyfriends were: the quasi-father, the supportive bio-
      logical father, the supportive companion, and the pimp. This stu-
      dy indicated that the role of the boyfriend was much more stable
      and considerably less exploitive than commonly depicted and that
      some men spent a considerable portion of their lives bargaining for
      a familial relationship as a quasi-father, concludes the author.

668a. Smith, Dennis Elliott. "Independence Training of Their Male Off-
      spring by Lower Class Black Mothers with High and Low Achievement
      Motivation." Unpublished Doctoral Dissertation, Wayne State Uni-
      versity, 1974. 85 pp.

      Dr. Smith compared two groups of Black mothers -- one high and
      one low achieving, to determine if independence training was re-
      lated to achievement motivation. The author's findings suggest
      that achievement motivation may influence reinforcements adminis-
      tered more so than independence training.

669. Vasquez, Albert M. "Race and Culture Variables in the Acceptance
      Rejection Attitudes of Parents of Mentally Retarded Children in
      the Lower-Socioeconomic Class." Unpublished Doctoral Disserta-
      tion, California School of Professional Psychology, Los Angeles,
      1973. 130 pp.

      The author investigates parental acceptance-rejection attitudes

Vasquez:

of mothers towards their mentally retarded children. Focused on
lower socioeconomic Mexican-American, Black, and white ethnic
groups. Prof. Vasquez wanted to determine if any significant
differences in ethnic group in acceptance of child, the socio adjustment of the child in school and correlations of attitudes of
mothers with social adjustment of child....

20. BLACK MALE'S ROLE IN THE FAMILY

670. Labrecque, Suzanne V. "Child-Rearing Attitudes and Observed Behaviors of Black Fathers with Kindergarten Daughters." Unpublished Doctoral Dissertation, Florida State University, 1976. 121 pp.

The present exploratory study of the interaction between Black fathers and their kindergarted daughters was conducted in order to
increase knowledge about the Black father-daughter relationship in
the early years. The study was concerned with the effect fathers'
reported child-rearing attitudes had on their own and their kindergarten daughters' actual behaviors as they interacted in completing a structured puzzle task. The sample was composed of 34
Black fathers and their five-year-old daughters. They were all
members of intact, financially self-supporting, Black families.
All the children were in regular attendance in public or private
kindergarten programs in Tallahassee, Florida. The data analysis
revealed the following statistically significant relationships:
(1) Black fathers' reported child-rearing attitudes concerning
their daughters' expressed independent and dependent behaviors
related to their observed behaviors when they interacted with
their daughters on completing an assigned task. (2) Black fathers' and their daughters' observed behaviors did reveal an association. When the child acted dependent the father tended to
intervene either physically by moving puzzle pieces, or verbally
by giving directions. (3) When five-year-old girls scored above
150 on the Characteristic Behavior Checklist, there was a relationship between the children's reported behaviors with their
fathers' reported child-rearing attitudes....

671. Melton, Willie, III. "Self-Satisfaction and Marital Stability
Among Black Males: Socioeconomic and Demographic Antecedents."
Unpublished Doctoral Dissertation, Washington State University,
1976. 107 pp.

This investigation is based on a secondary analysis of data from
a national five-year (1968-1972) panel study of family economic
patterns. The sample consists of 434 married Black male heads of
households with wives present in 1968. From 1969 to 1972 some
15% of the husbands experienced marital separation or divorce.
The two models prove to be poor predictors of variation in self-
satisfaction and marital stability. After examining the relative
effects of each antecedent variable on the respective dependent
variables, the major findings are that (1) wife's education has a
positive effect on husband's income: (2) the extent of labor

Melton:

force participation of wives in Black households has a substantial positive effect on family income; (3) steady employment is an
important source of self-satisfaction for Black husbands; (4)
wife's employment status has no effect on husband's self-esteem;
(5) level of educational attainment, independent of income and occupational prestige, has a slightly negative impact on husband's
self-esteem; (6) increases in the personal income of wives have
no consequences for the self-esteem of Black husbands; (7) marital stability among Black males increases with age; (8) husband's
sense of self-satisfaction has a small positive effect on the stability of his marriage; and (9) increases in the personal earnings
of wives produce a negative effect on marital stability. The number of children in the home is introduced belatedly as an antecedent variable and is found to be negatively related to husband's
self-satisfaction and marital stability, concludes Dr. Melton.

672.   Smith, John M., Jr. "The Husband/Father in the Intact Lower
        Class Urban Black Family." Unpublished Doctoral Dissertation,
        University of Georgia, 1972. 230 pp.

        The husband/father in the intact lower class urban Black family
        was studied from his perspective and that of his spouse in selec-
        ted roles associated with his position in the family. Those
        roles included the provider role, child-related roles, and family
        leadership roles. Selected attitudes pertaining to the family
        also were explored. The husband/fathers appeared to be more ac-
        tive in their families than the literature suggests; they not on-
        ly knew what was expected of them in their positions but also be-
        lieved that they were fulfilling the responsibilities associated
        with their positions, states the writer. However, further re-
        search is warranted on husband/father-wife/mother dyadic congru-
        ity concerning the husband/father, concludes Dr. Smith.

673.   Stearns, Richard Prescott. "Factors Related to Fertility Values
        of Low-Income Urban Black Males: A Case Study." Unpublished
        Doctoral Dissertation, Case Western Reserve University, 1974.
        138 pp.

        Study of demographic characteristics relating to fertility values
        of low income Black males 14-27. Found their fertility values
        below achieved fertility of their parents. General rejection of
        abortion and sterilization also present.

                    21. BLACK MIDDLE-CLASS FAMILY

674.   Alexander, Myrna B. "The Dynamics of a Black Middle-Class Family."
        Unpublished Doctoral Dissertation, George Washington University,
        1981. 201 pp.

        The researcher's findings focused on the husband-wife relation-
        ship, the children, parent-child relationships, extended family

Alexander:

and help systems, health, communication and metacommunication, and values and goals of the Black middle-class family. Hypotheses pertinent to Black middle-class family dynamics are summarized as follows: (1) Social exchange theory and husband-wife relations are integrally related, and the male's occupational status in the economic structure affects both. (2) The children's communication, interaction, and development emanate from parental role models and society. (3) Emphasizing entry into the white opportunity structure, Black parents stress academic achievement, financial attainment, and success as significant goals for their children. (4) The extended family provides valuable social, emotional, and material support for the upwardly mobile Black family. (5) The Black middle-class family practices sound health concepts. (6) Black family communication is a function of the family's interaction with white society. (7) Prominent family values emphasize education, achievement, hard work, and human relations. Based on generated hypotheses, it was generally concluded that Black middle-class family patterns largely converge with those of white society, where divergences do exist, they result mainly from racial discrimination against Blacks. Like the white achievement-oriented society, Blacks aspire to the American opportunity system, concludes Dr. Alexander.

675. Ballweg, John A. "Social Class Differences in Friend and Kin Relationships of the Negro Conjugal Unit." Unpublished Doctoral Dissertation, University of Nebraska, 1967. 132 pp.

This study provides insights into the origins, developments and composition of primary associations for middle class and working class Black couples. These findings indicate that Black couples have a number of primary relationships which they share with both relatives and friends. Dr. Ballweg indicates that the similarities in primary associations for middle and working class Black couples are greater than the differences.

676. Canonici, Paul Victor. "Characteristics Associated With Socio-Economic Success of an Emerging Black Middle Class of Mississippi: A Study in Need Gratification." Unpublished Doctoral Dissertation, Mississippi State University, 1970. 200 pp.

Dr. Canonici investigates characteristics associated with socioeconomic success of certain affluent, emerging middle class Black residents of Hinds County, Mississippi. Most possess the following characteristics: native Southerners, educated in south, had stable homes, high occupational status, their parents had socioeconomic status above general Black population, and their childhood modest but not severely deprived.

677. Semone, Ronald Cecil. "The Negro Middle-Class in the South: A Study of Race, Class, and Political Behavior." Unpublished Doctoral Dissertation, University of North Carolina at Chapel Hill, 1969. 149 pp.

Semone:

Using E. Franklin Frazier's thesis that he articulated in <u>Black Bourgeoisie</u> that the Black middle class ignores the plight of the Black masses, this researcher studied the Black middle class since the 1960's. Dr. Semone found that Frazier's theory did not fit the Black middle class of the South on the eve of the civil rights movement.

678.   Walters, Toni S. "A Study of Black Middle-Class Parents and Their Academically Successful Children." Unpublished Doctoral Dissertation, Oakland University, 1984. 275 pp.

The Black middle-class parents in this study unanimously feel it is realistic to expect that their children will attain either a four year college degree or a graduate degree because the children have the ability, interests, and academic performance record to achieve this educational goal. The parents also believe their children will be educationally equipped to make occupational choices. Ultimately, the parents want their children to enjoy a better adult economic life style than they had as children, states Dr. Walters. "Black middle-class parents perceive their academically successful children have acquired foundational literacy skills. Their children are continually developing and refining literacy skills as they progress through school. The parents believe the home environment is the single most important influence on their children's attitudes toward learning and they further believe that they are most responsible for the children's school success...," concludes Prof. Walters.

679.   Watts, Lewis G. "Attitudes Toward Moving of Middle-Income Negro Families Facing Urban Renewal." Unpublished Doctoral Dissertation, Brandeis University, 1964. 231 pp.

Despite opportunities to move into white neighborhoods most middle-income Blacks in this Boston ghetto remained there, declares the author. Younger Black families who had less tenure in the neighborhood were potential movers. These younger Blacks are also better educated and less affluent than the older members, concludes Dr. Watts.

680.   Wilkes, Robert Edward. "A Study of the Role of Husbands and Wives in the Decision Process of Selected Negro Families Purchasing Major Household Durable Goods." Unpublished Doctoral Dissertation, University of Alabama, 1971. 135 pp.

Decision process involved four states: problem recognition, search for information about alternative solutions, evaluation of alternative solution, and purchasing process, surmises Prof. Wilkes. Each family analyzed to determine activity involved during these stages and relative influence of husband-wife in that activity.

22. BLACK RURAL FAMILY

681.   Carson, Norma H.   "Informal Adoption Among Black Families in the
       Rural South." Unpublished Doctoral Dissertation, Northwestern
       University, 1981. 135 pp.

       This study illuminates the social and cultural context in which
       informal adoption takes place in the South. The data were collec-
       ted in Macon County, Alabama and include 75 interviews with pa-
       rent surrogates, natural mothers, informally adopted children, com-
       munity agency representatives, and additional information gathered
       through observation and analysis of relevant documents. Survival
       in the Black community is predicated on a network of mutual aid
       and support. Participants view the phenomenon of informal trans-
       actions in child care as an attempt to "help out". A small per-
       centage of the parent surrogates view the phenomenon as "adoption"
       and "giving the child away", states Prof. Carson. Natural mothers
       value informal adoption because they feel that their children will
       get a better foundation from parent surrogates. Children are in-
       formally adopted because of economic and emotional problems in
       the lives of their natural mothers. Natural mothers are usually
       young and attempting to maintain single parent families at the
       time of informal adoption, according to the researcher. The net-
       work of informal adoption can be viewed as an asset to the Black
       community in the absence of adequate resources. Informal adop-
       tion is an investment in the survival of the Black family, con-
       cludes Dr. Carson.

681a. Lucas, Katheryn L.   "The Quality of Marital Adjustment Between
       First and Second Marriages in Black Families." Unpublished Doc-
       toral Dissertation, Kansas State University, 1984. 124 pp.

       The population in this dissertation included only Black couples
       whose marriage licenses were recorded for the years 1980-1983 in
       the County of Hinds in Mississippi. A random sample of couples
       in first and second marriages was selected from this population.
       The subjects were well-educated and middle class. All had been
       married for less than five years. The statistical analysis in-
       dicated a significant difference between the perceptions of Black
       couples in first and second marriages as to the quality of mar-
       riage at the .05 level of significance. It was concluded that
       there are greater levels of marital adjustment and satisfaction
       for couples in first marriage than second marriage, thus null
       Hypothesis 1 was rejected....

682.   Samdani, Ghulan Mohammad.   "Migration and Modernization: A Study
       of Changing Values and Behavior Among Former Migrants from the
       Rural South to Upstate New York." Unpublished Doctoral Disserta-
       tion, Cornell University, 1970. 240 pp.

       A study of Southern rural Black migrant laborers who dropped out
       of the migrant stream to settle in the North. Examines process
       of migration and modernization. Found that economic reasons were
       a factor in locating in the North and the families had improved
       their financial conditions in the North.

23.   BLACK URBAN FAMILY

682a. Avery, Reginald S.   "The Impact of Court-Ordered Busing on Black
       Families in Boston, Massachusetts."   Unpublished Doctoral Disser-
       tation, Brandeis University, 1980.   396 pp.

       The purpose of this study is to examine the effects that court-
       ordered busing policy has had on Black families in Boston, Massa-
       chusetts. Specifically, the purpose of the study is to identify
       those variables or aspects of family life that are most affected
       by busing policy -- positively or negatively. While busing in
       itself did not seem to produce or cause most of the negative ef-
       fects reported by families, it is clear that it served to com-
       pound or aggravate existing problems that families may have had,
       states Dr. Avery. This was especially true for those families in
       lower income groups. In spite of the various negative effects of
       busing, the majority of families felt that busing was the most
       feasible was by which equality of educational opportunity could be
       obtained. Hence, they appeared to be "willing" to endure the ne-
       gative consequences of busing in order that their children could
       obtain what they perceived to be a better education, concludes the
       researcher.

683.   Brown, Addie W.   "Grandparents Perceived Roles in Urban Extended
       Black Family Relationships."   Unpublished Doctoral Dissertation,
       United States International University, 1983.   125 pp.

       The study examined the perceived roles of Black grandparents who
       resided in three-generation extended family homes. The purpose
       of the study was to describe, analyze and clarify these roles as
       they relate to family survival and stability. Also examined were
       similarities and differences between young and old, male and fe-
       male grandparents. Social and demographic characteristics of the
       subjects varied. There were thirty-four females, eleven of whom
       were married. Subjects ranged in age from thirty-two to seventy.
       Factors precipitating development of the three-generation house-
       hold were diverse. Many factors were created by circumstances,
       such as teenage unmarried mothers, economic necessity to double-
       up, separations, widowhood, and legal custody situations whereby
       the grandparent cared for grandchildren and their offspring.
       Nine roles were identified by the subjects which assisted their
       family's survival, asserts Prof. Brown. The shift to a three-
       generation family arrangement represented a dramatic change, with
       emotional overtones and economic problems for several grandparents.
       The roles described indicated that the subjects carried on the
       tradition of care and concern for their extended family as sug-
       gested by previous investigators, argues the writer.

684.   Gettys, Gloria D.   "Black Families Residential Choice and Quality
       of Life."   Unpublished Doctoral Dissertation, Bryn Mawr College,
       1980.   229 pp.

       This is a study of sixty-six Black families who pioneered by buy-
       ing homes in all-white neighborhoods in the suburbs of Philadelphia

Gettys:

during the period 1956-1976. The study focuses on the quality of
life as perceived by these families. Social and psychological
factors are examined to determine if the experience of moving into a predominantly white suburban neighborhood was felt to be a
satisfying experience in spite of the early obstacles and attitudinal rejections many of the Black families experienced in their
relocation. According to the author, although the majority of
the pioneer families initially experienced subtle hostility from
white neighbors, the pioneers enjoyed positive relations after a
period of time. The majority of families in this study now consider their residential environment to be highly satisfying in
fulfilling the needs and desires of family members, asserts Prof.
Gettys. The data did not demonstrate a need for special mental
health services for pioneering Black families nor a need for new
anti-discrimination laws. However, existing laws should be enforced more thoroughly, she declared.

685.   Slesinger, Doris Peyser. "The Utilization of Preventive Medical
        Services by Urban Black Mothers: A Socio-Cultural Approach." Un-
        published Doctoral Dissertation, University of Wisconsin, 1973.
        218 pp.

        Dr. Slesinger shows that preventive medical utilization varied di-
        rectly with socio-economic status, indirectly with social isola-
        tion and directly with positive medical orientation.

686.   Tate, Sandra J. "Well-Being of Informally Adopted Blacks in
        Wisconsin." Unpublished Doctoral Dissertation, University of
        Wisconsin-Madison, 1984.   174 pp.

        Many Black informally adopted children are being cared for by
        someone other than their natural parents. Since the practice is
        informal it tends not to come to the attention of the public.
        Therefore, relatively little is known about the quality of care
        these children receive and the effect it has on their Well-being,
        asserts the author. This study attempts to fill that void by
        examining the effect of selected background characteristics --
        surrogate income, education, marital status and parental visita-
        tion -- on Well-being. To study this effect, interviews were con-
        ducted with 59 informally adoptive Black families in Wisconsin.
        Surrogates responded to questions regarding themselves, their
        spouses, their informally adopted child and the child's natural
        parents....

687.   Weisman, Carol Sach. "An Analysis of Female Dominance in Urban
        Black Families." Unpublished Doctoral Dissertation, Johns Hopkins
        University, 1973.   219 pp.

        This study found no significant negative consequences of female
        dominance on the behavior or attitude of family members. Socio-
        economic status and not wives employment is responsible for

Weisman:

marital satisfaction because wives employment generally does not
affect family status, according to the author. Many results were
contrary to previous literature leading to the conclusion that
the role of female dominance in perpetuating Black inequality has
been greatly overrated in the literature.

688.   Winslow, Samuel W. "The Stability of a Selected Sample of Negro
Families in North-Central Philadelphia." Unpublished Doctoral
Dissertation, Temple University, 1963. 212 pp.

Dr. Winslow tried to determine the criteria of family stability,
incidence of stability in the families and the meaning of the
differences. Prof. Winslow's findings show much research needs
to be done especially in areas in which results were contrary to
expected norms based on previous studies.

689.   Young, Janet Spratlin. "Family Size, Income, and Housing Expenditure in Inner City Rental Market." Unpublished Doctoral Dissertation, University of Pennsylvania, 1973. 196 pp.

Income and family size interact to affect housing expenditure.
Dr. Young found that rental expenditures of large low income families is least responsive to changing income and most responsive
to changing family size. The opposite is true for small income
families, concludes the researcher.

24. BLACK WORKING CLASS

690.   Gillette, Thomas L. "The Working Class Mother: A Study of the Relationship Between Maternal Employment and Family Structure as Influenced by Social Class and Race." Unpublished Doctoral Dissertation, University of North Carolina at Chapel Hill, 1961. 300 pp.

This is a study of effects of maternal employment status, social
class and race on the performance and evaluation of certain family and family related roles. Working class mothers are more likely to see maternal employment as a means of achieving family oriented goals, middle class mothers are more likely to view it as
a method of gaining individual or self-oriented goals, concludes
Prof. Gillette.

691.   Grisby, Bill. "Family Structure and Family Behavior: A Consideration of Black Working-Class and Middle Class Families." Unpublished Doctoral Dissertation, University of Colorado, 1972. 273 pp.

Dr. Grisby investigates the effects of family skills and social
attributes on family members' behavior patterns of problem solving and the sources of help families use in solving these problems. Studied social class, family structure, and ethnicity. He
found that family attitudes and values are more important than
social class and family structure in predicting family problem-
solving behavior patterns.

692. Winters, Wilda G. "Black Mothers in Urban Schools: A Study of
      Participation and Alienation." Unpublished Doctoral Dissertation,
      Yale University, 1975. 167 pp.

      This study explores the participation of 160 Black mothers in the
      educational sector to determine if urban mothers who are active
      participants in their children's schools feel less alienated than
      mothers who are less active or inactive. Alienation was measured
      in terms of three components, subjective alienation, the degree
      of school activity, and perception of school. Alienation emerges
      as an indicator of an individual's dissatisfaction with the struc-
      tures of society, from which feelings of meaninglessness, normless-
      ness and powerlessness can result. School activity is explored and
      assessed. Mothers interviewed were from two urban elementary
      schools, an experimental school with a program of extensive parent
      participation and a control school with some parent activities
      which served as a low-intensity contrast. In accord with a parti-
      cipatory ethos, we have been able to demonstrate a methodology
      which engaged parents as urban educational consumers in the design
      and data gathering process, declares Prof. Winters. The author con-
      cludes that a highly significant association exists between mothers
      who have been active participants in their school and low aliena-
      tion. Participation in school life is a more powerful influence on
      feelings of alienation than a number of socio-demographic factions,
      contends Dr. Winters.

25. COMPARATIVE FAMILIES

693. Anthony-Welch, Lillian Doloris. "A Comparative Analysis of the
      Black Woman as Transmitter of Black Values, Based on Case Studies
      of Families in Ghana and Among Jamaicans and Afro-Americans in
      Hartford, Connecticut." Unpublished Doctoral Dissertation, Uni-
      versity of Massachusetts, 1976. 413 pp.

      The purposes of this investigation were to define (1) some of the
      viable cultural values of African people (the term "African peo-
      ple" refers to people of African descent living in the United
      States, the Caribbean, and on the African Continent) by focusing
      on the African Woman as one of the prime transmitters of those
      values, and with the data generated from the investigation (2)
      develop a model for studying the African Woman and (3) to develop
      a methodology to explore the relationship between values and cul-
      ture of the Black community and the American Schooling system.
      The primary question became, does the Black woman transmit viable
      cultural values? The results of this research provided three
      theories: (1) Theory: the Black woman is a Prime Transmitter of
      viable cultural values, (2) theory that viable cultural values
      exist, (3) theory that these viable cultural values transmitted

Anthony-Welch:

have an African origin. The results of this research also provided enough information for a model for studying the African woman and a methodology to explore the relationships between values
and culture of the Black community and the American schooling system, concludes the author.

694.   Bayer, Kurt Richard. "A Social Indicator of the Cost of Being
Black." Unpublished Doctoral Dissertation, University of Maryland,
1971. 162 pp.

Dr. Bayer investigates welfare position of Black families as compared to White families. He studied three areas where well-being
of Black is impaired: education, housing and crime. Prof. Bayer
found that the difference in well-being is greater than the difference in income since Blacks suffer more from discrimination....

695.   Calvin, Jasper. "Family Structure, Maternal Dominance, Educational and Occupational Achievement: A Black-White Comparative
Analysis." Unpublished Doctoral Dissertation, University of Kentucky, 1974. 175 pp.

This is a Black-white comparative analysis of maternal dominance,
the effects of maternal dominance upon educational achievement,
and the effects of family structure upon educational and occupational achievement. The primary purpose of this research was to
seek answers to a number of questions which have been stimulated
by the controversy over the Moynihan Report. The study constitu-
ted a partial test of the Moynihan thesis, which set forth the
proposition that an unstable family structure was the crucial factor which precluded the movement of Blacks into the mainstream of
American economic and political life. The theoretical problem was
as follows: How are family structure and maternal authority related to the life chances of Black Americans -- as reflected in
educational and occupational achievement, and to what extent is
the situation different from that of white Americans? The findings indicate that Blacks are higher on maternal dominance than
whites among respondents from stable families of orientation. The
proposition that maternal dominance would be related to educational achievement, and the prediction that the direction of the association would be positive for females and negative for males, were
not supported by the data, declares Prof. Calvin. Two significant
findings were: family instability had greater negative effects
upon the educational achievement of whites as compared with Blacks,
and family instability had a greater influence upon the educational
achievement of females as compared with males. Dr. Calvin came
to the following conclusions: (1) the Moynihan Report was characterized by a number of serious theoretical and methodological
weaknesses; (2) low educational achievement, especially among
Black males, is apparently not attributable to the matriarchal
pattern of family organization; (3) the failure of Blacks to succeed in American society is apparently not attributable to family
instability; and (4) other approaches, particularly social-psychological, should be used in future research on the Black family.

696.   Cohen, Roberta S.   "Analysis of Familial Effects in the Political
        Socialization of Black and White Youth." Unpublished Doctoral
        Dissertation, University of Illinois at Urbana-Champaign, 1973.
        193 pp.

        The politics of Illinois urban teenagers are examined for corres-
        pondences with the politics of their parents. The sample consists
        of 381 seventh through twelfth grade youth, responding to paper
        and pencil questionnaires administered in their classrooms, and
        the parents of the sampled youth, responding to telephone inter-
        views. Four dimensions of political orientations are examined
        for pair and group correspondence of generations and for the ef-
        fects of social setting criteria such as race and social class.
        The inter-generational correspondences among political interest
        and participation and political efficacy are found to be of rea-
        sonable magnitude; the parent's level of each is the best pre-
        dictor for the child's level. In contrast with earlier studies,
        the level of political party preference correspondence is rela-
        tively low among the families in this sample and race is found to
        account for as much variance in child's party choice as the choice
        of the parents accounts for. The investigator's knowledge of pa-
        rents' responses to specific political attitude items does not
        significantly contribute to prediction of child's responses, and
        group correspondences on attitude items are found to be relatively
        low. To account for the diminishing familial effects noted, a
        model of children's political choice and decision-making is pro-
        posed based on political self-interest, concludes Dr. Cohen.

697.   Crumbley, Joseph. "A Descriptive Analysis of Black and White
        Families Reported for Child Maltreatment." Unpublished Doctoral
        Dissertation, University of Pennsylvania, 1982. 280 pp.

        This study is an attempt to provide the child protective agency
        and staff with profiles of Black and white families reported for
        child maltreatment. The anticipated result is a more cross ra-
        cial knowledge base, from which culturally sensitive services can
        be developed, observes Dr. Crumbley. The study is organized by
        chapters devoted to providing: (1) A literature review of pro-
        files describing families in general reported for child maltreat-
        ment (Chapter 1). (2) A literature review of theoretical approa-
        ches to explaining the causes and factors associated with child
        maltreatment in general and in Black families specifically (Chap-
        ter 1). (3) A descriptive study of Black and white families re-
        ported for child maltreatment in Philadelphia, PA (Chapters II and
        III). (4) A discussion of the study's implications for assessing
        and intervening with Black families reported for child maltreat-
        ment (Chapter IV).

698.   Fortune, Hilda O. "A Study of the Power Position of Mothers in
        Contemporary Negro Family Life in New York City." Unpublished
        Doctoral Dissertation, New York University, 1963. 159 pp.

        The researcher investigates whether the Black mother is the deci-
        sion-maker in the Black family, if she has more power than her

Fortune:

husband, and if her position in the home conforms to that of the
White mother. She found that the decision-making process was
equalitarian in nature for the Black family.

699.   Groff, William Harold. "An Analysis of White and Negro Fertility
        Differences." Unpublished Doctoral Dissertation, Brown Universi-
        ty, 1968. 215 pp.

        This analysis lends tentative support to the hypothesis that ra-
        cial fertility differences are associated with the differential
        effects of racial segregation. The findings point to the com-
        plexity of factors impinging upon racial fertility differences
        and direct attention toward the possible significance of racial
        segregation in the evaluation of racial fertility differences and
        the prediction of future trends, concludes Dr. Groff.

700.   Guillory, Barbara Marie. "The Black Family: A Case for Change
        and Survival in White America." Unpublished Doctoral Disserta-
        tion, Tulane University, 1974. 441 pp.

        Dr. Guillory rejects the placing of responsibility of deviance
        solely upon Blacks themselves and also rejects any facile compari-
        son of Black and White families. She stresses that the Black fa-
        mily has had to be uniquely flexible in its structure, role and
        values, than the white family.

701.   Harris, Joan R. "Black/White and Socioeconomic Status as Factors
        in Maternal Attitudes Toward Childrearing Practices and the Use
        of Health Care in Families with and without an Educable Mentally
        Retarded Child." Unpublished Doctoral Dissertation, Brandeis
        University, 1976. 225 pp.

        One basic problem with which the study has been concerned is the
        separation of ethnic (Black and white) and socioeconomic status
        (SES) differences in patterns of maternal childrearing attitudes
        and the use of prenatal, postnatal, and pediatric medical care.
        Involved also was the examination of mothers of educable mentally
        retarded (EMR) children to see if the ethnic and SES differences
        found held regardless of the presence or absence of an EMR child.
        Since the sex of the child might have an effect on maternal atti-
        tudes, effort has been made to ascertain differences based on sex
        of child. Thus, four independent variables, SES, ethnicity, sex
        of child, and type of child, were tested against two dependent
        variables, maternal attitudes toward childrearing practices and
        toward the use of health care, surmises Prof. Harris. The conclu-
        sions indicated that ethnicity was most strong in regard to two
        childrearing factors, out of four extracted, and accounted for
        minimal explained variance. Factor I, Control of the Child's Be-
        havior, accounted for an overwhelming amount of the total explain-
        ed variance and SES was the strong main effect while ethnicity was
        not significant. SES occurred as a major effect throughout the

Harris:

analyses of maternal attitudes toward childrearing practices. Similar results were obtained for attitudes toward the use of health
care for pre- and post-natal and pediatric medical care except
there was a strong interaction effect between SES and ethnicity
(low SES demonstrated "less good" medical care and was even worse
for Black low-SES families) which leads to questions regarding the
lack of parity in the measurement of SES for Blacks and whites,
states the researcher. The basic issue involved in whether low-
SES is comparable for both ethnic categories. Type of child and
sex of child revealed few main or interaction effects on the dependent variables of attitudes toward childrearing practices and
use of health care. Overall, SES outweighed ethnicity although
these two variables were confounded in other instances, asserts
Dr. Harris.

702. Hill, Richard Child. "Urban Income Inequality." Unpublished
      Doctoral Dissertation, University of Wisconsin, 1973. 362 pp.

      This is a study of inequality in the distribution of income among
      families, classes and racial status groups in urban areas, espe-
      cially Black families. Prof. Hill found that inequality varies
      with location of urban area in the South, low levels of urban em-
      ployment in manufacturing industries; high levels of unionization,
      high percentage of non-whites in the area and low average incomes

703. Hughes, Blanche R. "Abortion: Perception and Contemporary Geno-
      cide Myth: A Comparative Study Among Low-Income Pregnant Black
      and Puerto Rican Women." Unpublished Doctoral Dissertation, New
      York University, 1973. 178 pp.

      In this study about half (50.5%) of the sample were single and
      37.5 percent were married, and the remainder were separated, wid-
      owed, or divorced. Approximately one-half of the Puerto Rican
      sample (49%) were married as compared with about one-fourth (26%)
      of the Blacks. Puerto Ricans reported no divorces while Blacks
      had 3 percent. Among clinical groups about one-half of the pre-
      natals were married as compared with about one-fourth of the
      abortion seekers. More Blacks (25%) than Puerto Ricans (18%) liv-
      ed with husbands or males despite the reverse occurring in groups
      reported married, states Dr. Hughes. Both ethnics were different
      in how they perceived of abortion for Medical-social and Reli-
      gious-ethical reasons, but there was no probable difference be-
      tween their perception of abortion in genocidal terms. There was
      a probable difference between prenatal and abortion seekers per-
      ceptions of abortion, asserts the author. Dr. Hughes concludes:
      "Neither ethnic or clinic group perceived of abortion as signifi-
      cantly associated with genocide. The male ethnics appeared to
      pose the greatest threat to these females' interruption of preg-
      nancy. Progeny appeared to represent a thrust for survival and
      power for some minority males."

704. King, Karl B., Jr. "Comparison of Power Structure of the Negro and the White Family by Socioeconomic Class." Unpublished Doctoral Dissertation, Florida State University, 1964. 108 pp.

The results of the tests of significant differences between races for each question with sex controlled revealed that there were eighteen out of a possible twenty-one categories for the males and twenty out of twenty-one for the females that contained significant racial differences. When the socioeconomic correlates were applied to the male and female sample, the racial differences all but vanished, states Prof. King. For the males there were sixty-five significant differences reported out of a possible 231 categories that had significant differences. The results suggest that even though there were significant differences by race when sex was controlled, the differences in power structure are not related in any consistent or significant way to the correlates of social class used in this study, concludes Dr. King.

705. Mack, Delores Eliza. "The Husband-Wife Power Relationship in Black Families and White Families." Unpublished Doctoral Dissertation, Stanford University, 1970. 117 pp.

These results show that it is not possible to make simple statements about power in the husband-wife relationship. Results obtained in questionnaires differed from those obtained in discussion and bargaining situations. No important racial differences were found between working class Black and white couples and middle class Black and white couples, concludes Prof. Mack.

706. Martin, Barbara Thompson. "A Study of Achievement Oriented Behaviors of Poverty Black and White Mothers with Their Preschool Sons." Unpublished Doctoral Dissertation, Claremont Graduate School and University Center, 1970. 114 pp.

The focus of this study was on maternal behavior related to achievement motivation as observed in the interaction of mother and child in the home. Achievement motivation was one factor in the failure of many lower class children to achieve in school and later on in society.

707. Porterfield, Ernest. "Black-White Families: A Midwestern Study." Unpublished Doctoral Dissertation, University of Illinois at Urbana-Champaign, 1972. 215 pp.

Dr. Porterfield focuses on intrafamilial relations and their interpersonal relationships with larger society of 20 Black-White families. Interracial dating and marriage was found on the increase. There is a level of mild acceptance and/or tolerance to extreme opposition in their relations with larger community, states the author. Most couples felt that things were getting better and that America will increasingly become devoid of racial prejudices, concludes the researcher.

708. Riemer, Robert J. "Child-Spacing and Economic Behavior in a Black
      Community." Unpublished Doctoral Dissertation, University of
      Notre Dame, 1971. 164 pp.

      Dr. Riemer studied four aspects of economics in a Black community:
      family income, occupation of head of family, employment of family
      head and family debt. Rate of family growth has a consistent re-
      lationship with the socio-economic position of Black couples. His
      findings indicate that the relationship between the rate of family
      growth and economic behavior apparently cuts across racial lines....

709. Rubenstein, Daniel Irving. "The Social Participation of the Black
      Elderly." Unpublished Doctoral Dissertation, Brandeis University,
      1972. 357 pp.

      Dr. Rubenstein explores well being and social participation of
      Black elderly. Until recently Blacks were excluded from parti-
      cipation and even in studies of the elderly. Black elderly usu-
      ally live with a family member whereas white elderly usually live
      alone.

710. Scott, Patricia Bell. "Correlations of Concensus in the Area of
      Financial Priorities Among Black and White College Student Cou-
      ples." Unpublished Doctoral Dissertation, University of Tennessee,
      1975. 115 pp.

      This data revealed that presence of children was a significant
      factor of value consensus. Selected aspects of the caring or af-
      fective relationship were also significant predicators of value
      consensus. No significant differences in Black and white couples
      in financial priorities were found, concludes Dr. Scott.

711. Sizemore, Ray B., Jr. "Comparison of Family Background, School
      Context, and Teacher Effects on Reading Achievement of White and
      Black Students." Unpublished Doctoral Dissertation, Florida
      State University, 1972. 165 pp.

      Dr. Sizemore states that his research on white students indicates
      that family background explains more of the variation in their
      achievement than student body or teacher characteristics. This
      held true in all residential locations. In most instances, the
      latter two variables explained a minimal amount of the variation.
      For Blacks, student body characteristics explained more of the
      variation than either of the other two variable groups, and fami-
      ly background explained the least, according to the author. This
      is true when residential location is controlled. He concludes:
      "One possible interpretation of these results is that Blacks are
      more 'sensitive' than whites to their school environment. In
      general, the three variable groups together explain more of the
      variation for persons living in metropolitan areas."

712.   Walker, Lewis. "Matricentricity and Delinquency: A Study of the
       Female-Based Households and White Boys." Unpublished Doctoral
       Dissertation, Ohio State University, 1964. 99 pp.

       Dr. Walker found that families of Negro delinquents are no more
       matricentric than those of white delinquents, while families of
       white non-delinquents are no less matricentric than those of Ne-
       gro non-delinquents. However, significant differences do exist
       between delinquents' families and non-delinquents' families in
       the degree of matricentricity, states the researcher. It was al-
       so found that Negro and white delinquents are less favorably so-
       cialized than Negro and white non-delinquents. Coefficients of
       correlation were substantial enough to show that matricentricity
       is directly related to the incidence of juvenile delinquency in
       both Negro and white families. Prof. Walker concludes that it
       appears that the relation of female-based households to delinquen-
       cy and non-delinquency is a general lower-class pattern rather
       than a phenomenon characteristic of lower-class Negro families,
       and this relation is significant enough to be regarded as a major
       factor involving the ever-increasing rate of juvenile delinquency
       in modern America.

713.   Wermuth, Robert Fred. "Relationship of Musical Aptitude to Fami-
       ly and Student Activity in Music, Student Interest in Music, So-
       cioeconomic Status, and Intelligence Among Caucasian and Negro
       Middle School Students." Unpublished Doctoral Dissertation, Ohio
       State University, 1971. 177 pp.

       This study investigates whether significant relationships and
       differences exist between musical aptitude and family activity in
       music, student activity in music, student interest and intelli-
       gence quotient and status among Black and white middle school
       students from culturally advantaged and disadvantaged environ-
       ments....

26.   CONTEMPORARY BLACK FAMILIES

714.   Bieber, Toby B. "A Comparison of Negro Wed and Unwed Mothers."
       Unpublished Doctoral Dissertation, Columbia University, 1963.
       138 pp.

       These findings show that unwed mothers showed evidence of shame
       and guilt but nevertheless accepted the child. Unwed girls ten-
       ded to come from fatherless homes and evidence of conflict about
       having a permanent relationship with the putative father appeared
       in a tendency to resist marriage.

715.   Hemmons, Willa Mae. "Towards an Understanding of Attitudes Held
       by the Black Women on the Women's Liberation Movement." Unpub-
       lished Doctoral Dissertation, Case Western Reserve University,
       1973. 173 pp.

       Social psychological investigation of attitudes of Black women

Hemmons:

toward the women's liberation movement, and the social pressures involved in and goals of this kind of collective behavior were discussed. Dr. Hemmons hypothesizes that endorsement of the traditional female role is negatively related to female liberalism. The Black Power Movement is more positively associated with female liberalism and lack of group integration is incompatible with female liberalism, concludes the author. It also discusses the effects that the women's liberation movement has on the Black family.

716. Jones, Levi. "The Black Family: Its Process of Survival." Unpublished Doctoral Dissertation, Vanderbilt University, 1974. 321 pp.

Dr. Jones describes influences of the social environment upon internal functions and processes of the family. The interplay social environment and family coping elements suggest that the Black family is complex, strong and durable. This is reflected in their innovations and flexibilities in coping with racially hostile social environments, concludes Prof. Jones.

717. Strong, Ethelyn Ratcliff. "The Meaning of Childlessness to Childless Negro Couples." Unpublished Doctoral Dissertation, Catholic University of America, 1967. 261 pp.

The author's results show two interpretations of significance of childlessness to the couples: some had negative family experiences and wanted to remain childless, while the others were involuntarily childless but refused to adopt a child. It was revealed that the attitude of childless couples toward adoption is linked to belief about the meaning of childlessness.

718. Wheeler, William Henry, III. "The Black Family in Perspective." Unpublished Doctoral Dissertation, Arizona State University, 1973. 326 pp.

The author feels current literature on Black family life styles is lacking in cultural perspective. It reveals the effects of Africa, American slavery, and institutional racism on the development of a Black life style. Better research literature will help professionals (counselors and social workers) facilitate more effective programs serving Blacks, concludes Dr. Wheeler.

27. RESEARCH AND THE BLACK FAMILY

719. Ball, Richard E. "Expressive Functioning and the Black Family: Life and Domain Satisfaction of Black Women." Unpublished Doctoral Dissertation, University of Florida, 1980. 233 pp.

It was concluded from the findings that for these Black women,

Ball:

satisfaction levels were as high for the widowed and the divorced as for the married. Among this population, being single may have been considered indicative of unattractiveness and rejection, rather than choice, resulting in lower satisfaction. Separation may have resulted in trauma, temporarily lowering satisfaction. Family/household extension or augmentation, while sometimes instrumentally necessary, may have been inimical to nonmarried mothers' satisfaction. This may have been due to crowding, and violation of the norm of neolocality. Children appeared to have no impact on aggregate satisfaction levels. The effect on satisfaction of the instrumental burden of nonproductive children may have been countered by the expressive fulfillment they brought to their mothers, suggests Dr. Ball.

720.   Douglass, Melvin I. "The Black Family as a Matrix of Achievement: The Historical Case of Dr. William Montague Cobb." Unpublished Doctoral Dissertation, Columbia University Teachers College, 1981. 132 pp.

This dissertation is a historical study that focuses on Dr. William Montague Cobb and members of his family spanning several generations, to see why/how certain factors within this family helped to mold or shape the life of a key figure in the Black organizational movement. The researcher found that in each instance certain traditions played a major role in the lives of the subjects under investigation. All of the subjects received and handed down certain beliefs, legends, and customs from generation to generation. The traditional values that were passed on were: piety, thrift, respect for education, and race pride. He found several external factors in the family: the family's history of manumission, the history of the family being able to read and write, the family's good financial base, the family's small size, the strong parental figures, and the family's attitude and support of learning. These contributed to the academic achievement of each person. Dr. Douglass found several factors within the community that were equally important to the subjects under investigation: public and private learning institutions, religious institutions, and educational climate of the communities. He concludes: "In addition to the above being of major importance, I found that good fortune played a role in the academic achievement of individuals in this research report. In other words, they were at the right place at the right time."

721.   Morgan, Elizabeth R. "The Process of Parenting Among Twenty-Four Black Families in Berkeley, California." Unpublished Doctoral Dissertation, University of California, Berkeley, 1981. 150 pp.

This paper is a report of a descriptive study of twenty-four Afro-American families in Berkeley, California. The process of parenting is described from the perspective of the primary social parents who direct such process. The research reported herein utilizes a bicultural approach which includes historical, anthropological, and sociological data, including data derived in interview

Morgan:

with families included in the sample. Consideration of such process in historical context suggests that parenting processes in
this Berkeley sample are responsive to cultural trends which are
not shared by the wider society, suggests Dr. Morgan. To the degree that other Afro-American families are affected in similar
manner, studies of Afro-American family life which depend primarily on frameworks used for study of the wider society may not
yield reliable findings, concludes the author.

722. Norris, Wessie Lavon. "A Path Model for Feelings of Personal Ef-
      ficacy for Black Employed Male and Female Family Heads, Employed
      Female Non-Family Heads and Housewives." Unpublished Doctoral
      Dissertation, University of Michigan, 1980. 138 pp.

      Dr. Norris states that 2097 Black respondents, interviewed for a
      study of racial attitudes in fifteen American cities in 1968, com-
      prised the sample population. There were 792 employed male family
      heads, 262 employed female family heads, 469 employed female non-
      family heads, and 574 housewives. The respondents were between
      the ages of 16 and 69. A six-stage path model was proposed to
      explain feelings of personal efficacy for these four groups. The
      variables at each stage were: (1) family of origin characteris-
      tics and age, (2) respondent's education and marital status, (3)
      respondent's occupation, (4) income, (5) perceived social class,
      and (6) perceptions of racial discrimination. The writer states
      that the results of the analysis show that the model explained
      twice the amount of the variance in the efficacy of employed fe-
      male family heads and non-family heads as for male family heads
      and housewives. If sources of efficacy are conceived on a conti-
      nuum ranging from vicarious to environmental, housewives have
      mostly vicarious sources (family income, marital status, perceiv-
      ed social class), and female non-family heads have a combination
      of vicarious (family income and marital status) and environmental
      sources (occupation, age, education, personal experiences with
      discrimination), argues Prof. Norris. Male and female family
      heads have all environmental sources of efficacy. For both groups,
      age, education and perception of current opportunities are impor-
      tant. In addition, for women, evaluation of change is important,
      while for men, income is crucial to efficacy, concludes Dr. Norris.

Index

Including authors, joint authors, and editors. Numbers refer to individual entry numbers.

Hunt, Annie Mae, 156
Hunter, C.L., 493
Hunton, Addie, 361
Hyman, Herbert H., 13
Hynes, Winifred Joyce, 646
Hypertension, 633

Illegitimacy, 52, 80, 124, 131,
  253-254, 300, 403-404, 552, 634
Indianapolis, IN, 129
Iowa State University College of
  Home Economics, 175
Irvine, Russell W., 379

Jackson, Jacqueline J., 93, 271,
  441-443, 508
Jackson, James S., 90
Jackson, Viola, 309
Jacques, Jeffrey M., 495
Jeffers, Camille, 69
Jenchek, Margaret P., 487
John Hay Homes, 393
Johnson, Charles S., 13, 70-71,
  416
Johnson, Daniel M., 72
Johnson, Everett, 509
Johnson, Joan E., 4
Johnson, Kathryn, P., 168, 366
Johnson, Leanor B., 90, 574
Johnson, Marilyn, 114
Johnson, Robert C., 380
Johnson, Willa D., 73
Jones, Barbara Ann Posey, 638
Jones, Bobby Frank, 594
Jones, Curtis J., 664
Jones, Enrico E., 251
Jones, Eugene Kinckle, 510
Jones, Jacqueline, 74, 332
Jones, Levi, 716
Jones, Reginald L., 176
Jones, Robert R., 212
Juvenile Delinquency, 354, 368,
  533, 602

Kain, John F., 399, 511
Kaiser, Ernest, 187
Kamii, Constance K., 362, 425,
  663
Kandal, Denise B., 363
Kanno, Nellie B., 546
Kanter, Rosabeth Moss, 184
Kardiner, Abram, 75
Karlson, Alfred L, 241
Kass, Edward H., 315
Keller, Ella T., 636
Keniston, Kenneth, 263

Kennedy, Theodore R., 76
Kephart, William M., 77, 512
Kilpatrick, Alice C., 473
King, Charles E., 333
King, James R., 334
King, Jerry G., 606
King, Karl B., 364-365, 546a,
  704
King, Lewis M., 4
King, Mae C., 547
King, Margaret A., 241
King, Martin Luther, Jr., 3, 280
King, Ruth E.G., 103
Kingston, Jamaica, 424
Kiser, Clyde Vernon, 296
Klagsbrun, Francine, 177
Klebanow, Diana, 264
Kleiner, Robert J., 106, 152a,
  315, 484
Korchin, Sheldon J., 251
Kornweibel, Theodore, Jr., 297
Kriesberg, Louis, 78
Kronus, Sidney, 79
Ku Klux Klan, 76
Kulikoff, Allan, 55
Kunstader, Peter, 417

LaBarre, Maurine, 400
Labrecque, Suzanne V., 670
Ladner, Joyce, 80, 513
Lake, Robert W., 81
Lammermeier, Paul J., 514
Lamphere, Louise, 191
Lansing, MI, 647
Lantz, Herman, 335-336
LaPoint, Velma DeVonne, 135, 647
Larner, Jeremy, 178
Lawden, Elizabeth A., 82
Lawrence, Margaret Morgan, 83
Lee, A.L., 231
Leggon, Cheryle B., 103
Leigh, James W., 84
Leman, Paul, 89
Leslie, Gerald R., 179, 281
Levine, Elaine S., 520
Levita, Sar A., 180
Lewis, Diane K., 431, 277
Lewis, Hylan, 13, 85, 181, 204,
  315
Lewis, Jerry M., 86
Lewis, Ronald L., 337
Liberia, 94
Lichtman, Allen J., 271
Liebow, Elliot, 13, 87
Lim, Perry, 4
Lincoln, C. Eric, 446